THE ENCYCLOPEDIA OF TEAM-DEVELOPMENT ACTIVITIES

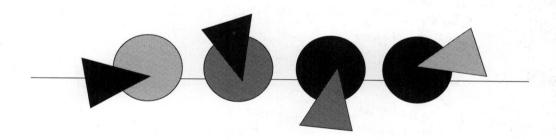

EDITED BY

J. WILLIAM PFEIFFER, Ph.D., J.D.

ASSOCIATE EDITOR
CAROL NOLDE

Pfeiffer
& COMPANY

Amsterdam • Johannesburg • Oxford
San Diego • Sydney • Toronto

Copyright © 1991 by University Associates, Inc.
ISBN: 0-88390-258-3
Library of Congress Catalog Card Number 90-22868
Printed in the United States of America

Library of Congress Cataloging-in-Publication Data
The Encyclopedia of team-development activities / edited by J. William Pfeiffer.
     p.   cm.
    Includes bibliographical references.
    ISBN 0-88390-258-3 (acid-free paper)
    1. Work groups.   I. Pfeiffer, J. William
HD66.E524 1991
658.4'02—dc20
                                         90-22868
                                           CIP

Content and Copy Editing:	*Carol Nolde*
Typesetting:	*Judy Whalen*
Cover Design / Art:	*Paul Bond*
Editorial Assistance:	*Val Eddingfield*
	Jennifer O. Bryant
	Steffany N. Parker

Pfeiffer & Company
8517 Production Avenue
San Diego, CA 92121
(619) 578-5900

This book is printed on acid-free, recyled stock that meets or
exceeds the minimum GPO and EPA specifications for recycled paper.

Contents

Introduction for the Leader 1

Team Effectiveness

Introduction to Team Effectiveness 11
Useful Feedback: Establishing the Process 13
Seven Questions: Encouraging Feedback 17
Getting Started: Setting the Stage for Team Building 21
Leadership Functions: An Assessment Activity 23
Task Delegation: A Team Approach 27
Project Selection: Collaborating to Identify Problems 31
The Team Audit: Identifying and Evaluating Skills 37
Team-Development Needs: Setting Objectives 45

Values/Mission

Introduction to Values/Mission 55
The Girl and the Sailor: Value Clarification 57
Personal Values: Sharing in the Team 63
Purpose of the Team: The What, How, Who, and Why 67
Mission Statement: Formulating a Team Mission 71
Team Mission and Individual Objectives: Discovering Strengths
    and Opportunities 75
Team Blasphemies: Clarifying Values 81
Looking at Change: An Assessment of Values 85

Problem Solving/Decision Making

Introduction to Problem Solving/Decision Making 89
Effective Problem Solving: A Survey for Assessing Skills 91
Identification and Resolution: Isolating Common Problems 95
Brainstorming: A Problem-Solving Technique 99
Nominal Group Technique: Applied Team Problem Solving 103
Bricks: Using Creativity in Solving Problems 109
Force-Field Analysis: Problem Solving 113
Shoe Store: Communication in Problem Solving 123
Circles of Influence: Widening a Team's Horizons 127
Team Decisions: Examining and Changing the Process 131
Decision Making: Learning Effective Processes 137
Reviewing Objectives and Strategies: An Action-Planning Task 141

Stress Management

Introduction to Stress Management 147
Enhancing Personal Energy: Identifying Resources and Depleters . . . 149
Burnout Remedies: Strategies for Managing Energy and Time 155
The Trouble with Marti: Managing Complex Tasks 161
Role Mapping: Dealing with Role-Related Stress 167

Team-Member Relationships

Introduction to Team-Member Relationships 177

Alphabet Names: Achieving Synergy 179
Process Observation: Analyzing How a Team Operates 183
Widget Engineering Corporation: Examining Team Commitment 189
Dos and Don'ts: Evaluating Team Norms 193
Team Communications: Identifying and Correcting Difficulties 195
Conflict Management: Developing a Procedure 197
Team-Climate Assessment: Action Planning for Improvement 201

Meetings

Introduction to Meetings 205
Recognition: Starting Meetings Appropriately 207
News Bulletin: Focusing the Team 211
Lowlights and Highlights: A Warmup for Team Meetings 213
Meeting Evaluation: Increasing Awareness of Procedures 215
Successful Meetings: Clarifying and Evaluating 217
Creating Agendas: Using a Check List 219
Checkpoints: Creating a Check List for Team Meetings 225

Inventories and Forms

Introduction to Inventories and Forms 229
Postmeeting Reaction Form 231
Postmeeting Evaluation Form 233
The Team-Effectiveness Critique 235
Survey of Team Development 243
Team-Profile Questionnaire 247
Team-Development Rating Form 249
Teamwork Survey 251
Team-Development Scale 259
Team-Observation Guide 263
Behavior-Frequency Observation Guide 273
Team-Behavior Questionnaire 275
Interpersonal-Skills Questionnaire 277

Supplemental Materials

Introduction to Supplemental Materials 279
Characteristics of an Effective Team 281
Characteristics of Effective Team Leaders 283
Characteristics of Effective Team Members 285
Symptoms of Team Problems 287
Team-Building Agenda 289
Hidden Agendas 291
Win-Lose Situations 293
Responsibility in Communication 297
Communicating Communication 299
Defensive and Supportive Communication 305
Conflict-Resolution Strategies 311
Constructive Conflict in Discussions 317
Decision-Making Styles 323
Encouraging Others to Change Their Behavior 327
Dealing with Disruptive Individuals in Meetings 333
A Positive Approach to Resistance 339
Humor and the Effective Team 345

Introduction for the Leader

THE IMPORTANCE OF TEAMS AND TEAM BUILDING

Although the technology of team building is not new, it is especially important today. Contemporary organizations are less hierarchical and more participative than they once were—both in composition and in operating philosophy. Organizations have long been aware of the phenomenon of synergy, that a team can accomplish much more than its individual members can by working alone. In fact, the team is replacing the individual as the primary unit of focus in innovative organizations. With this emphasis on teams has come the realization that a team takes on a life of its own, that efforts must be made regularly to nurture and maintain it, just as these efforts are made in behalf of individual employees.

Not all groups are teams. Reilly and Jones (1974) defined the four essential elements that differentiate a team from a group:

1. The group members must have shared goals or a reason for working together;

2. The group members must be interdependent (that is, they perceive that they need one another's experience, ability, and commitment in order to arrive at mutual goals);

3. The group members must be committed to the idea that working together leads to more effective decisions than working in isolation; and

4. The group must be accountable as a functioning unit within a larger organizational context.

Turning a group into a team, however, means more than assuring the presence of the four elements of shared goals, interdependence, commitment, and accountability. The aim of team building is to help a group evolve into a cohesive unit whose members not only share the same high expectations for accomplishing group tasks but also trust and support one another and respect one another's individual differences as persons. Kormanski and Mozenter (1987) note that a great deal of attention has been paid to team leadership—the assumption being that a team's effectiveness is primarily based on the quality of its leadership—while so little attention has been paid to followership. Most team members have received little if any training in how to be followers. Kormanski and Mozenter characterize an effective follower as one who:

- Understands and is committed to team goals;
- Is friendly, concerned, and interested in others;
- Acknowledges and confronts conflict openly;
- Listens to others with understanding;
- Includes others in the decision-making process;
- Recognizes and respects individual differences;

- Contributes ideas and solutions;
- Values others' ideas and contributions;
- Recognizes and rewards team efforts; and
- Encourages and appreciates feedback about team performance.

As the aim of team building and the characteristics of an effective follower imply, teamwork is demanding of the individual members. Anyone who works with teams needs to be sensitive to this fact and to appreciate the effort required of group members as they strive to develop into an effective team.

THE BASICS OF TEAM BUILDING

An effective team is one that can solve its own problems, and the ability to solve problems is predicated on an ability to identify and remove obstacles that deflect energy from those problems. When the team members are expending energy on hidden agendas, internal conflicts, role ambiguity, confusion about the team's values or mission, or how to give one another essential feedback, they cannot focus their best efforts on solving the work-related problems that continually arise. Therefore, team building seeks to improve the members' problem-solving ability by enabling them to confront and manage the issues that hinder their functioning as a unit. During the process of team building, the team members identify these issues by examining the team's *"real-time"* data, which is information derived from what is actually occurring in the team at the moment (current norms concerning disclosure, feedback, openness, trust, leadership, membership, competition and collaboration, conflict resolution, and so on).

In addition to real-time data, two other types of data can be useful in team building: (1) *collected data,* information on the team's history, which can be obtained from various sources, including interviews and the personal accounts of team members and others; and (2) *simulation data,* information derived from team-member interactions in role plays and other simulations. These two types of data are used only as a means of preparing the team members to confront and manage their real-time data.

Typically there are four primary phases to the team-building process: sensing, diagnosing, resolving identified issues, and following through.[1]

1. *Sensing.* Prior to the team-building session, the consultant who will conduct that session interviews each of the team members (including the team leader) privately, indicating the purpose of the interview, the limits of confidentiality, and the plans for using the interview data. The purpose of the interviews is to obtain information about issues involving the team that are of concern to the team members, to clarify this information so that the consultant understands it, and to

---

[1] Much of this discussion has been adapted from "Team-Building: A Feedback Experience," in *A Handbook of Structured Experiences for Human Relations Training* (Vol. III, Rev.), edited by J.W. Pfeiffer and J.E. Jones, 1974, San Diego, CA: University Associates.

increase the team members' ownership of the information (in that they are the ones who generated it). Ownership of the information leads to commitment to the outcomes of the team-building session.

An alternative to individual interviews is the sensing meeting. The team leader calls and leads the meeting, eliciting information and recording it on newsprint. The consultant is present and helps the team leader to listen, to avoid defensive reactions, and to record the information as accurately as possible.

2. **Diagnosing.** The consultant analyzes the information received in the interviews, noting common themes, and prepares a series of newsprint posters presenting the following kinds of data: (1) information pertaining to each team member, (2) information on the team's process (decision-making patterns, communication, and so on), (3) information on goal statements, (4) information on objectives for the team-building session, and (5) any other miscellaneous information (or separate data categories as appropriate).

If Phase 1 consisted of a sensing meeting instead of separate interviews, at the end of that meeting the team leader commits to a definite course of action for resolving the issues that concern the members.

3. **Resolving identified issues.** The entire team meets in a room that affords privacy and freedom from interruptions. The consultant explains the goals of the team-building session, lists and posts objectives on newsprint, and then posts the previously prepared newsprint posters. The consultant reviews each poster's content, explaining his or her analysis and eliciting and answering questions of clarification. For the duration of the session, the consultant assists the team members in working through the posted information—reinforcing openness, risk taking, trust, and interdependence. The consultant also may suggest another meeting between the team leader and the members; if this is the case, the consultant should ensure that the team leader is capable of giving and receiving feedback nondefensively. In addition, the consultant helps the team members learn how to observe their team's process. The decisions made are formulated into an action plan, including the names of those responsible for performing particular actions, deadline dates for acting, and the names of any people outside the team who need to be involved and what the roles of these people will be. The consultant may encourage the team members to contract with one another for follow-through. In any case the consultant carefully records all elements of the action plan on newsprint; at the conclusion of the session, a volunteer is asked to collect this newsprint, turn its contents into a handout, and distribute copies of this handout to all team members. Before adjourning the session, the consultant schedules a follow-through meeting to review progress.

If the sensing-meeting alternative was chosen, a series of meetings is scheduled and subsequently attended by the team leader, the team members, and possibly by other interested parties (the consultant, "experts" who can provide information that the team needs in order to solve problems and make decisions, and/or representatives of upper management whose approval the team needs before acting). At these meetings the team considers the identified issues one by one, following much the same process as that described in the preceding paragraph.

4. ***Following through.*** At the scheduled follow-through meeting the team leader and the members review their action plan to determine what has been done, what still needs to be done, and what elements of the plan need to be revised or abandoned. (Events since the action-planning session may have necessitated changes that could not have been foreseen.) The consultant may or may not attend this meeting, depending on the team's preferences and level of experience with follow-through. Arrangements are made as necessary for any new assignments and deadline dates, and all revisions to the action plan are given to one member to reproduce and distribute in handout form. (Several such follow-through meetings may be held before the team completes all items on its action plan.)

THE DIFFERENCE BETWEEN TEAM BUILDING AND TEAM DEVELOPMENT

In the past, *team building* has been facilitated almost exclusively by a professional consultant in the field of human resource development (HRD). Many team-building activities[2] are relatively intense in terms of the affect they produce and the extent to which the participants must stretch their abilities as team members. In addition, many require that the facilitator deliver lecturettes or handle "props" (complex handouts or materials required by the activity design). A professional is trained to deal appropriately with intensity, to convey information in lecture format, and to handle props effectively, whereas a nonprofessional—such as the team's formal leader—might not be. In addition, a team leader who tries to engage in some of these facilitative behaviors may violate the team members' expectations of him or her. Consequently, the value of the team-building assistance provided by a professional is inestimable; a professional can introduce a team to the process of team building and to group dynamics and can help a team to get on track in a way that few nonprofessionals could.

However, relying exclusively on a professional for help in handling issues is incongruous with the goals of team building. As organizations look more and more to teams to accomplish tasks, to solve problems, and to make decisions, there is greater need for teams to be responsive and action oriented, relying as much as possible on the resources of their own members. Thus, a new phenomenon has arisen that we term *team development.* Its objective is the same as that of team building: to enhance problem-solving ability by dealing with issues that stand in the way. However, the team-development facilitator is not a professional, but the team's own formal leader, a designated member of the team, or someone else in the organization who has been asked to perform this function. The activities that can

---

[2] See *The Encyclopedia of Team-Building Activities,* edited by J.W. Pfeiffer, 1991, San Diego, CA: University Associates.

be conducted by a nonprofessional facilitator are, of necessity, different from those designed for a professional: they are less intense, produce less affect, and demand less of the facilitator and of the team members as participants.

After a team's members have been introduced to team building by an HRD professional, that professional can suggest that they follow up with team-development activities to enhance their ability to resolve their own issues. It is preferable that the individual facilitating a team-development activity also participate fully. However, for more complex activities, it may be necessary for the individual who is facilitating to reduce or eliminate his or her participation.

CLASSIFICATION OF THE ACTIVITIES AND MATERIALS IN THIS BOOK

The activities in this book emphasize team development rather than team building, as defined previously in this introduction. Therefore, they are constructed in such a way that they can be conducted by a nonprofessional facilitator who has a reasonable degree of knowledge and experience in the HRD field. (Throughout the book this person is referred to as the activity's "leader.") However, these activities can easily be adapted for use by a professional HRD consultant, if the team leader or members prefer this approach.

In addition to the activities contained in the first six sections, this book offers a number of other useful materials. The topics addressed in both the activities and the materials are representative of the kinds of issues typically addressed by teams in their development efforts. Each activity has been placed into a particular category or section according to its most probable use; the other materials have been assembled into the two final sections. Tabbed divider pages are included to separate the sections. The contents of these sections are described briefly in the following paragraphs and in greater detail in the introductory pages that designate the section divisions.

1. *Team Effectiveness.* These activities delve into various aspects of team functioning that contribute to effectiveness. They cover such diverse topics as feedback, task delegation, and assessment of leadership functions within the team.

2. *Values/Mission.* The activities in this category help the team members to clarify their values or to specify the team's mission.

3. *Problem Solving/Decision Making.* These activities deal with the team's skills in isolating, analyzing and solving problems; in making decisions; and in planning to take action.

4. *Stress Management.* The activities in this category offer techniques and methods for identifying personal resources, managing energy and time, managing complex tasks, and dealing with role-related stress.

5. *Team-Member Relationships.* These activities are aimed at examining, clarifying, and/or improving the team members' relationships with one another as well as their approach to working together.

6. *Meetings.* This category offers activities that seek to improve the effectiveness of the team's meetings.

7. *Inventories and Forms.* These materials are questionnaires and forms that team members will find useful in observing and evaluating the team's skills, procedures, stage or level of development, and effectiveness.

8. *Supplemental Materials.* The materials in this category offer information on a variety of subjects of interest to team leaders and members.

ACTIVITY FORMAT

The basic format of the activities in this encyclopedia includes the following sections: goals, time required, materials, physical setting, process, variations, and any handouts required (work sheets, for example). If there is no pertinent information for a particular section (if, for example, an activity requires no materials), the heading for that section has been omitted.

Each of the sections is described in detail in the following paragraphs.

Goals

In this section the leader will find the chief or primary goal of the activity and others that apply. A good goal is specific in that it states exactly what will occur; it is less specific in terms of the result of that occurrence, in order to permit inductive learning (learning through discovery). For example, if a goal is "to examine" or "to explore" the effects of a particular procedure, the activity will involve the dynamics of examining or exploring. What is learned, however, may differ from person to person or from team to team, depending on the team members' backgrounds and their unique experiences during the activity. A goal is performance oriented, to guide the team members toward what they are going to do; it involves the team members in the goal objective; it is observable, so that others can see the result; and, most important, it is realistic. For maximum effectiveness, a goal must be attainable.

When looking for an activity to use with a specific team and for a specific purpose, the leader may want to start by reviewing the goals of several activities. In this way the leader can become familiar with all of the goals served. For example, an activity appearing in the "Meetings" section because its primary goal has to do with meetings may have a secondary goal associated with increasing the level of trust within the team.

Time Required

The time listed for an activity includes adequate time not only for following the steps indicated but also for completing the Experiential Learning Cycle (see Figure 1). Experiential learning occurs when a person engages in some activity ("experiencing"), shares reactions to that activity with the other participants ("publishing"), examines that activity critically and "talks it through" with the other participants ("processing"), abstracts some useful insight that could be used outside the activity setting ("generalizing"), and puts that insight to work by determining how it could be used in actual situations ("applying").

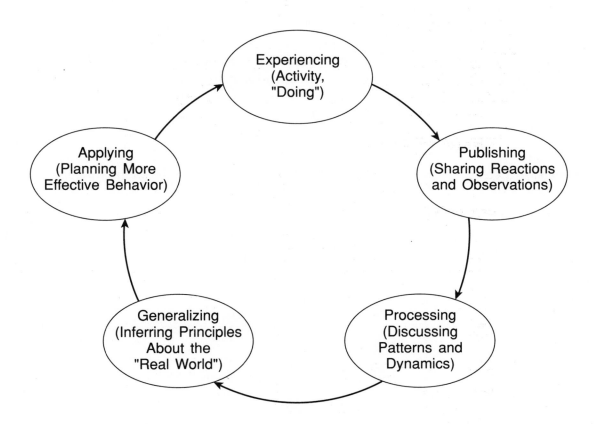

Figure 1. The Experiential Learning Cycle

Materials

This section specifies any handouts required and the quantities of each. Other materials (such as blank paper, pencils, newsprint flip charts, and felt-tipped markers) also are listed if the activity design requires them.

Physical Setting

This section deals with the team members' needs in connection with an activity. For example, the design may call for a room with a table and chairs for the team members; any room in which the team regularly meets; a room with plenty of wall space for posting newsprint; a room that allows the team members to move around in an unrestricted fashion; and so on. Occasionally an activity will note that writing surfaces should be provided; if this is the case, the leader either may distribute clipboards or other portable writing surfaces or may use tables or desks, whichever is preferable.

Process

In this section the step-by-step procedure is presented in terms of what the leader does and says and what the team members do in the appropriate sequence. These steps are presented in specific terms. Often the process includes a list of questions that the leader may want to ask in a concluding discussion.

Variations

This section presents adaptations that may vary the activity's content, sequence, time, materials, complexity of process, and so on. Of course, not all adaptations could be listed for any activity. In addition, if no variations are specified, the leader should not assume that none should be tried. If the leader wants to try a variation that is not listed in the activity design and that is considerably different from the original activity, he or she might want to discuss this possibility with an HRD professional before proceeding; the professional should be able to tell the leader what to expect in using the proposed variation.

Credit Line

A credit line appears at the end of each activity, immediately before any handouts that are included. The credit line designates the author or authors and *should be copied along with the design itself if the activity is reproduced for training purposes.* (Information about reproducing the activities is included on the copyright page in the front of the book.) The details about reproducing items from the Inventories and Forms section and from the Supplemental Materials section are specified at the bottom of the first page of each of those items.)

Handouts

All handouts required to conduct the activities are printed on separate pages included at the end of the activity format. They are presented in this manner so that they can be reproduced easily for distribution to team members in training events.

THE EFFECTIVE USE OF GROUP ACTIVITIES

Certain questions need to be contemplated by the person who will serve as the leader of an activity. Determining answers to these questions can help in the process of selecting designs that are both relevant and effective.

1. ***What are the goals of this team?*** Structured activities are designed for a variety of purposes, but their most effective use is within programs that are aimed at specific learning goals. The leader needs to keep these goals in mind at all times.

2. ***At what stage is the team in its development or what stage is it likely to reach?*** Different issues surface at various stages of group development, and some activities are particularly useful at some points in a team's life. For example, a feedback design may be inappropriate in the earliest stages but highly beneficial after the team has a brief history.

3. ***Why is it important that I intervene?*** It is important that the leader assess his or her own motives for intervening in the interaction among team members. Useful distinctions can be made between making things happen, letting things happen, and being a part of what is happening. One useful guideline is "When in doubt, wait." Another approach is to obtain an HRD professional's opinion about what should be done in a given situation.

4. ***Why does this particular intervention appeal to me?*** It may be that the activity seems appropriate because it would be enjoyable, but the overriding consideration should be the learning needs of the team members at a particular point in the team's development.

5. ***How ready are these team members to take risks, to experiment?*** Some activities may be threatening to some team members and therefore may evoke anxiety and defensiveness rather than the intended openness to learning. It is useful, however, ιo establish an experimentation norm; team members should be expected to "stretch" somewhat. Again, the opinion of an HRD professional may be helpful.

6. ***What modifications can I make for an effective, appealing design?*** Local issues and concerns (roles, goals, company policies, issues, cases, and so on) can be incorporated into activity materials and processes in order to heighten the possibility of the transfer of training. Such advance preparation can have a high payoff in developing work norms and avoiding "game playing." If the leader is in doubt about incorporating specific materials, an HRD professional and/or the organization's management should be consulted.

7. ***What advance preparations need to be made?*** Appropriate rooms, with the right kinds of furniture, should be scheduled. Other people outside the team may need to be notified. If any materials are needed, they must be duplicated

and/or assembled. Sometimes it is helpful to prearrange the furniture in a particular configuration.

8. *How rigid are the time constraints for the session?* It is important not to generate more data than can be adequately processed within the session. It is better not to use an activity than to leave too much data "hanging" at the end. One consideration is to anticipate which elements of the design can be speeded up or expanded, if necessary. (An HRD professional or others who have experience in leading activities can help in making this determination.)

9. *How am I going to set up the processing?* Since the processing of the data generated by the activity is more important than the experience itself, this planning phase should be carefully considered. A number of strategies can be used, such as process observers (who have been briefed and who are using observations, check lists, or guides); inventories that yield information, and subgrouping (when the team is large). Some of the data may be saved for use in future sessions.

10. *How am I going to evaluate the effectiveness of the design?* Because structured activities are best employed in an atmosphere directed toward specific goals, some assessment of the extent to which the goals of a given activity were met is necessary. Such a study may be based on the leader's and the team members' subjective impressions or on some objective criteria, but it needs to be planned beforehand. The leader needs to decide the basis for judging whether or not or to what degree the aims of a particular intervention were accomplished.

REFERENCES

Kormanski, C., & Mozenter, A. (1987). A new model of team building: A technology for today and tomorrow. In J.W. Pfeiffer (Ed.), *The 1987 annual: Developing human resources* (pp. 255-268). San Diego, CA: University Associates.

Pfeiffer, J.W. (Ed.). (1990). *The encyclopedia of team-development activities.* San Diego, CA: University Associates.

Pfeiffer, J.W., & Jones, J.E. (1974). Team-building: A feedback experience. In J.W. Pfeiffer & J.E. Jones (Eds.), *A handbook of structured experiences for human relations training* (Vol. III, rev. ed.) (pp. 73-77). San Diego, CA: University Associates.

Reilly, A.J., & Jones, J.E. (1974). Team-building. In J.W. Pfeiffer & J.E. Jones (Eds.), *The 1974 annual handbook for group facilitators* (pp. 227-237). San Diego, CA: University Associates.

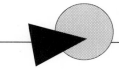

Introduction to
Team Effectiveness

The activities in the Team Effectiveness section help the team members to assess and work on improving their effectiveness in working together as a unit. Assessing a team's effectiveness consists of gathering information about how the team is presently functioning, analyzing that information, and pinpointing problem areas. Once the problems have been identified, they can be worked on.

One critical aspect of team effectiveness has to do with the team members' degree of skill and comfort in giving and receiving feedback. In order to build themselves into an effective team, the members must be able to discuss freely with one another how their team is functioning, how they interact, and what processes they use to fulfill their responsibilities. Consequently, the activities in this section concentrate on such topics as establishing a feedback process, encouraging feedback among team members, setting the stage for a team-building intervention, assessing leadership functions, task delegation, collaborating to identify issues that the team wants to work on, identifying and evaluating team-member skills, and setting team-development objectives.

USEFUL FEEDBACK: ESTABLISHING THE PROCESS

Goal

To help the team members to establish their own guidelines for giving and receiving personal feedback.

Time Required

One hour to one hour and fifteen minutes.

Materials

I. A copy of the Useful Feedback Characteristic Sheet for each team member.

II. A copy of the Useful Feedback Ranking Sheet for each team member.

III. A pencil for each team member.

IV. A newsprint flip chart and a felt-tipped marker.

V. Masking tape for posting newsprint.

Physical Setting

A room with a table and chairs for the team members. If a table is not available, the leader may substitute clipboards or other portable writing surfaces. Plenty of wall space should be available for posting newsprint.

Process

I. The leader distributes copies of the characteristic sheet, copies of the ranking sheet, and pencils. Each team member is instructed to read the characteristic sheet and then to complete the ranking sheet by choosing the five most significant characteristics from the characteristic sheet, listing these in order according to their importance, and writing statements explaining why the chosen characteristics are important. (Fifteen to twenty minutes.)

II. The leader asks the team members to take turns presenting their chosen characteristics and explaining briefly why each is important. As the team members share this information, the leader records it on newsprint and posts each newsprint sheet after it is filled. (Fifteen minutes.)

III. The leader reviews the posted information with the team members and assists them in achieving consensus[1] about which feedback characteristics they want to use as guidelines for their own team; which they would like to omit, if any; and the order of importance of the retained characteristics.

IV. When the team members have agreed about the guidelines for giving and receiving feedback in their team and the order of importance of these guidelines, the leader records the final, numbered guidelines on newsprint and writes these words at the top of the list: *For this team, good feedback is:....* Then the leader gives the newsprint list to a volunteer to reproduce and distribute to all team members. The leader also suggests posting a copy in the room where the team usually holds its meetings. (Ten minutes.)

V. Before adjourning, the leader elicits reactions to the activity and then makes appropriate concluding comments.

By Dave Francis and Don Young. Adapted from *Improving Work Groups: A Practical Manual for Team Building,* by D. Francis and D. Young, 1979, San Diego, CA: University Associates.

---

[1] A consensus decision is one that all team members can accept, regardless of how satisfied they are with it. Each member's opinion must be heard; no "majority-rule" voting, bargaining, or averaging is allowed.

❖ *Useful Feedback Characteristic Sheet*

Useful feedback is:

1. *Given with care.* To be useful, feedback requires the giver to feel concern for and to care for the person receiving the feedback—to want to help rather than hurt the recipient.

2. *Given with attention.* It is important for the giver to pay attention to what he or she is doing while giving feedback. This promotes a two-way exchange with some depth of communication.

3. *Invited by the recipient.* Feedback is most effective when the recipient has invited the comments. This provides a platform for openness and some guidelines; it also gives the recipient an opportunity to identify and explore particular areas of concern.

4. *Directly expressed.* Good feedback is specific and deals clearly with particular incidents and behavior. Dancing around the issue or making vague comments is of little value. The most useful help is direct, open, and concrete.

5. *Fully expressed.* Effective feedback requires more than a bald statement of facts. Feelings also need to be expressed so that the recipient can judge the full impact of his or her behavior.

6. *Uncluttered by evaluative judgments.* Feedback is most helpful when it does not consist of judgments or evaluations. If judgments must be included, the giver should first state clearly that these are matters of subjective evaluation, then describe the situation as he or she sees it, and finally let the recipient make the evaluation.

7. *Well timed.* The most useful feedback is given when the recipient is receptive to it and is sufficiently close to the particular event being discussed for it to be fresh in his or her mind. Storing comments over time can lead to a build-up of recriminations that reduces the effectiveness of the feedback when it is finally given.

8. *Readily actionable.* The most useful feedback centers around behavior that can be changed by the recipient. Feedback concerning matters outside the recipient's control is less useful. Often it is helpful to suggest alternative ways of behaving that allow the recipient to think about new ways of tackling old problems.

9. *Checked and clarified.* If possible, the recipient of the feedback should check with other people to determine whether the giver's perceptions are shared by others. Different viewpoints can be collected and assimilated, points of difference and similarity clarified, and a more objective picture developed.

❖ *Useful Feedback Ranking Sheet*

Characteristic	Why I Think It Is Important
1.	
2.	
3.	
4.	
5.	

SEVEN QUESTIONS: ENCOURAGING FEEDBACK

Goals

I. To encourage the team members to provide one another with feedback.

II. To assist the team members in clarifying their relationship patterns.

III. To help the team members to determine areas of strength and avenues for growth in their relationships with one another.

Time Required

Approximately one to one and one-half hours.

Materials

I. A copy of the Seven Questions Form for each team member.

II. A pencil for each team member.

III. A newsprint flip chart and a felt-tipped marker.

IV. Masking tape for posting newsprint.

Physical Setting

A room with plenty of wall space for posting newsprint.

Process

I. The leader introduces the activity by announcing its goals.

II. Each team member is given a copy of the Seven Questions Form and a pencil and is asked to complete the form. (Five minutes.)

III. The leader collects the completed forms. This procedure is followed for each of the seven questions:

1. The leader posts a sheet of newsprint on the wall and labels it according to the content of the question. (For example, the newsprint sheet for the first question may be labeled "Important Mission.")

2. The leader goes through the collected forms one at a time, recording on the newsprint the members' choices for the particular question being considered. In each case the leader writes the name of the person who completed

the form on the left, then draws an arrow from left to right, and writes the name of the choice just to the right of the arrow tip:

Chris ⟶ **Terry**

3. After all choices have been recorded, the leader asks these questions: (a) What does this information tell us? (b) How do you feel about this information?

Each question is covered in this manner before the leader proceeds to the next question. Each newsprint sheet remains posted throughout the activity. (Thirty minutes to one hour.)

IV. The team members are instructed to travel around the room, looking at the seven newsprint sheets and determining the patterns that emerge for themselves and others. (Ten minutes.)

V. The leader leads a concluding discussion by asking questions such as these:

1. What patterns did you see?
2. As a result of completing this activity, what can you identify as our team's strengths? What might be some avenues of growth for the team?
3. How do you feel about the team at this moment?
4. What can you personally do to improve relationships in this team?

Variation

The leader may continue the activity by asking the team members to choose partners for the purpose of contracting to experiment with new behaviors and associations.

By Cyril R. Mill. Adapted from *Activities for Trainers: 50 Useful Designs,* by C.R. Mill, 1980, San Diego, CA: University Associates.

❖ *Seven Questions Form*

Your Name_____

Instructions: Read each of the following seven questions, determine which team member you would choose, and write that person's name in the blank to the right. You may choose any team member for more than one item.

Which team member would you choose...

1. To send on an important mission?   _____

2. To discuss a new idea with?   _____

3. As a companion for recreation?   _____

4. To ask for help if you were in serious trouble?   _____

5. To be marooned with on a tropical island?   _____

6. To escort your spouse/significant other
   across the country?   _____

7. For a boss?   _____

GETTING STARTED: SETTING THE STAGE FOR TEAM BUILDING

Goals

I. To assist the team members in creating an agenda for a team-building session and in rank ordering the items on that agenda.

II. To generate ownership of and commitment to commonly perceived problems that face the team.

III. To develop the team members' listening skills.

Time Required

Approximately one hour.

Materials

I. Blank paper and a pencil for each team member.

II. A newsprint flip chart and a felt-tipped marker.

III. Masking tape for posting newsprint.

Physical Setting

A room large enough so that pairs of team members can meet privately without disturbing one another. Writing surfaces and movable chairs should be provided.

Process

I. The leader discusses the goals of the activity and gives a brief overview of the design.

II. The team members are given paper and pencils and are instructed to form pairs. The leader stipulates that each team member should select a person with whom he or she has not talked recently.

III. When the pairs have assembled in separate places in the room, the leader tells the partners to take turns interviewing each other on the topic "What problem situations should we work on in our upcoming team-building session?" The leader states that each interview should last five minutes and that the interviewer should make notes on the content of the interview. Then the team members are told to begin.

IV. After the interviewing phase has been completed, the team is reassembled in a circle. The members take turns reporting what their partners said, and the leader lists on newsprint each member's suggested problem situations (in the member's own words.) Each member whose comments appear on newsprint then adds anything that the interviewer left out and/or corrects any misperceptions. During this phase, the team members are told that they may respond only by asking questions for clarification.

V. The lists of problem situations are posted, and the items are numbered. Duplicates are combined or are given the same number.

VI. The leader instructs each team member to select, by number, the three problem situations that he or she believes are most important. Then the leader tallies on the newsprint the number of members who have indicated each of the items.

VII. The leader posts a new list of the items with the highest frequencies in the tally.

VIII. Each team member is instructed to rank order these problem situations independently, in terms of which are most important. The rank of 1 is to be assigned to the item that the member believes *must* be discussed if the team-building session is to be successful. The second-most pressing situation is to be ranked 2, and so on.

IX. The leader tallies the ranks assigned to the items by asking how many members ranked each item as 1, 2, 3, and so on. (If there are more than six or seven items, the tally may be based on a ranking of high, medium, or low.)

X. The leader posts the final agenda on newsprint and then leads a discussion of reactions to the agenda-setting process.

Variation

If the team-building session is to be held immediately after this activity, the interview time may be varied as necessary. If the agenda-setting time is limited, the interviewers may ask for the one problem situation that needs to be faced by the team.

By John E. Jones. Adapted from *A Handbook of Structured Experiences for Human Relations Training* (Vol. V), edited by J.W. Pfeiffer and J.E. Jones, 1975, San Diego, CA: University Associates.

LEADERSHIP FUNCTIONS: AN ASSESSMENT ACTIVITY

Goals

I. To help the team members to understand how leadership functions are currently carried out in the team.

II. To assist the team members in determining the best ways of carrying out leadership functions in the future.

III. To provide the team members with a means for giving and receiving feedback on their leadership behaviors.

Time Required

Approximately two hours.

Materials

I. A copy of the Leadership Functions Check Sheet for each team member. *Important note:* A few days before conducting the activity, the leader distributes copies of the Leadership Functions Check Sheet with a cover note asking whether the team members have reservations about participating in an activity based on this handout. The leader proceeds with plans to conduct the activity only if all team members express willingness to participate. Once voluntary participation has been affirmed, the team session is scheduled.

II. A pencil for each team member.

III. A newsprint flip chart and a felt-tipped marker.

IV. Masking tape for posting newsprint.

Physical Setting

Any room in which the team regularly meets.

Process

I. At the beginning of the team session, the members are instructed to complete the check sheet. (Five to ten minutes.)

II. The team members take turns sharing their individual responses from the check sheet. As the team members respond, the leader charts each item separately on newsprint and tallies the individual responses.

III. The leader leads a discussion of each item, concentrating on areas that seem to require some change in methods of work or behavior. Highlights are recorded on newsprint. (Thirty minutes.)

IV. The leader makes a newsprint list of all items suggested for change and posts this list prominently. Then the leader helps the team members to achieve consensus[1] on which items must be changed, who will be responsible for the leadership behaviors represented in the items to be changed, and what the team members will do to help those who take on these new responsibilities. All agreed-on information is recorded on newsprint. (One hour.)

V. Arrangements are made for a follow-up meeting to discuss progress on the changes. The leader asks for a volunteer to devise a handout from the newsprint generated during the previous step and to distribute this handout to all team members.

VI. The leader concludes the activity by leading a discussion based on questions such as these:
   1. What have you learned about yourself as a member of this team?
   2. What have you learned about your fellow team members?
   3. What have you learned about team leadership?
   4. How do you feel about the way we worked together during this session?
   5. How do you feel about the decisions we made?

Variations

I. The team members may be asked to complete their check sheets prior to attending the session.

II. If any team member has reservations about openly sharing his or her check-sheet responses, the team members may submit their sheets anonymously.

III. The activity may be repeated periodically as the team develops maturity and flexibility of operation.

By Dave Francis and Don Young. Adapted from *Improving Work Groups: A Practical Manual for Team Building,* by D. Francis and D. Young, 1979, San Diego, CA: University Associates.

---

[1] A consensus decision is one that all team members can accept, regardless of how satisfied they are with it. Each member's opinion must be heard; no "majority-rule" voting, bargaining, or averaging is allowed.

❖ Leadership Functions Check Sheet

Instructions: The following items represent the kinds of leadership behavior that are important to a team's functioning. Read each item carefully and make a check mark (✔) under the phrase that most accurately describes whoever performs that function in your team. If you select "Team Member(s)," make a check mark and then write the name(s) of the member(s).

	No One	Formal Leader	Team Member(s) (Write Names)
1. Who usually brings together individual contributions?			
2. Who ensures that the team makes decisions?			
3. Who begins our meetings or starts our work?			
4. Who keeps a check on whether objectives are set?			
5. Who ensures that we follow an effective method of working together?			
6. Who puts energy into the team to start us off or help us when we seem stuck?			
7. Who lets us know if our procedures are not working?			
8. Who finds and brings in external information to help our work stay relevant?			
9. Who represents us as a team with other groups or teams?			

	No One	Formal Leader	Team Member(s) (Write Names)

10. Who summarizes and clarifies after our discussions?

11. Who encourages contributions from team members?

12. Who supports other members in difficult situations?

TASK DELEGATION: A TEAM APPROACH

Goals

I. To provide the team leader and the team members with an opportunity to negotiate the delegation of tasks within the team.

II. To increase the leader's and the members' awareness of attitudes about task delegation.

III. To offer the team leader an opportunity to receive feedback from the team members about his or her delegation skills.

Time Required

A minimum of two hours and fifteen minutes; a maximum of four and one-half hours. If the team has more than eight members, the leader may want to conduct the activity in two sessions.

Materials

I. Each member's three task lists, assigned as prework and copied onto sheets of newsprint prior to the activity:

1. The specific tasks that the leader presently delegates to the team member;
2. The specific tasks that the team member does not presently perform but would like to be responsible for; and
3. The specific tasks that the team member presently has but would not mind giving up.

II. The leader's three task lists, prepared and copied onto sheets of newsprint prior to the activity:

1. The specific tasks that the leader presently delegates;
2. The specific tasks that the leader presently delegates but would not mind performing himself or herself; and
3. The specific tasks that the leader does not presently delegate but would like to.

III. Several sheets of blank paper and a pencil for each team member, including the leader.

IV. A clipboard or other portable writing surface for each team member, including the leader.

V. A newsprint flip chart and several felt-tipped markers.

VI. Masking tape for posting newsprint.

Physical Setting

A room with movable chairs for the team members. Plenty of wall space should be available for posting newsprint.

Process

I. After introducing the goals of the activity, the leader assists the team members in devising two lists: one for situations in which delegation is advisable and one for situations in which it is not. During this procedure the leader explains his or her personal views about delegation and encourages all team members to express theirs. The leader stresses the importance of reaching consensus[1] on the situations to be included in the lists. As final decisions are made about situations, the leader records the two lists on newsprint and posts these lists. (Thirty minutes.)

II. All team members, including the leader, post the newsprint lists that they prepared in advance.

III. The team members are given blank paper, pencils, and clipboards or other portable writing surfaces and are asked to spend twenty minutes perusing all lists, testing them against the lists devised in Step I and making notes about pertinent ideas or about any clarification needed. The leader also views the lists and makes notes. (Twenty to thirty minutes.)

IV. After all team members have completed their reviews, the leader leads a discussion of the contents of the lists, focusing on one team member at a time. At the beginning of the discussion, the leader encourages creative thinking and reminds the team members to consider each member's individual wants as well as the team's needs. During the discussion the leader encourages the team members to ask for clarification where needed, to contribute ideas, to consider the lists of advisable and inadvisable delegation situations, and to trade or negotiate task responsibilities where appropriate. All changes in task responsibility that are agreed to are recorded on the appropriate newsprint lists; each team member is responsible for recording changes to his or her lists. (One to three hours.)

V. The leader leads a concluding discussion by asking questions like these:

---

[1] A consensus decision is one that all team members can accept, regardless of how satisfied they are with it. Each member's opinion must be heard; no "majority-rule" voting, bargaining, or averaging is allowed.

1. How comfortable are you with the tasks that have been delegated to you?
2. How did you feel about trading and negotiating task responsibilities?
3. What have you learned about delegation?
4. What have you learned about the various attitudes toward delegation that are represented in this team?
5. How can you use what you have learned in the future?
6. When you consider my delegation habits, what would you like me to keep doing? What would you like me to do differently that would be helpful to you and/or the rest of the team?

By T.F. Carney. Adapted from *A Handbook of Structured Experiences for Human Relations Training* (Vol. VIII), edited by J.W. Pfeiffer and J.E. Jones, 1981, San Diego, CA: University Associates.

PROJECT SELECTION: COLLABORATING TO IDENTIFY PROBLEMS

Goals

I. To introduce a process that a team can use to identify and select work-related problems as projects.

II. To allow the team members to practice behaviors that are associated with effective teamwork: participating collaboratively, listening to other team members, and withholding judgment while considering issues that are before the team.

Time Required

Approximately one and one-half hours.

Materials

I. A copy of the Project Selection Work Sheet for each team member.

II. A copy of the Project Selection Procedure Sheet for each team member.

III. A pencil for each team member.

IV. A newsprint flip chart and a felt-tipped marker.

Physical Setting

A room with a chair and a writing surface for each team member.

Process

I. The leader introduces the activity as offering a process whereby the team members can identify and select work-related problems as projects.

II. Each team member is given a copy of the Project Selection Work Sheet and a pencil and is instructed to complete the sheet. (Ten minutes.)

III. The team members are instructed to share their work sheets with one another and to select the one problem of those listed that they would most like to solve as a team project. As they work on this step, the leader records highlights on newsprint. (Fifteen minutes.)

IV. The leader distributes copies of the Project Selection Procedure Sheet and asks the team members to read this sheet. (Five minutes.)

V. The leader briefly discusses the content of the procedure sheet and elicits and answers any questions that the team members may have. The team members are told that although it will not be possible within the course of the activity to complete the entire problem-solving procedure, the remaining time will be spent on the first two steps described in the handout. (Ten minutes.)

VI. The team is instructed to repeat the process of selecting one work-related problem as a project, but this time the members are to take a different approach and follow Step 1[1] and Step 2 of the procedure described in the handout. The leader emphasizes that the members should practice the behaviors cited in the procedure sheet: collaborative participation, careful and thoughtful listening, and withholding judgment until it is time to make a final decision. (Twenty minutes.)

VII. After the team has chosen a problem as a project, the leader processes the activity by asking questions such as these:

1. What were the differences in the two procedures used to complete the task?
2. Which of these two procedures proved to be more satisfying to you?
3. Did the second procedure change the chosen problem? If so, how?
4. What appear to be the advantages of the process described in the procedure sheet? What are the disadvantages?
5. What additional behaviors besides those listed in the procedure sheet might be useful to our team as it addresses work-related problems?
6. In your experience, how and by whom are work-related problems usually solved? What is your general level of satisfaction with the outcome? What steps could you personally take to increase your level of satisfaction with the team's problem-solving process and the outcomes of that process?

Variations

I. During Step IV the leader may lead a discussion by eliciting the team members' feelings about and satisfaction with the first procedure chosen to complete the task.

II. The activity may be continued by asking the team to complete additional steps of the problem-solving process described in the procedure sheet.

By Michael J. Miller. Adapted from *The 1984 Annual: Developing Human Resources*, edited by J.W. Pfeiffer and L.D. Goodstein, 1984, San Diego, CA: University Associates.

---

[1] See also the activity entitled "Brainstorming: A Problem-Solving Technique."

❖ *Project Selection Work Sheet*

Instructions: In the spaces provided below, list the *work-related problems* that are currently plaguing your team. Think of a problem as a situation or condition for which you can identify a difference between how things are and how you would like them to be. Be *as specific as possible* in stating each problem.

1.

2.

3.

4.

5.

❖ *Project Selection Procedure Sheet*[2]

Many teams hold meetings for the particular purpose of identifying, analyzing, and solving problems related to their work and work area. They develop recommendations for solving these problems, present their recommendations to management (if necessary), implement solutions, and then evaluate the impact of the implemented solutions.

In order to function effectively, the members of such a work team must develop certain behaviors that allow them to complete the problem-solving procedure. These behaviors include not only participating collaboratively in the team's problem-solving efforts, but also listening carefully to fellow members and withholding judgment about various ideas and suggestions until it is time to select a final solution.

The problem-solving procedure that calls for the use of these behaviors includes the following steps:

1. *Identifying problems*. To identify work-related problems, the team members use a technique called brainstorming in which they take turns making contributions of problems that might make worthwhile projects. When used effectively, brainstorming works in the following way:

- As ideas are contributed, they are listed on newsprint or a chalkboard.
- Each member offers only one idea per turn. If a member does not have a contribution to make on any particular turn, he or she simply says "pass."
- No opinions about ideas, either positive or negative, may be stated. The withholding of judgment at this point is important so that creativity is not stifled.
- The process continues until all contributions have been exhausted.

2. *Selecting a problem*. A team works on solving only one problem at a time. The members discuss all problems identified in Step 1 and then choose one. The process used to arrive at this choice is governed by the following principles:

- No voting, bargaining, or lobbying is permissible.
- Each member must be offered an opportunity to express his or her opinion and the reasons for holding this opinion.
- No member may say that the opinions of another member are "wrong."
- All members must care about the problem that is finally chosen; they must be willing to commit themselves to its resolution.

The members must be able to do something about the chosen problem. Problems that the team cannot possibly solve either on its own or with help provided by management constitute inappropriate projects.

---

[2] Adapted from *How to Train and Lead a Quality Circle* by R.G. James and A.J. Elkins, 1983, San Diego, CA: University Associates, and from *Installing Quality Circles: A Strategic Approach* by L. Fitzgerald and J. Murphy, 1982, San Diego, CA: University Associates.

3. ***Analyzing the problem.*** After a problem has been selected, it must be defined in writing in precise, detailed terms. Defining includes specifying why the situation or condition is a problem; where and when the problem exists; and the impact of the problem on productivity, morale, and so forth. Another task to be completed is determining the causes of the problem, which may necessitate obtaining data from experts.

4. ***Generating and evaluating possible solutions.*** During this step the team members think as creatively as possible to come up with a wide range of alternative solutions. Brainstorming is the technique that is generally used for this process. Subsequently, the benefits, costs, and possible ramifications of each alternative are considered.

5. ***Selecting a solution.*** After each alternative has been analyzed, the team members choose the one that seems most appropriate.

6. ***Implementing the solution.*** A detailed plan to guide the implementation is essential. When developing this plan, the team members outline what should be done, when the work should begin, and who should do it. They also consider potential problems and ways to deal with these problems. Finally, they develop a plan for evaluating the solution by determining what they will accept as evidence that the solution has worked, how they will collect this evidence, who will collect it, and when it will be collected.

THE TEAM AUDIT:
IDENTIFYING AND EVALUATING SKILLS

Goals

I. To help the team members to identify the social and technical skills required by the team.

II. To help the team members to evaluate their present skills.

III. To help the team members to select the skill areas most in need of development.

Time Required

Approximately three hours.

Materials

I. A copy of The Team Audit Evaluation Sheet for each team member.

II. A copy of The Team Audit Rank-Order Sheet for each team member.

III. A pencil for each team member.

IV. A newsprint flip chart and a felt-tipped marker.

V. Masking tape for posting newsprint.

Physical Setting

A room with a chair and a writing surface for each team member. Each member should be seated so that he or she can see the other team members as well as the leader and the newsprint flip chart.

Process

Important note: Because this activity may highlight some issues that are sensitive to the whole team or to individual team members, all of the team members must voluntarily agree to participate prior to the activity.

I. The leader introduces the activity by explaining its goals.

II. Each team member is given a copy of The Team Audit Evaluation Sheet and a pencil and is asked to read this handout. (Five minutes.)

III. The leader discusses the instructions on the evaluation sheet with the team members, eliciting and answering questions as necessary. (Five minutes.)

IV. The leader asks each team member to work independently to complete the evaluation sheet. While the team members are working on this task, the leader prepares a copy of the evaluation sheet on newsprint and posts it. (Fifteen minutes.)

V. After all team members have completed the task, the leader asks them to take turns reading their scores for the skills that are printed on the evaluation sheet. The leader totals the individual scores for each skill and enters the average individual score for each skill on the newsprint copy. (Ten minutes.)

VI. The leader asks the team members to take turns reading the skills they added to the list and records these on newsprint. The leader helps the team to reach consensus on which of these skills should be added to the list. (Fifteen minutes.)

VII. The leader asks each member to write down a personal score for each of the agreed-on additional skills and to take turns reading the scores. The leader records the average scores on newsprint. (Five minutes.)

VIII. The leader discusses with the team members any significant differences between their individual scores and the average scores and helps them to reach a consensus on the score for each skill. The leader lists the consensus scores in the "Team Score" column of the newsprint evaluation sheet and instructs the team members to write these scores in the "Team Score" column of their own evaluation sheets. (Thirty minutes.)

IX. Each team member is given a copy of The Team Audit Rank-Order Sheet and is asked to read the instructions. While the team is reading, the leader rank orders the top fifteen skills (as determined by the consensus scores) on the newsprint evaluation sheet.

X. The leader discusses the instructions with the team members, eliciting and answering questions as necessary, and then asks them to work independently on the task. While the team is working, the leader makes a copy of The Team Audit Rank-Order Sheet on newsprint and posts it. (Fifteen minutes.)

XI. When all team members have completed the task, the leader uses the same procedure as before to obtain average ratings and to record them on the newsprint rank-order sheet. (Ten minutes.)

XII. The leader discusses with the team members any significant differences between their individual ratings and the average ratings and helps them to reach a consensus on the rating for each skill. The leader lists the consensus ratings in the "Team Rating" column of the newsprint rank-order sheet and instructs the team members to write these ratings in the "Team Rating" column of their own evaluation sheets. (Thirty minutes.)

XIII. The leader discusses with the team members the five skills with the highest group ratings to arrive at an action plan for developing or improving the skills. The leader lists the action steps on newsprint, along with names of team members responsible for the actions and deadline dates. This newsprint sheet is given to one member of the team for reproduction and distribution to the other members for follow-up.

Variations

I. The team members may consider only the skills printed on The Team Audit Evaluation Sheet.

II. The team members may agree in advance on the skills to be added to those printed on The Team Audit Evaluation Sheet.

III. The team members may create their own list of skills for The Team Audit Evaluation Sheet.

IV. On The Team Audit Evaluation Sheet, the "Personal Score" column may be used for a self-rating; the "Team Score" column, for a rating of the team as a whole.

By Dave Francis and Don Young. Adapted from *Improving Work Groups: A Practical Manual for Team Building,* by D. Francis and D. Young, 1979, San Diego, CA: University Associates.

❖ *The Team Audit Evaluation Sheet*

Instructions: Evaluate the following skills in relation to the needs of your team. Using the key shown below, assign a priority number to each skill and write the number in the "Personal Score" column. If your team needs skills that are missing, add these to the list (next page) and assign a priority number to each of them.

KEY

3 = Vital to the success of the team

2 = Important to the success of the team

1 = Useful to the success of the team

0 = Irrelevant to the success of the team

Type of Skill	Personal Score	Team Score
1. Skillful and positive leadership		
2. Clear identification of objectives		
3. Creative and innovative ideas		
4. Realistic planning		
5. Ability to accomplish things		
6. Good conceptual and theoretical ability		
7. Effective troubleshooting		
8. Persuasive communication		
9. Imaginative design skills		
10. Technical expertise		
11. Financial expertise		
12. Production expertise		
13. Personnel expertise		
14. Marketing expertise		
15. Editorial expertise		
16. Problem-solving abilities		
17. Diplomacy		
18. Human relations skills		

KEY

3 = Vital to the success of the team

2 = Important to the success of the team

1 = Useful to the success of the team

0 = Irrelevant to the success of the team

Type of Skill	Personal Score	Team Score
19.		
20.		
21.		
22.		
23.		
24.		
25.		

❖ The Team Audit Rank-Order Sheet

Instructions: After the top fifteen skills on The Team Audit Evaluation Sheet have been rank ordered, copy them in rank order in the spaces provided below. Evaluate each skill in relation to the needs of your team. Using the key provided, assign a number to each skill and write that number in the "Personal Rating" column.

KEY

1 = The team has adequate skills in this area.

2 = There is a need to improve skills in this area.

3 = The team has little or no skill in this area and needs to develop some.

Top 15 Skills	Personal Rating	Team Rating
1.		
2.		
3.		
4.		
5.		
6.		
7.		
8.		
9.		
10.		

KEY

1 = The team has adequate skills in this area.

2 = There is a need to improve skills in this area.

3 = The team has little or no skill in this area and needs to develop some.

Top 15 Skills	Personal Rating	Team Rating
11.		
12.		
13.		
14.		
15.		

TEAM-DEVELOPMENT NEEDS: SETTING OBJECTIVES

Goals

I. To help the team members to clarify their team-development needs.

II. To assist the team members in determining criteria for judging the success of the team's development.

III. To offer the team members an opportunity to set objectives for team-development progress.

IV. To assist the team members in creating an action plan for a team-development program.

Time Required

Two hours and fifteen to thirty minutes.

Materials

I. A copy of the Team-Development Needs Questionnaire for each team member.

II. A copy of the Team-Development Needs Answer Sheet for each team member.

III. A copy of the Team-Development Needs Interpretation Sheet for each team member.

IV. Several sheets of blank paper and a pencil for each team member.

V. A newsprint flip chart and a felt-tipped marker.

VI. Masking tape for posting newsprint.

Physical Setting

A room with chairs and writing surfaces for the team members.

Process

I. The leader introduces the activity by explaining the goals.

II. Each team member is given a copy of the Team-Development Needs Questionnaire, a copy of the Team-Development Needs Answer Sheet, and a pencil. The leader asks the team members to read the instructions on the questionnaire. (Five minutes.)

III. The leader discusses the instructions, eliciting and answering questions, and asks the team members to work independently on the task. (Twenty to thirty minutes.)

IV. After all team members have completed the answer sheet, the leader distributes the Team-Development Needs Interpretation Sheet and asks each team member to transfer his or her totals from the answer sheet to the appropriate boxes in the "My Score" column on the interpretation sheet. (Five minutes.)

V. The leader asks each team member to circle the three categories on his or her interpretation sheet that received the highest scores.

VI. The leader asks the team members to take turns announcing their three highest-scored categories and records these categories on newsprint, using tick marks to denote how many times each category is announced. The leader then computes the average score for each category and instructs the members to record the averages in the appropriate boxes in the "Team Average" column on their interpretation sheets. (Five minutes.)

VII. The leader leads a discussion based on questions such as these:

1. To what extent do the results of the survey accurately mirror our team's position?
2. To what extent do we want to develop our team in the identified areas?

The leader helps the team members to reach consensus[1] on which three categories represent the team's most important needs; the members write the numbers 1, 2, and 3, respectively, in the appropriate boxes in the "Team's Three Priorities" column on their interpretation sheets. (Thirty minutes.)

VIII. The leader leads a discussion of the team's top three priorities based on questions such as these:

1. How will we know when our needs have been met?
2. What will success look like?
3. How can we set measurable criteria for success?

The leader helps the team members to reach consensus on criteria for judging degrees of success and records these criteria on newsprint. The newsprint is given to one member of the team for reproduction and distribution to the other members. (Twenty minutes.)

IX. Each team member is given several sheets of blank paper and is asked to write two or three objectives for each of the team's top three priorities. (Ten minutes.)

X. The leader asks the team members to take turns sharing their objectives and helps them to reach consensus as they select objectives for the team. The

---

[1] A consensus decision is one that all team members can accept, regardless of how satisfied they are with it. Each member's opinion must be heard; no "majority-rule" voting, bargaining, or averaging is allowed.

leader records the objectives on newsprint and gives them to a member of the team for reproduction and distribution to the other members. (Fifteen minutes.)

XI. The leader leads a discussion based on questions such as these:

1. What are the first steps to reaching our objectives? Where do we go from there?
2. How do we determine who is responsible for each element of our action plan?
3. What is the general time frame for our objectives?

The leader records on newsprint any action steps identified, the names of the team members responsible for the actions, and the deadline dates. The leader reviews the action steps with the team to determine if the action plan is complete. The newsprint is given to one member of the team for reproduction and distribution to the other members.

Variation

The Team-Development Needs Questionnaire and the Team-Development Answer Sheet may be completed prior to the activity.

By Dave Francis and Don Young. Adapted from *Improving Work Groups: A Practical Manual for Team Building,* by D. Francis and D. Young, 1979, San Diego, CA: University Associates.

❖ Team-Development Needs Questionnaire

Instructions: As you read each of the statements in this questionnaire, consider whether or not it is descriptive of your work team. If you believe that a statement is basically true, look at the answer sheet, find the box that contains that statement number, and mark an X through that box. If you believe that the statement is not generally true for your work team, leave the corresponding box blank on the answer sheet.

Work methodically through the statements, answering each one as you reach it. If you have great difficulty deciding whether or not a particular statement is true, use your best judgment and then write a question mark by the statement and in the corresponding box on the answer sheet; you may want to discuss these statements later with your team.

This questionnaire is not a scientific survey; it is meant to serve as a tool to provoke thought and discussion. Therefore, the quality of the result is directly related to your openness when responding to the following statements.

1. The leader and members of our team spend little time in clarifying what they expect and need from one another.

2. The work of our team would improve if the members upgraded their technical qualifications.

3. Most members feel that the aims of our team are hardly worthwhile.

4. People in our team often are not really frank and open with one another.

5. The objectives of our team are not really clear.

6. Members of our team are unsure about the team's contribution to the wider organization.

7. We rarely achieve much progress in team meetings.

8. The objectives of some individual team members do not correlate with those of other members.

9. When team members are criticized, they often feel that they have lost face.

10. New members often are just left to find their own place in our team.

11. Not many new ideas are generated by our team.

12. Conflicts between our team and other groups are quite common.

13. Our team leader rarely tolerates leadership efforts by other team members.

14. Some members of our team are unable to handle the current requirements of their work.

15. The team members are not really committed to the success of our team.

16. In team discussion the members often hide their real motives.

17. Our team rarely achieves its objectives.

18. Our team's contribution is not clearly understood by other parts of the organization.

19. When our team is having a meeting, the members do not listen to one another.

20. The team members are uncertain about their individual roles in relation to our team.

21. Members of our team often restrain their critical remarks to avoid "rocking the boat."

22. The potential of some team members is not being developed.

23. Members of our team are wary about suggesting new ideas.

24. Our team does not have constructive relationships with some of the other teams within the organization.

25. Members of our team are uncertain of where they stand with our team leader.

26. Our mix of skills is inappropriate to the work we are doing.

27. I do not feel a strong sense of belonging to our team.

28. It would be helpful if our team could have sessions to "clear the air" more often.

29. In practice the members of our team accept low levels of achievement.

30. If our team were disbanded, the organization would not feel the loss.

31. Our team meetings often seem to lack a methodical approach.

32. There is no regular review of individual objectives and priorities.

33. Our team is not good at learning from its mistakes.

34. Members of our team tend not to show initiative in keeping up to date or in developing themselves.

35. We have the reputation of being "sticks in the mud."

36. Our team does not respond sufficiently to the needs of other teams in the organization.

37. Our team leader gets little information about how the members of the team view his or her performance.

38. People outside our team regard us as unqualified to meet the requirements of our jobs.

39. I am not prepared to put myself out for our team.

40. Important issues are often "swept under the carpet" and not worked through.

41. Individuals are given few incentives to stretch themselves.

42. There is confusion between the work of our team and the work of others.

43. Our team members rarely plan or prepare for meetings.

44. If some of our team members are missing, their work just does not get done.

45. Attempts to review events critically are seen by our team as negative and harmful.

46. Our team spends little time and effort on individual development and training.

47. Our team seldom innovates anything.

48. We do not actively seek to develop our working relationships with other teams.

49. Our team would reach better-quality decisions if the team members took the initiative.

50. Our team's total level of ability is too low.

51. Some team members find it difficult to commit themselves to doing their jobs well.

52. In our team there is too much emphasis placed on conformity.

53. In our team energy is absorbed in unproductive ways and does not go into getting results.

54. The role of our team is not clearly identified within the organization.

55. Our team does not set aside time to consider and review how it tackles problems.

56. Much improvement is needed in communication among the members of our team.

57. Our team would benefit from an impartial assessment of how the members work.

58. Most of our team members have been trained only in their technical disciplines.

59. Good ideas seem to get lost.

60. Some significant mistakes would have been avoided if we had better communication with other teams.

61. Our team leader often makes decisions without talking them through with the team.

62. We need an input of new knowledge and skills to make our team complete.

63. I wish I could feel more motivated by working in our team.

64. Differences between team members are rarely worked through properly.

65. No time is devoted to questioning whether our efforts have been worthwhile.

66. We do not have an adequate way to establish our team's objectives and strategy.

67. We often seem to get bogged down when a difficult problem is being discussed in team meetings.

68. Our team does not have adequate administrative resources and procedures.

69. We lack the skills to review our effectiveness constructively.

70. Our team does not take steps to develop its members.

71. New ideas from outside our team are seldom accepted.

72. In this organization teams and departments tend to compete rather than collaborate.

73. Our team leader does not adapt his or her style to changing circumstances.

74. New people coming into our team sometimes lack the necessary qualifications.

75. No one is trying hard to make ours a winning team.

76. Individuals in our team do not really get to know one another as people.

77. Our team seems more concerned about giving a good appearance than achieving results.

78. The organization does not use the vision and skills that our team has to offer.

79. We have team meetings but do not properly examine their purpose.

80. We function in a rather rigid manner and are not sufficiently flexible in using team resources.

81. Our team's performance would improve if constructive criticism were encouraged.

82. Members of our team who are shy or uncertain are often overridden.

83. It would be fair to say that our team has little vision.

84. Some of the other teams/departments seem to have a low opinion of us.

85. Our team leader is not sufficiently sensitive to the different needs of each team member.

86. Some team members are not adapting to the needs of the team, despite efforts to help them.

87. If a team member gets into difficulties, he or she usually is left to cope with them alone.

88. There are cliques and political maneuvering in our team.

89. Nothing that we do could be described as excellent.

90. Our team's objectives have not been systematically related to the objectives of the whole organization.

91. Decisions made at meetings are not properly recorded or activated.

92. Team members could collaborate much more if they examined the possibilities of doing so on a person-by-person basis.

93. Little time is spent on reviewing what our team does, how it works, and how to improve the team.

94. Anyone who questions established practices in our team will be quickly put in his or her place.

95. Only a few team members suggest new ideas.

96. We do not get to know the people working in other teams in the organization.

97. I do not know whether our team is adequately represented at higher levels.

98. Some of our team members need considerable development to do their work effectively.

99. Team members are committed to individual goals at the expense of our team.

100. Disagreements between members of our team are seldom worked through thoroughly, and individual viewpoints are not fully heard.

101. Our team often fails to finish things satisfactorily.

102. We do not work within clear strategic guidelines.

103. Our team meetings do not properly resolve all the issues that should be dealt with.

104. We do not examine how our team spends its time and energy.

105. We make resolutions, but basically we do not learn from our mistakes.

106. Individuals are not encouraged to go outside the team to widen their personal knowledge and skills.

107. Our team members often do not follow creative ideas through to definite action.

108. If we worked better with other teams, it would help us all to be more effective.

❖ Team-Development Needs Answer Sheet

Instructions: After you have responded to all statements according to the instructions on the questionnaire, count the number of X's in each vertical column and write the totals in the appropriate boxes in the "Totals" row. The total for each vertical column (A through L) should be some number between zero and nine.

	1	2	3	4	5	6	7	8	9	10	11	12
	13	14	15	16	17	18	19	20	21	22	23	24
	25	26	27	28	29	30	31	32	33	34	35	36
	37	38	39	40	41	42	43	44	45	46	47	48
	49	50	51	52	53	54	55	56	57	58	59	60
	61	62	63	64	65	66	67	68	69	70	71	72
	73	74	75	76	77	78	79	80	81	82	83	84
	85	86	87	88	89	90	91	92	93	94	95	96
	97	98	99	100	101	102	103	104	105	106	107	108
Totals												
	A	B	C	D	E	F	G	H	I	J	K	L

❖ *Team-Development Needs Interpretation Sheet*

Instructions: When you have totaled all X's in the twelve vertical columns on the answer sheet (labeled with letters "A" through "L"), transfer each total to the "My Score" column of the following grid, next to the appropriate letter of the alphabet. Each of the lettered columns on the answer sheet represents nine questionnaire statements, all of which concern a particular team problem. For example, questionnaire statements 1, 13, 25, 37, 49, 61, 73, 85, and 97, which form the vertical column labeled "A" on the answer sheet, all have to do with *inappropriate leadership*. Similarly, questionnaire statements 2, 14, 26, 38, 50, 62, 74, 86, and 98, which form the vertical column labeled "B" on the answer sheet, all have to do with *unqualified membership*.

Letter	My Score	Team Average	Team's Three Priorities	Category
A				Inappropriate Leadership
B				Unqualified Membership
C				Insufficient Team Commitment
D				Nonconstructive Climate
E				Low Achievement Orientation
F				Undeveloped Corporate Role
G				Ineffective Work Methods
H				Inadequate Team Organization
I				Soft Critiquing[1]
J				Stunted Individual Development
K				Lack of Creative Capacity
L				Negative Intergroup Relations

[1]Members are unable/unwilling to effectively identify, discuss, and resolve team and individual errors; therefore, the team cannot learn from its mistakes.

Introduction to
Values/Mission

The activities in the Values/Mission section help team members to clarify the process by which they choose or act, both individually and as a team, and to determine their specific mission or purpose as a unit. Through these activities the team members can learn what motivates them; this information can be used, in turn, to help clarify how they are inclined to behave in response to the work environment and to situations that arise in team life.

The team members' individual values affect all levels of their behavior at work: their task orientation, the level of both speed and quality that they strive for, the degree of interpersonal connection that they require, the points at which they feel compromised by certain activities, the extents to which they need to know why a certain task must be performed, and—certainly of great importance to any team—the degree to which they can relinquish individual goals for the good of the team. In exchanging information about their values, team members can learn the significance that they individually attach to their own points of view; they can learn to set priorities and make decisions more effectively; they can examine their growth as individuals and as members of a team. They can even identify what career goals they might want to focus on in the future. Often relationships among team members are improved immensely when those members share and develop an understanding of one another's values. In fact, value clarification is often essential when the team members need to understand themselves and one another better in order to work toward common goals.

In addition, when the team members determine what they value *as a team* and what their team's mission is, they define what they expect of themselves and one another as a functioning unit. They can then work more effectively together, establish clear goals more easily, expedite their problem-solving and decision-making processes, and determine how to respond to many given situations in a way that promotes the good of the team.

The activities in this section include the topics of clarifying and sharing personal values, specifying the purpose of the team, formulating a team mission, identifying team strengths and opportunities, clarifying what the team stands for, and assessing viewpoints toward change.

THE GIRL AND THE SAILOR: VALUE CLARIFICATION

Goals

I. To provide an opportunity for the team members to practice identifying and clarifying values.

II. To develop the team members' awareness of some of the factors that affect their own value judgments as well as those of their fellow team members.

III. To demonstrate how values affect relationships as well as personal and team decisions.

Time Required

One hour and thirty to forty-five minutes.

Materials

I. A copy of The Girl and the Sailor Case History Sheet for each team member.

II. A pencil for each team member.

III. A sheet of newsprint prepared in advance with the following questions written on it:

1. What values seemed to underlie the choices that were made?

2. What similarities in team members' values became apparent? What differences became apparent? How do you account for the similarities and differences?

3. What feelings did you experience when a team member agreed with your values? What feelings did you experience when a team member disagreed with them?

4. How did differences in values affect the relationships among the team members during this activity? How did these differences affect the effort to achieve consensus?

5. What conclusions can you draw about the effects of values on decisions? What generalizations can you make about the effects of values on relationships with others and on teamwork?

IV. A sheet of newsprint and a felt-tipped marker for the team's use as it works on its task.

V. Masking tape for posting newsprint.

Physical Setting

A room where the team can work without interruptions.

Process

I. The leader introduces the activity and its goals.

II. The team members are given copies of The Girl and the Sailor Case History Sheet and pencils.

III. The leader asks the team members to read the case history sheet and to work individually to complete the task instructions at the end of the handout. (Ten minutes.)

IV. The team members are instructed to share their rankings, disclosing their rationales and articulating their associated values and beliefs as clearly as possible. The leader emphasizes that during this sharing no one is to express an opinion regarding another member's decisions or beliefs; requests for clarification are the only permissible comments. (Fifteen minutes.)

V. The team is given a sheet of newsprint, a felt-tipped marker, and masking tape. The leader explains that the members are to spend twenty minutes trying to reach a consensus[1] regarding the ranking of any or all of the characters. If a consensus is reached, one member should be appointed to record the decisions on newsprint and post the newsprint on the wall in view of all the team members; if no consensus is possible, nothing is posted. (Twenty minutes.)

VI. The leader posts the newsprint that was prepared in advance with questions written on it (see the Materials section, III) and then leads a discussion based on these questions. (Twenty minutes.)

VII. Each team member is asked to identify and discuss with fellow members one or two significant factors that influence his or her judgment in assessing similar situations involving value conflicts. (Twenty to thirty minutes.)

VIII. The leader summarizes the general themes expressed during the discussion in Step VII and then elicits comments from the team members about how they might apply what they have learned. The following types of questions may be asked:

1. How can you use what you have learned from this activity to deal more productively with value conflicts you experience?

2. How can you use this information to improve a situation at work or in this team? What will be your first step?

---

[1] A consensus decision is one that all team members can accept, regardless of how satisfied they are with it. Each member's opinion must be heard; no "majority-rule" voting, bargaining, or averaging is allowed.

3. What consequences do you expect from taking that first step? How will you manage those consequences? What support would you like from your fellow team members?

Variations

I. In Step VIII the team members may be asked simply to offer statements about back-home applications.

II. If the team has more than six members, Step VII may be completed in subgroups. Subsequently, the results are reported to the total team.

III. To heighten the experience of value conflict, the team members may be told that they *must* arrive at a consensus on the ranking of characters in the case history sheet.

This structured experience is adapted from *The 1989 Annual: Developing Human Resources,* edited by J.W. Pfeiffer, 1989, San Diego, CA: University Associates. The version that appears in the 1989 *Annual* is an adaptation of "Louisa's Problem: Value Clarification" (Structured Experience 283) by C.E. Amesley, 1981, in *The 1981 Annual Handbook for Group Facilitators* by J.E. Jones and J.W. Pfeiffer (Eds.), San Diego, CA: University Associates, and of "The Promotion: Value Clarification" (Structured Experience 362) by J.L. Mills, 1983, in *A Handbook of Structured Experiences for Human Relations Training* (Vol. IX), by J.W. Pfeiffer (Ed.), San Diego, CA: University Associates. The case of the girl and the sailor is part of the folklore of value clarification; the version adapted here is from "Cog's Ladder: A Process-Observation Activity" (Structured Experience 126) by G.O. Charrier, 1974, in *The 1974 Annual Handbook for Group Facilitators,* by J.W. Pfeiffer and J.E. Jones (Eds.), San Diego, CA: University Associates.

❖ *The Girl and the Sailor Case History Sheet*

The Dilemma

A ship sank in a storm. Five survivors scrambled aboard two lifeboats: a sailor, a girl, and an old man in one boat; the girl's fiance and his best friend in the second.

That evening the storm continued, and the two boats separated. The one with the sailor, the girl, and the old man washed ashore on an island and was wrecked. The girl searched all night in vain for the other boat or any sign of her fiance.

The next day the weather cleared, and still the girl could not locate her fiance. In the distance she saw another island. Hoping to find her fiance, she begged the sailor to repair the boat and row her to the other island. The sailor agreed, on the condition that she sleep with him that night.

Distraught, she went to the old man for advice. "I can't tell you what's right or wrong for you," he said. "Look into your heart and follow it." Confused but desperate, she agreed to the sailor's condition.

The next morning the sailor fixed the boat and rowed her to the other island. Jumping out of the boat, she ran up the beach into the arms of her fiance. Then she decided to tell him about the previous night. In a rage he pushed her aside and said, "Get away from me! I don't want to see you again!" Weeping, she started to walk slowly down the beach.

Her fiance's best friend saw her and went to her, put his arm around her, and said, "I can tell that you two have had a fight. I'll try to patch it up, but in the meantime I'll take care of you."

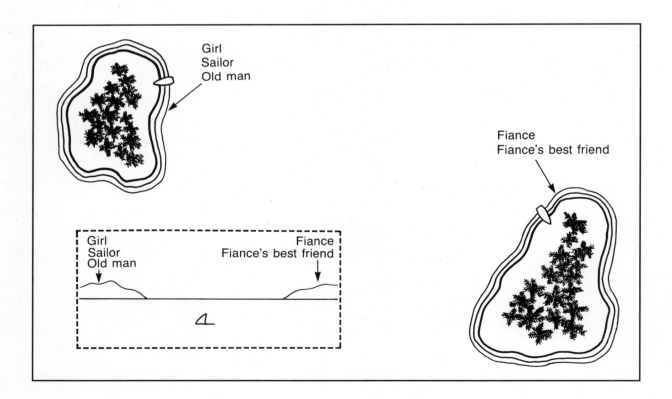

Task Instructions

Rank order the following characters from 1 (the person you liked best or valued most) to 5 (the person you liked or valued least):

_____ The sailor

_____ The girl

_____ The old man

_____ The girl's fiance

_____ The fiance's best friend

PERSONAL VALUES: SHARING IN THE TEAM

Goals

I. To offer the team members an opportunity to disclose their personal values and how strongly they feel about those values.

II. To assist the team members in establishing a value profile for the team.

III. To help the team members to assess the implications of their individual values and of the team's value profile.

Time Required

One and one-half to two and one-half hours.

Materials

I. A copy of the Personal Values Work Sheet for each team member.

II. A pencil for each team member.

III. A newsprint flip chart and a felt-tipped marker.

Physical Setting

A room that is free from interruptions. Comfortable chairs should be provided for the team members.

Process

I. The leader introduces the goals of the activity, distributes copies of the work sheet and pencils, and instructs the team members to complete their work sheets. (Ten minutes.)

II. The leader draws a matrix on newsprint, listing the ten values vertically down the sheet and the team members' initials horizontally across the top (see Figure 1). The team considers the values separately, completing the following procedure for each:

    1. The members take turns calling out their rankings. The leader records these rankings under the appropriate initials.

    2. The members discuss the value thoroughly, explaining their individual interpretations of the value and why they ranked it as they did. The leader

assists during this discussion by asking for clarification when appropriate and by encouraging the team members to explain their rationales thoroughly.

3. The leader averages the team members' rankings and records this number on the extreme right of the newsprint sheet under the column heading "Average Ranking" (see Figure 1).

(One to one and one-half hours.)

	CN	MK	JB	MP	VE	AB	RT	DB	Average Ranking
Getting along with colleagues									
Professional reputation									
Achieving business goals									
Excitement									
Leisure time for family or fun									
Material wealth									
Respect of peers									
Contributing to society									
Pleasing others									
Accomplishing personal goals									

Figure 1. Sample Matrix for Recording Rankings of Values

III. After all values have been discussed, the leader points out the average rankings of the values, states that these rankings can be construed as a value profile for the team, and elicits the members' reactions to this profile. (Ten minutes.)

IV. The leader leads a concluding discussion by asking questions such as these:

1. What have you learned about your personal values? How did you feel about sharing your personal values with your fellow team members?

2. What have you learned about your fellow team members' values? What were your reactions to hearing the values that the other team members hold?

3. What similarities do you see between your personal goals and the goals of this team? How do you feel about those similarities?

4. What differences do you see between your personal goals and the team's goals? What are your feelings about those differences?

5. How might this knowledge about your own and one another's values affect the way you work together? How might it affect the actual work that the team does? How might it affect the team's contribution to the organization?

V. The leader asks a volunteer to devise a handout based on the contents of the newsprint sheet and to distribute this handout to the team members for future reference.

Variations

I. If this activity is used with a top-management group, the resulting value profile may be reproduced in the form of a values statement for the organization and distributed to all employees.

II. The leader may wish to post the value profile in the team's main meeting room so that the members can refer to it while deliberating team problems and decisions.

III. The leader may use this activity as a precursor to creating a team mission statement.

By J.W. Pfeiffer.

❖ *Personal Values Work Sheet*

Instructions: Read each of the ten values listed below, and think about their relative importance to you. Rank the ten values on a scale from 1 to 10, where 1 is *most important to you personally* and 10 is *least important to you personally.* Record each value's rank in the blank on the left.

_____ Getting along with colleagues

_____ Professional reputation

_____ Achieving business goals

_____ Excitement

_____ Leisure time for family or fun

_____ Material wealth

_____ Respect of peers

_____ Contributing to society

_____ Pleasing others

_____ Accomplishing personal goals

PURPOSE OF THE TEAM: THE WHAT, HOW, WHO, AND WHY

Goals

  I. To assist the team members in understanding the purpose of their team.

  II. To assist the team members in discovering the reason for their team and their values associated with the reason.

Time Required

One and one-half hours.

Materials

  I. A copy of the Purpose of the Team Triangle for each team member.

  II. Several sheets of blank paper and a pencil for each team member.

  III. A newsprint flip chart and a felt-tipped marker.

  IV. Masking tape for posting newsprint.

Physical Setting

A room with a chair and a writing surface for each team member. Each member should be seated so that he or she can see the other team members as well as the leader and the newsprint flip chart.

Process

  I. The leader introduces the activity by explaining its goals.

  II. Each team member is given a copy of the Purpose of the Team Triangle, several sheets of blank paper, and a pencil.

  III. The leader draws a large copy of the triangle on newsprint and explains that it represents the work of the team: the three points represent what the team does, how it does it, and for whom it does it; at the heart of the triangle is the team's reason for its work. This sheet of newsprint is posted. (Five minutes.)

  IV. The leader asks each team member to work independently to write down what products or services the team produces and/or what functions it fills. (Five minutes.)

V. The leader asks the team members to take turns sharing their answers and records them on newsprint. The leader helps the members to reach consensus on the answer and records it on the newsprint triangle near the top point. The leader instructs the team members to write the answer in the corresponding spot on their copies of the triangle. (Ten minutes.)

VI. The leader asks each team member to work independently to write down the ways in which the team produces its products or services and/or the ways in which the team's functions are fulfilled. (Five minutes.)

VII. Step V is repeated, except the answer is recorded near the *left* point of the triangle. (Ten minutes.)

VIII. The leader asks each team member to work independently to write down the names or categories of people for whom the team's work is done. (Five minutes.)

IX. Step V is repeated, except the answer is recorded near the *right* point of the triangle. (Ten minutes.)

X. The leader asks each team member to work independently to write down the team's reasons for its work—the motivation behind the team members' work. (Five minutes.)

XI. Step V is repeated, except the answer is recorded inside the heart. (Ten minutes.)

XII. The leader leads a discussion based on questions such as the following:

1. Now that you have agreed on answers to each of the four questions (what, how, for whom, and why), how do the answers correlate with one another? What conflicts exist among the answers? What changes are necessary as a result of these conflicts?

2. How will your answers to the what, how, and for-whom questions help you to make day-to-day decisions in this team?

3. What does your answer in the heart (the why) reveal about your values?

If the team members agree that changes are needed for their answers on the triangle, the leader helps them to reach consensus[1] on new answers.

Variations

I. This activity may be used as a preamble to a mission-formulation activity.

II. Rather than working independently, the team members may work together on a first draft of their answers.

---

[1] A consensus decision is one that all team members can accept, regardless of how satisfied they are with it. Each member's opinion must be heard; no "majority-rule" voting, bargaining, or averaging is allowed.

By J. William Pfeiffer.

❖ *Purpose of the Team Triangle*

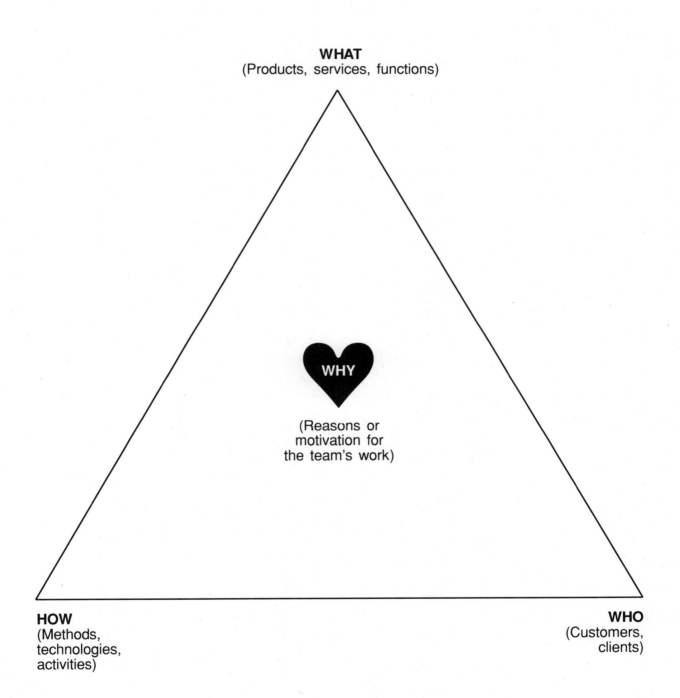

WHAT
(Products, services, functions)

WHY

(Reasons or
motivation for
the team's work)

HOW
(Methods,
technologies,
activities)

WHO
(Customers,
clients)

MISSION STATEMENT:
FORMULATING A TEAM MISSION

Goal

To assist the team members in drafting a mission statement for their team.

Time Required

A *minimum* of one and one-half hours. The leader should note that writing a mission statement is often a slow process requiring a good deal of discussion; consequently, this activity may extend well beyond the minimum time requirement stated. The leader needs to encourage discussion that helps push similarities and differences in points of view while helping the team avoid becoming "stuck."

Materials

I.   A copy of the Mission Statement Criteria Sheet for each team member.

II. A copy of the organization's mission statement (if such a statement exists) for each team member.

III. Several sheets of blank paper and a pencil for each team member.

IV. A newsprint flip chart and a felt-tipped marker.

V.   Masking tape for posting newsprint.

Physical Setting

A room with a chair and a writing surface for each team member. Each member should be seated so that he or she can see the other team members as well as the leader and the newsprint flip chart.

Process

I.   The leader introduces the activity by explaining its goal.

II. Each team member is given a copy of the Mission Statement Criteria Sheet and is asked to read this handout. (Five minutes.)

III. The leader discusses the handout contents with the team members, eliciting and answering questions as necessary. (Fifteen minutes.)

IV. The leader distributes blank paper and pencils and asks each team member to work independently to draft a mission statement for the team. (A minimum of twenty minutes.)

V. After all team members have completed the task, the leader asks them to take turns reading their statements. As the statements are read, the leader records key elements and phrases on newsprint and posts the newsprint.

VI. The leader helps the team members to reach a consensus on which elements and phrases should be incorporated in their mission statement. When the agreed-on statement has been recorded on newsprint, the leader assists the team in determining whether or not it meets the ten criteria on the handout and in making any necessary changes. During this phase of the activity, copies of the organization's mission statement are distributed and discussed in terms of consistency with the team's mission statement; if such a statement does not exist, this part of the discussion is based on the team members' best understanding of organizational values and mission. (A minimum of thirty minutes.)

VII. A volunteer is asked to turn the team's mission statement into a handout and to ensure that each team member, including the leader, receives a copy. The leader announces that the mission statement will be revised in about a year (or sooner if the team's purpose appears to change significantly).

Variations

I. In Step IV the team members may be instructed to work in pairs.

II. The leader may make arrangements for distributing the team's mission statement to other interested parties within the organization.

Adapted from *Applied Strategic Planning: A How To Do It Guide,* by J.W. Pfeiffer, L.D. Goodstein, and T.M. Nolan, 1986, San Diego, CA: University Associates.

❖ *Mission Statement Criteria Sheet*

1. The team's mission statement is clear and understandable to all team members.
2. The mission statement is brief enough for most team members to keep it in mind.
3. The mission statement clearly specifies what the business of the team is:

    a. What customer or client needs the team is attempting to fill, not what products or services are offered;

    b. Who the team's primary customers or clients are; and

    c. How the team plans to go about its business, that is, what its primary technologies are.

4. The mission statement should focus primarily on a single thrust of team effort.
5. The mission statement should reflect the team's distinctive competence.
6. The mission statement should be broad enough to allow flexibility in implementation but not so broad as to permit a lack of focus.
7. The mission statement should serve as a template and be the means by which the team leader and members can make decisions.
8. The mission statement must be consistent with the values, beliefs, and philosophy of both the organization and the team.
9. The mission statement should reflect attainable goals.
10. The mission statement should be worded so as to serve as an energy source and rallying point for the team.

TEAM MISSION AND INDIVIDUAL OBJECTIVES: DISCOVERING STRENGTHS AND OPPORTUNITIES

Goals

   I. To assist the team members in clarifying the team's mission.

  II. To help the team members to discover their strengths in relating their individual objectives to the team's overall mission.

 III. To help the team members to discover areas of opportunity in relating their individual objectives to the team's overall mission.

Time Required

A minimum of one and one-half hours. Time must be allowed for each member of the team to discuss three objectives (see Process, Step VI).

Materials

   I. A copy of the Team Mission and Individual Objectives Work Sheet A for each team member.

  II. A copy of the Team Mission and Individual Objectives Work Sheet B for each team member.

 III. A pencil for each team member.

 IV. A newsprint flip chart and a felt-tipped marker.

  V. Masking tape for posting newsprint.

Physical Setting

A room with a chair and a writing surface for each team member. Plenty of wall space should be available for posting newsprint.

Process

   I. The leader introduces the activity by explaining its goals.

II. Each team member is given a pencil and a copy of the Team Mission and Individual Objectives Work Sheet A, and the leader explains that each member should work independently to draft at least three major reasons for the existence of the team. (Five minutes.)

III. After all team members have completed the task, the leader asks them to take turns reading their reasons. The leader records the reasons on newsprint and posts the sheets for reference during the next task. (Ten minutes.)

IV. The leader helps the team to reach a consensus[1] on which reasons are most pertinent. The leader then asks the team members for suggestions to combine these relevant reasons into a statement of the team's mission and notes these suggestions on newsprint. When the team members agree on the wording, the mission statement is recorded on newsprint and posted. (Ten minutes.)

V. Each team member is given a copy of the Team Mission and Individual Objectives Work Sheet B, and the leader explains that each member should work independently to complete the first three columns of the work sheet. (Five minutes.)

VI. After all team members have completed the task, the leader asks them to take turns reading their objectives as stated in the first column of the work sheet and explaining how they will know when they have succeeded. As each objective is presented, the leader helps the team to reach consensus regarding the part of the mission statement that the objective relates to. The team member who presented the objective then completes the fourth column of his or her work sheet. Before continuing with the next objective, the leader leads a discussion based on questions such as these:

1. How is this objective a strength in accomplishing the team's mission? How might it be a hindrance?

2. How could the objective become an opportunity for accomplishing the team's mission?

The leader records salient points on newsprint as these questions are discussed. Any appropriate action steps are listed, along with the names of the team members responsible for the actions and deadline dates. (Fifteen minutes per team member.)

VII. The leader gives the newsprint sheets containing the action steps to a team member for reproduction and distribution to the other members of the team for follow-up.

---

[1] A consensus decision is one that all team members can accept, regardless of how satisfied they are with it. Each member's opinion must be heard; no "majority-rule" voting, bargaining, or averaging is allowed.

Variations

I. The team members may complete the Team Mission and Individual Objectives Work Sheets A and B prior to the meeting.

II. Steps V through VII may follow—either directly or at a later date—any activity in which the team's mission statement is created.

By Dave Francis and Don Young. Adapted from *Improving Work Groups: A Practical Manual for Team Building,* by D. Francis and D. Young, 1979, San Diego, CA: University Associates.

❖ Team Mission and Individual Objectives Work Sheet A

Instructions: List three to five major reasons that your team exists. Focus on the things that your team should achieve.

1.

2.

3.

4.

5.

❖ Team Mission and Individual Objectives Work Sheet B

Instructions: Complete the first three columns by stating three objectives that you personally have for your job, the dates by which you hope to achieve these objectives, and how you will know that you have succeeded in achieving them. Leave the fourth column blank until your team discusses the appropriate answer.

My Objective	Date for Achievement	How I Will Know	How Related to Team's Mission
1.			
2.			
3.			

TEAM BLASPHEMIES: CLARIFYING VALUES

Goals

I. To provide an opportunity for the team members to be creatively open about the characteristics of their team.

II. To assist the team members in identifying and comparing their values with regard to the team.

III. To allow the team members to explore the match between their own goals or values and those of the team.

Time Required

One and one-half to two hours.

Materials

I. Several sheets of blank paper and a pencil for each team member.

II. Newsprint and a felt-tipped marker.

III. Masking tape for posting newsprint.

Physical Setting

A room with a chair and a writing surface for each team member.

Process

I. The leader introduces the activity by stating that it is useful for the members of a team to think from time to time about the team's objectives and whether they, as individuals, are working toward those objectives.

II. The leader explains that in the next step of the activity each team member will be writing a "team blasphemy"[1]—a phrase or slogan so alien to what the team represents that the members will squirm in their seats when they hear it. The leader then gives examples of blasphemies for other teams:

---

[1] The idea of an "organizational blasphemy" was suggested in *The Corporation Man* by Anthony Jay, Penguin Books, Ltd., 1975.

- Accounting Department: "What difference does it make if we keep accurate records?"
- Human Resource Development (HRD) Department: "You can't teach an old dog new tricks."
- Marketing Department: "Let the customers solve their own problems; we have our own needs to attend to."

(Five minutes.)

III. The team members are given blank paper and pencils, and each team member is instructed to spend five minutes inventing a blasphemy for this team and writing this blasphemy on one of the sheets of paper. (Five minutes.)

IV. The leader calls time, collects the blasphemies, and reads them aloud while a member of the team records them on newsprint. This newsprint list remains posted throughout the activity. (Ten minutes.)

V. The team discusses the activity so far. The following topics may be included in this discussion:

1. How did it feel to consider and write down ideas of this nature?
2. Why did team members select these particular blasphemies?
3. What common theme runs through the blasphemies? What might this theme mean in terms of the way the members perceive the team?
4. What blind spots or biases in the team might these blasphemies indicate?
5. What taboos are there within the team that appear clearly in the list of blasphemies?
6. What do the blasphemies imply about the goals of the team? What do they imply about the way in which the team works?
7. Does any team member's blasphemy differ significantly from the rest? If so, what might be the reason?
8. What implications do the results of this activity have for the team? for the individual members? for the fit between the team and the individual members?

(Fifteen to thirty minutes.)

VI. The leader states that blasphemies often highlight beliefs or aspects of behavior that have been "socialized out" of the team members by the team's processes. The team members then are invited to contribute their own examples of how this process of socialization has operated, if at all, within their team. (Ten minutes.)

VII. The leader states that a team is a culture within its organization's culture and that the values of these two cultures can differ to a great extent. The leader then replicates Figure 1 on newsprint and posts this figure prominently. The leader explains that the larger the shaded area, the more "comfortable" individuals are likely to feel in the organization or team. If the shaded area is large, the individual is confronted by less value conflict. The leader says that tension can be present whenever the individual perceives a clash between the values of one culture and the values of another culture to which it is connected (for example, personal and work or team and organization) and that these values may conflict more than one realizes. (Five minutes.)

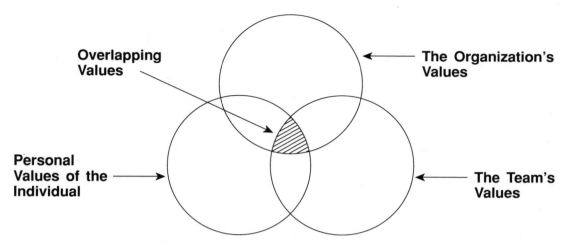

Figure 1. The Sets of Values That Exist Within an Organization

VIII. The leader asks the team members to think about themselves in relation to the team and the organization and, using the diagram of the three circles as a model, to draw circles (of approximately the same size) to represent their own values in relation to the values of their team and the values of the organization. Each member is also told to list the respective values in the three circles (his or her own values in the "personal" circle, the team's values in the "team" circle, and the organization's values in the "organization" circle). (Ten minutes.)

IX. The members are asked to take turns presenting their drawings to the total team and explaining the rationales behind these drawings. (Fifteen to thirty minutes.)

X. The leader leads a discussion of the experience, asking questions such as these:

1. What do the shaded areas on our drawings indicate about the match between the individual members and the team?

2. How do our team's goals match the organization's goals? How do we feel about the match? How might it affect our team? What, if anything, do we want to do about the match?

3. What values are seen as common (as shown in the shaded areas of the drawings)? What values outside the common areas are shared by individual team members?

4. How can an awareness of individual, team, and organizational values help us in our work?

5. How can we turn the blasphemies around and state them in terms of agreed-on goals?

Variations

I. The activity may be ended after Step V.

II. The team members may be asked to complete their drawings on sheets of newsprint and post them in various places in the room. Subsequently, the members travel from "poster" to "poster" for the presentations in Step IX.

III. If the team is large, Step IX may be done in pairs.

By Tony McNulty. Adapted from *The 1983 Annual for Facilitators, Trainers, and Consultants,* edited by L.D. Goodstein and J.W. Pfeiffer, 1983, San Diego, CA: University Associates.

LOOKING AT CHANGE: AN ASSESSMENT OF VALUES

Goals

   I. To help the team members to discover their values that affect their attitudes toward change.

  II. To assist the team members in evaluating their resistance to and acceptance of change.

Time Required

One hour.

Materials

    I. A copy of the Looking at Change Work Sheet for each team member.

   II. A pencil for each team member.

 III. A newsprint flip chart and a felt-tipped marker.

 IV. Masking tape for posting newsprint.

Physical Setting

A room with a chair and a writing surface for each team member. Each member should be seated so that he or she can see the other team members as well as the leader and the newsprint flip chart.

Process

    I. A pencil and a copy of the Looking at Change Work Sheet are given to each member of the team.

   II. The leader asks each member to work independently in listing ten words or phrases to describe "change." (Five minutes.)

 III. After all members have completed the task, the leader asks each member to review the ten words or phrases on his or her sheet and to draw a plus (+) next to the words or phrases that seem positive and a minus (-) next to those that seem negative. If a word or phrase is truly neutral, the team member should write a zero (0) by it. (Five minutes.)

IV. After all members have completed the task, the leader asks them to take turns sharing the positive words or phrases they used. The leader records these on newsprint. The leader then asks them to share the negative words or phrases and records these on newsprint. In the same manner, any neutral terms are recorded on newsprint. The leader counts the positive terms and writes the total at the bottom of the list. The same is done for the negative and neutral lists. (Twenty minutes.)

V. The leader posts the newsprint and leads a discussion based on questions such as the following:

1. What do the terms you used to describe change reveal about your values regarding change?
2. What might the proportion of positive-to-negative terms indicate?
3. Which terms might indicate that you are in favor of change? Why?
4. What types of change within this team (or department or organization) can be seen as positive? How are they positive? How do you feel about these types of change?
5. What do the neutral terms you used to describe change reveal about your attitude toward change?
6. What types of change would have a neutral effect on this team? Why?
7. What types of change within this team (or department or organization) can be seen as negative? How are they negative? How do you feel about these types of change?
8. Which terms indicate resistance to change?
9. In what ways can you prepare to accommodate changes that feel like negative moves?
10. What have you learned in this activity about your resistance to and acceptance of change? How can this knowledge help in your work with this team?

The leader records salient points on newsprint. If action steps are needed, they are recorded along with the names of members responsible for the actions and deadline dates. The leader gives the newsprint to a member for reproduction and distribution to the other members.

By Mary Kitzmiller.

❖ *Looking at Change Work Sheet*

Instructions: List ten words or phrases that you would use to describe "change." Do not *define* the word; that is, do not say it means "to make something different." Your description may, however, relate to how you feel about change or to the effects of change in your work team or organization.

1. _____

2. _____

3. _____

4. _____

5. _____

6. _____

7. _____

8. _____

9. _____

10. _____

Introduction to
Problem Solving/
Decision Making

Problem solving and decision making are the essence of a work team. The crux of team development is to remove obstacles to effective problem solving and decision making. The basic problem-solving process employed by teams (with variations/ additions as appropriate) consists of the following steps:

1. Define the problem in specific terms.
2. Determine goals to be met in solving the problem.
3. Generate alternative solutions.
4. Select the most viable solution.
5. Develop an action plan for implementing the chosen solution: identify *who* will do *what* and *by when*.
6. Implement the solution.
7. Follow through (1) by ensuring that the proposed action steps were carried out and (2) by evaluating the effectiveness of the solution and its repercussions at intervals.

The ability to make effective decisions is an integral part of this problem-solving process; team members must decide and agree on the problem definition, the goals for the solution, the solution itself, and how and by whom and by when the solution will be implemented. Ineffective procedures during any part of this process can significantly alter the quality of the team's decisions. Even teams characterized by harmonious internal relationships can fall prey to poor problem solving and decision making; if members do not voice their differences of opinion, they may find that critical information is inaccessible, that the issues involved cannot be clarified, or that they consistently opt for the easiest or most apparent solution without exploring alternatives.

The activities in the Problem Solving/Decision Making section address these concerns. They concentrate on issues such as assessing problem-solving skills; isolating common problems; learning processes like brainstorming, the nominal group technique, and force-field analysis; using creativity in solving problems; enhancing communication during problem solving; examining and changing the process by which the team makes decisions; and action planning.

EFFECTIVE PROBLEM SOLVING: A SURVEY FOR ASSESSING SKILLS

Goals

I. To identify strengths and weaknesses in team problem solving.

II. To set agendas for strengthening the weakest characteristics.

Time Required

One hour.

Materials

I. A copy of the Effective Problem Solving Survey for each team member.

II. Blank paper and a pencil for each team member.

III. A newsprint flip chart and a felt-tipped marker.

IV. Masking tape for posting newsprint.

Physical Setting

A room with a chair and a writing surface for each team member. Each member should be seated so that he or she can see the other team members as well as the leader and the newsprint flip chart.

Process

I. The leader introduces the activity by explaining its goals.

II. Each team member is given a copy of the Effective Problem Solving Survey, a sheet of paper, and a pencil and is asked to read the survey. (Five minutes.)

III. The leader discusses the survey instructions and contents with the team members, eliciting and answering questions as necessary. (Five minutes.)

IV. The leader asks each team member to complete the survey independently. (A minimum of five minutes.)

V. After all team members have completed the task, the leader asks them to take turns reading the ratings they assigned to each item on the survey. As the members respond, the leader records the ratings for each item on newsprint. This information is posted for reference throughout the activity. (Ten minutes.)

VI. When all responses have been recorded, the leader adds the scores for each item and identifies the two items that have the highest scores and the two that have the lowest scores. The leader helps the team members to acknowledge their high scores and leads a brief discussion on their successes. (Five minutes.)

VII. The team members' attention is directed to the two items with the lowest scores. The leader states that for each of these problem areas, each member is to write two action steps that the team could take to improve in that area. (Ten minutes.)

VIII. The leader asks the team members to report their suggested action steps and leads a discussion about them, helping the team to arrive at a consensus[1] about which actions they will take. The leader records the agreed-on steps on newsprint, along with the names of the people responsible for taking action on each step and the deadline dates for the action. The leader gives this newsprint to one member of the team to reproduce and distribute to the other members for follow-up action.

By Dave Francis and Don Young. Adapted from *Improving Work Groups: A Practical Manual for Team Building,* by D. Francis and D. Young, 1979, San Diego, CA: University Associates.

---

[1] A consensus decision is one that all team members can accept, regardless of how satisfied they are with it. Each member's opinion must be heard; no "majority-rule" voting, bargaining, or averaging is allowed.

❖ *Effective Problem Solving Survey*

Instructions: Give your candid opinion of your team's most recent problem-solving session by rating its characteristics on the seven-point scales shown below. Circle the appropriate number on each scale to represent your evaluation.

1. Order

1	2	3	4	5	6	7

Lacked order and poorly controlled   Orderly and well controlled

2. Objectives

1	2	3	4	5	6	7

Confusion about objectives   Clear and shared objectives

3. Organization

1	2	3	4	5	6	7

Organization was inappropriate to task   Organization was flexible, appropriate to task

4. Criteria

1	2	3	4	5	6	7

Criteria for success not established   Clear criteria for success established

5. Information

1	2	3	4	5	6	7

Information was
poorly evaluated

Information was
well analyzed

6. Planning

1	2	3	4	5	6	7

Planning was
inadequate

Planning was
effective, thorough

7. Action

1	2	3	4	5	6	7

Action was
ineffective

Action was
effective, thorough

8. Learning

1	2	3	4	5	6	7

No attempt to learn
from the experience

Thorough review
to help team learn
from the experience

9. Time

1	2	3	4	5	6	7

Time was wasted

Time was well used

10. Participation

1	2	3	4	5	6	7

People withdrew or
became negative

Everyone
participated
positively

IDENTIFICATION AND RESOLUTION: ISOLATING COMMON PROBLEMS

Goals

I. To assist the team members in identifying the kinds of problems they commonly face as a team.

II. To acquaint the team members with a useful procedure for resolving problems.

III. To offer the team members an opportunity to practice this procedure.

Time Required

One hour and thirty to forty-five minutes.

Materials

I. A newsprint flip chart and a felt-tipped marker.

II. Masking tape for posting newsprint.

Physical Setting

A room with plenty of wall space for posting newsprint.

Process

I. The leader asks the team members to brainstorm[1] problems that they believe are being experienced by at least two members. As these problems are mentioned, the leader records them on newsprint, reproducing the original wording as accurately as possible. (Five to ten minutes.)

---

[1] Brainstorming is a technique used by groups to generate a number of creative ideas in a short time. The group members take turns contributing one idea at a time until all ideas have been exhausted. No criticism, evaluation, or judgment of ideas is allowed until the brainstorming phase has been completed. For further instructions see the activity entitled "Brainstorming: A Problem-Solving Technique."

II. After all ideas have been exhausted, the leader asks each member to identify privately which problem is the most significant and which is the next-most significant.

III. The members are instructed to take turns stating their choices for the most significant and the next-most significant problems. The leader tallies their choices on newsprint, isolates the one problem that received the most votes, and announces that the team will explore and resolve this problem. (If two or more problems are tied for the greatest number of votes, the leader helps the team members to achieve consensus[2] regarding the problem they wish to resolve during this activity.) (Five to ten minutes.)

IV. The leader elicits examples of the selected problem and lists these examples on newsprint. (Five minutes.)

V. The leader asks the team members to review the listed examples and choose a representative example—one that, if it were resolved, would also resolve most other occurrences of the problem. (Five minutes.)

VI. The leader assists the team in analyzing the wording of the representative example and formulating a new problem statement if necessary. (The final wording must be such that the team can work on resolution by brainstorming the problem's consequences *or* causes and ways to eliminate those consequences or causes.) (Ten minutes.)

VII. After the team members have arrived at a satisfactory problem statement, they brainstorm consequences or causes. While they work, the team leader records their ideas on newsprint. (Five to ten minutes.)

VIII. The team members brainstorm ways to resolve the problem by eliminating the identified consequences or causes. The leader records the results on newsprint. (Five to ten minutes.)

IX. The team evaluates the options from the previous step and chooses the resolution or combination of resolutions that is most worthy of implementation. (Fifteen minutes.)

X. The team creates an action plan for implementation, specifying *who* will do *what* and *by when*. (Twenty minutes.)

XI. The team reviews the other examples of the problem (from Step IV) and eliminates any that will be resolved by implementing the action plan. (Five minutes.)

XII. The team members make plans to meet again soon to repeat the procedure of Steps VI through X for each identified problem that they still want to address (including any examples not eliminated in Step XI).

---

[2] A consensus decision is one that all team members can accept, regardless of how satisfied they are with it. Each member's opinion must be heard; no "majority-rule" voting, bargaining, or averaging is allowed.

By William R. Daniels. Adapted from *Group Power I: A Manager's Guide to Using Task-Force Meetings,* by W.R. Daniels, 1986, San Diego, CA: University Associates. This procedure is based on one learned while the author was studying under Charles A. Waters of Organization Dynamics, Inc., Berkeley, California.

BRAINSTORMING:
A PROBLEM-SOLVING TECHNIQUE

Goals

I. To introduce brainstorming as a problem-solving technique.

II. To offer the team members an opportunity to practice brainstorming.

III. To develop the team members' skills in creative problem solving.

Time Required

Approximately one hour.

Materials

I. A copy of the Brainstorming Rule Sheet for each team member.

II. A newsprint flip chart and a felt-tipped marker.

Physical Setting

A room with movable chairs for the team members.

Process

I. The leader explains that the team members will be generating ideas to solve an imaginary problem.

II. The leader announces that the technique the team members will use to solve the problem is called "brainstorming," distributes copies of the Brainstorming Rule Sheet, asks the members to read this sheet, and elicits and answers questions about the brainstorming procedure. (Ten minutes.)

III. The team members are instructed to sit in a circle. The leader announces that each team member is to imagine being cast ashore on a desert island, nude and with nothing but a belt. The problem is to figure out what can be done with the belt. The leader tells the members that they have fifteen minutes to generate ideas and asks them to begin. The leader records every idea on newsprint, reproducing phraseology as closely as possible.

IV. At the end of the generating phase, the leader tells the team members that the ban on criticism is over and helps them to establish criteria for evaluating their ideas. These criteria are written on newsprint and posted prominently so that all members can see them throughout the evaluation phase. (Ten minutes.)

V. The team members discuss and evaluate their ideas and select the most viable single idea or combination of ideas. (Fifteen minutes.)

VI. The leader leads a discussion of brainstorming, eliciting the team members' ideas about how they can use the technique to their best advantage in future problem-solving efforts.

Variations

I. The leader may wish to follow this activity with a problem-solving session involving a real problem facing the team.

II. An object other than a belt may be used in the problem. For example, the team members may brainstorm uses for a flashlight, a rope, an oar, or a corkscrew.

Adapted from *A Handbook of Structured Experiences for Human Relations Training* (Vol. III, Rev.), edited by J.W. Pfeiffer and J.E. Jones, 1974, San Diego, CA: University Associates.

❖ *Brainstorming Rule Sheet*

1. The team members sit in a circle.

2. They agree to a specific statement of a simple problem.

3. One person contributes the first idea about how to solve the problem. Then the individual to that person's left contributes an idea, and so on around the circle until no one has any ideas left to contribute. The objective is to generate as many ideas as possible.

4. While the team members are contributing ideas, someone records them on newsprint in full view of all members. Phraseology is duplicated as closely as possible.

5. No criticism, evaluation, or judgment is allowed while the members are contributing ideas.

6. Anyone may pass on a particular round if he or she has nothing to contribute.

7. Anyone may "piggyback" or build on a previously stated idea (by adding to it, improving on it, or using it as a springboard to another idea).

8. Quantity is more important than quality. No idea is too "crazy" to mention. Far-fetched ideas may trigger more practical ones.

9. After all ideas have been exhausted, the team members establish criteria for evaluating the recorded ideas.

10. The members discuss and evaluate all ideas and select the single idea or combination of ideas that represents the most viable solution.

NOMINAL GROUP TECHNIQUE: APPLIED TEAM PROBLEM SOLVING

Goals

I. To increase creativity and participation in team meetings involving a problem-solving and/or fact-finding task.

II. To develop or expand the team members' perception of critical issues within a specified problem area.

III. To obtain the input of as many individual team members as possible without the dysfunction of unbalanced participation.

Time Required

Two hours.

Materials

I. A copy of the Nominal Group Technique Task Form for each team member.

II. Twenty 3" x 5" cards for each team member.

III. Blank paper and a pencil for each team member.

IV. A newsprint flip chart and several felt-tipped markers.

V. Masking tape for posting newsprint.

Physical Setting

A room with a table and chairs for the team members. Plenty of wall space should be available for posting newsprint.

Process

I. The leader states that the role of everyone present is to contribute his or her perceptions, expertise, and experience to defining the critical issues within the problem at hand (in this case, the problem stated at the beginning of the Nominal Group Technique Task Form). The leader stresses that the theme of the experience is "problem centering" rather than "solution finding." After announcing that the approach to be used during this session is the "nominal group technique," the leader defines a nominal group as one in which individuals work in the presence of others but do not interact verbally with one another except at specified times.

II. The leader distributes copies of the Nominal Group Technique Task Form and pencils, explains the task, clarifies that the "problem" to be addressed is printed at the beginning of the form, gives an example of the kind of response desired, and then asks the team members to complete the form. (Twenty-five to thirty minutes.)

III. After all team members have completed their task forms, the leader asks for a volunteer to record the team's ideas on newsprint and to help them clarify their ideas later. The leader then instructs the team members to take turns presenting items from their forms, until no one has anything left to contribute. The leader specifies that no discussion or comments about the contributions is allowed at this time; however, the members are encouraged to contribute new ideas that are inspired by previously stated ones. As each sheet of newsprint is filled, the recorder posts it in prominent view before starting a new sheet. (Thirty minutes.)

IV. After all ideas have been exhausted, the recorder goes through all of the newsprint lists, numbering each item and leading a discussion of each so that the team members can ask questions, clarify, or elaborate where necessary and so that they can add new items if they wish. *Note:* Items are not to be condensed or collapsed into categories at this point. (Fifteen minutes.)

V. Each team member is given ten 3" x 5" index cards and is asked to review all newsprint items, to select the ten that he or she feels are most critical to the solution of the problem, and to write these ten items and their corresponding numbers on 3" x 5" cards (a separate card for each item). The leader adds that after all ten cards have been completed, the team member should place the cards in front of him or her on the table, rank them from 1 to 10 in order of importance, and write each card's rank in the upper-right corner. (Fifteen minutes.)

VI. When all team members have completed the ranking task, the recorder collects the 3" x 5" cards from each member and tabulates the results on a newsprint tally sheet, which is set up as shown in Figure 1. As each sheet of newsprint is filled, it is posted prominently before a new sheet is begun.

VII. The recorder leads a brief discussion of each item recorded during the previous step, ensuring that the team members understand what is meant by each. (Ten minutes.)

VIII. Each team member is given ten more 3" x 5" index cards and is asked to review the original newsprint list (the one generated in Steps III and IV), to select ten items that he or she now considers most important, to write these ten items and their corresponding numbers on 3" x 5" cards (a separate card for each item), to rank them from 1 to 10 in order of importance, and to write

Item Number	Ranks Assigned by Team Members	Average of Ranks
1.		
2.		
3.		
4.		
5.		
6.		
7.		
8.		
9.		
10.		

Figure 1. Example of Newsprint Tally Setup (Step VI)

each card's rank in the upper-right corner. The leader stipulates that this task must be completed silently and independently and that any changed opinions resulting from the previous team discussion should be reflected in the new cards. (Fifteen minutes.)

IX. Each team member is instructed to assign a value of 100 to his or her highest-priority item and a value between 0 and 100 to each of the remaining nine items to indicate relative differences in importance among the ten items. The leader specifies that each value is to be recorded immediately under the rank number in the upper-right corner.

X. The recorder collects and tallies on newsprint the new rankings and the corresponding ratings.

XI. The leader leads a discussion about the entire experience, asking questions such as these:

1. How would you describe your understanding of the issues affecting the problem before we used the nominal group technique? How would you describe your understanding of those issues now?

2. What kinds of problems that we typically face as a team might be candidates for using the nominal group technique? Which might not be?

3. What did you like about the technique? What did you dislike about it? What can you generalize about the advantages and disadvantages of the nominal group technique?

Variations

I. The leader may use the nominal group technique with a real problem that the team currently faces.

II. The leader may wish to present a problem (not necessarily the one on the task sheet), use another problem-solving technique to generate one set of responses, and then lead into this activity with a different problem. Subsequently, the team can compare the results of the two methods in terms of number of items generated, acceptance of high-priority items by all members, and so on.

By David L. Ford, Jr. Adapted from *The 1975 Annual Handbook for Group Facilitators,* edited by J.E. Jones and J.W. Pfeiffer, 1975, San Diego, CA: University Associates. The version of this activity that appeared in the 1975 *Annual* was adapted from "A Team Process Model for Problem Identification and Program Planning" by A. Delbecq and A. Van de Ven, 1971, *Journal of Applied Behavioral Science, 7,* pp. 466-491. Used in this book by permission of the *Journal of Applied Behavioral Science.*

❖ *Nominal Group Technique Task Form*

Instructions: List all of the facts and resources that your team will need to solve the problem stated below. Do not discuss this task with anyone; work silently and independently. If you complete the task with time to spare, please sit quietly and reconsider your list until everyone has finished and you have been given further instructions.

Problem: How would you compile and produce an informational brochure on your organization?

1. _____
2. _____
3. _____
4. _____
5. _____
6. _____
7. _____
8. _____
9. _____
10. _____
11. _____
12. _____
13. _____
14. _____
15. _____
16. _____
17. _____
18. _____
19. _____
20. _____

BRICKS: USING CREATIVITY IN SOLVING PROBLEMS

Goals

I. To provide the team members with an opportunity to practice creative problem solving.

II. To allow the team members to experience the dynamics that are involved in group-task accomplishment.

Time Required

Approximately one and one-half hours.

Materials

I. A copy of the Bricks Task Sheet for each team member.

II. A newsprint flip chart and a felt-tipped marker.

Physical Setting

A room in which the team members can work without interruptions.

Process

I. Each team member is given a copy of the Bricks Task Sheet and is asked to read this handout.

II. The leader elicits and answers questions about the task and reads the following guidelines for creative problem solving:[1]

1. Adopt a questioning attitude.
2. Establish an environment of acceptance in which ideas are considered before they are judged.
3. Examine the problem from new angles; try stating it in atypical ways.

---

[1] Adapted from "Creativity and Creative Problem Solving" by M.B. Ross, 1981, in *The 1981 Annual Handbook for Group Facilitators*, edited by J.E. Jones and J.W. Pfeiffer, San Diego, CA: University Associates.

4. Break the problem into its components and list as many alternatives as possible for each component; combine the alternatives to create new variations.

After providing a newsprint flip chart and a felt-tipped marker to record ideas, the leader tells the team members that they have fifteen minutes to accomplish the task and invites them to begin.

III. After fifteen minutes the team members are told to stop their work. The leader leads a discussion of the activity by eliciting answers to questions such as these:

1. What method did the team use to generate ideas? What was helpful about this method? What was not helpful?
2. How was the team's approach "creative"?
3. Did everyone participate equally? If not, why did some members participate more than others? What effect did the members' levels of participation have on the team's ability to solve the problem creatively?
4. How might this activity relate to real problems that the team attempts to solve?
5. What might be a first step toward incorporating creativity into the team's problem-solving process?

Variations

I. The team may be asked to generate uses for a specified quantity of a different material. Such materials may include packages of licorice whips, balls of yarn, can openers, and boxes of uncooked spaghetti.

II. The leader may specify that the team members use brainstorming[2] to accomplish the task.

III. If the team has six or more members, the leader may ask the members to form subgroups of three to complete the task described in the task sheet. Subsequently, each subgroup prepares and makes a five-minute presentation of its ideas for the total team, creating and using newsprint posters as visual aids. The leader then leads the discussion described in Step III.

By J. Allan Tyler. Adapted from *A Handbook of Structured Experiences for Human Relations Training* (Vol. IX), edited by J.W. Pfeiffer, 1983, San Diego, CA: University Associates.

---

[2] For instructions on brainstorming, see the activity entitled "Brainstorming: A Problem-Solving Technique."

❖ *Bricks Task Sheet*

Your team has just been stranded without provisions on a deserted island. In your search for supplies, you and your fellow members locate a little food and two thousand bricks. In discussing the situation, the group determines that rescue probably will not occur for at least two weeks and that the food is insufficient to support everyone for that period. Therefore, the members decide that the task of immediate importance is to generate creative ways of using the bricks to increase chances for survival.

FORCE-FIELD ANALYSIS: PROBLEM SOLVING

Goal

To offer the team members an opportunity to study dimensions of a work-related problem and to devise a strategy for solving that problem through analysis.

Time Required

A minimum of two and one-half hours.

Materials

I. A copy of the Force-Field Analysis Inventory for each team member.

II. A copy of the Force-Field Analysis Theory Sheet for each team member.

III. A pencil for each team member.

IV. A newsprint flip chart and a felt-tipped marker.

Physical Setting

A chair and a writing surface for each team member. The team members should be seated so that all of them can see the newsprint flip chart.

Process

I. The leader explains the goal of the activity and assists the team members in selecting a work-related problem that they would like to concentrate on solving during this session. (Ten minutes.)

II. Each team member is given a copy of the Force-Field Analysis Inventory and a pencil. The leader announces that the team is to complete Parts I and II of the inventory, focusing on the problem selected in Step I. As the group works, the leader assists as necessary and records the inventory information on newsprint; the team members are encouraged to make notes that they feel will be useful to them as they complete the problem-solving process. (A minimum of one hour.)

III. After Parts I and II have been completed, the leader distributes copies of the Force-Field Analysis Theory Sheet and asks the team members to read this handout. After all members have read the sheet, the leader leads a discussion on its content, eliciting and answering questions. During this discussion the following points are emphasized:

In planning specific changes to deal with a problem, one should be aware that increasing the driving forces to change the status quo also produces increased tension. One should also be aware that whatever change in status quo has been accomplished will be lost if the driving force is reduced. A change in the status quo, then, can best be accomplished by reducing the strengths of the restraining forces while maintaining the force of the drive. If the driving forces are not maintained, the tension will be reduced without any change in the status quo.

(Twenty minutes.)

IV. The leader assists the team members in completing Part III of the inventory and records the information on newsprint. (A minimum of thirty minutes.)

V. At the conclusion of the problem-solving process, the leader reassembles the total team and leads a discussion about the entire experience by asking questions such as these:

1. How satisfied are you with the outcome of this problem-solving process?
2. How does the process of solving a problem with force-field analysis compare with the way we usually solve problems in this team?
3. What are the advantages of force-field analysis? What are the disadvantages?
4. On what kinds of problems might we use force-field analysis in the future?

(Twenty minutes.)

VI. The leader asks for a volunteer to reproduce the newsprint information in handout form and to distribute a copy of the handout to each team member for future reference.

Variations

I. If the team is large, the members may complete the inventory process in subgroups of three or four. Subsequently, the subgroups present summaries of their change strategies to the total team; then the members select the strategies that they feel are best.

II. The team members may select the problem in advance. Also, they may be given copies of the inventory in advance so that they can make notes on Parts I and II prior to the session.

Adapted from *A Handbook of Structured Experiences for Human Relations Training* (Vol. II, Rev.), edited by J.W. Pfeiffer and J.E. Jones, 1974, San Diego, CA: University Associates.

❖ *Force-Field Analysis Inventory*[1]

Part 1: Problem Specification

Instructions: Think about a problem that is significant for you. Respond to each of the following items as fully as necessary for another team member to understand the problem.

1. We understand the specific problem to be that...

2. The following people with whom we must deal are involved in the problem:

   Their roles in this problem are...

   They relate to us in the following manner:

3. We consider these other factors to be relevant to the problem:

4. We would choose the following aspect of the problem to be changed if it were in our power to do so (choose only one aspect):

---

[1] This inventory is based in part on materials developed by Warren Bennis and draws in part on material developed by Saul Eisen.

Part II: Problem Analysis

5. If we consider the present status of the problem as a temporary balance of opposing forces, the following would be on our list of forces driving toward change. (Fill in the spaces to the right of the letters. Leave the spaces to the left blank.)

_____ a. _____

_____ b. _____

_____ c. _____

_____ d. _____

_____ e. _____

_____ f. _____

_____ g. _____

_____ h. _____

6. The following would be on our list of forces *restraining* change:

_____ a. _____

_____ b. _____

_____ c. _____

_____ d. _____

_____ e. _____

_____ f. _____

_____ g. _____

_____ h. _____

7. In the spaces to the left of the letters in Item 5, rate the driving forces from 1 to 5, according to this scale:

1—It has *almost* nothing to do with the drive toward change in the problem.
2—It has *relatively little* to do with the drive toward change in the problem.
3—It is of *moderate importance* in the drive toward change in the problem.
4—It is an *important factor* in the drive toward change in the problem.
5—It is a *major factor* in the drive toward change in the problem.

8. In the spaces to the left of the letters in Item 6, rate the forces restraining change, using the number scale in Item 7.

9. In the following chart, diagram the forces driving toward change and restraining change that you rated in Items 7 and 8: first write several key words to identify each of the forces driving toward change (a through h); then repeat the process for forces restraining change. Then draw an arrow from the corresponding degree of force to the status-quo line. For example, if you considered the first on your list of forces (letter a) in Item 5 to be rated a 3, draw your arrow from the 3 line in the "a" column indicating drive up to the status-quo line.

Restraining Forces

| | a | b | c | d | e | f | g | h |

5
4
3
2
1

Status Quo

1
2
3
4
5

| | a | b | c | d | e | f | g | h |

Driving Forces

Part III: Change Strategy

10. Select two or more restraining forces from your diagram and then outline a strategy for reducing the potency of each.

11. Apply the following goal-setting criteria (the SPIRO model) to your change strategy:

    S — Specificity: Exactly what are we trying to accomplish?
    P — Performance: What behavior is implied?
    I — Involvement: Who is going to do it?
    R — Realism: Can it be done?
    O — Observability: Can others see the behavior?

❖ *Force-Field Analysis Theory Sheet*[2]

Bringing about change in a team or an organization means altering the way things are done. This may mean changes in compensation methods, sales and production levels, leadership styles, or interpersonal functioning, among other factors. Kurt Lewin's (1969) technique of force-field analysis provides a framework for solving problems and for implementing planned-change efforts. One way to explain this technique is to review the way in which a particular group of managers applied it when they met to discuss their effectiveness as a team.

In talking with one another, the team members soon recognized that their day-to-day effectiveness and their ability to improve it were hampered by the degree to which they felt free to confront one another on relevant task and interpersonal issues. The members agreed that they needed to talk more openly with one another, but each individual now waited for someone else to "be open." They became frustrated with this situation and began to wonder why they could not change the way they worked together.

Definition of the Problem

As the managers began to examine the climate in which they were operating, they identified some factors or pressures that strongly supported changes in the direction of more openness:

- The team members wanted to perform effectively for the sake of their own careers as well as for the good of the organization;
- They were functionally interdependent and had to work together to accomplish their goals;
- Existing work-related problems were having an impact on their effectiveness (for example, responsibility without authority and unclear job definitions); and
- Some interpersonal tension already existed in the system (for example, destructive competition and both passive and overt hostility).

As they continued their analysis, the managers also identified pressures that acted as powerful obstacles to change:

- Several team members lacked experience and skills in dealing with conflict and more open feedback;
- The risk of the unknown was high in terms of "What will we open up?" and "Will we hurt one another?";
- There was concern that if certain issues were brought up, things could get worse; and

---

[2] Adapted from "Kurt Lewin's 'Force Field Analysis'" by M. Spier, 1973, in J.E. Jones and J.W. Pfeiffer, *The 1973 Annual Handbook for Group Facilitators,* San Diego, CA: University Associates.

- There were questions about whether the organization's top management would support a more open climate or would instead respond with "That's not the way things are done around here."

Thus, the definition of the problem took the form of recognizing that opposing forces like these in the environment determined the existing level of interpersonal functioning in the team.

Figure 1 summarizes this "diagnosis" of the problem. The top and bottom of the figure represent opposite ends of a continuum of a team's functioning in terms of its interpersonal climate. The environmental conditions and pressures supportive of more openness in the system are the *driving forces* represented by the arrows pushing upward, which also act as barriers to the team's backward movement toward a more closed system. The arrows pushing downward represent the *restraining forces,* which are keeping the system from moving toward a higher degree of openness as well as driving forces toward a climate of lower interpersonal risk.

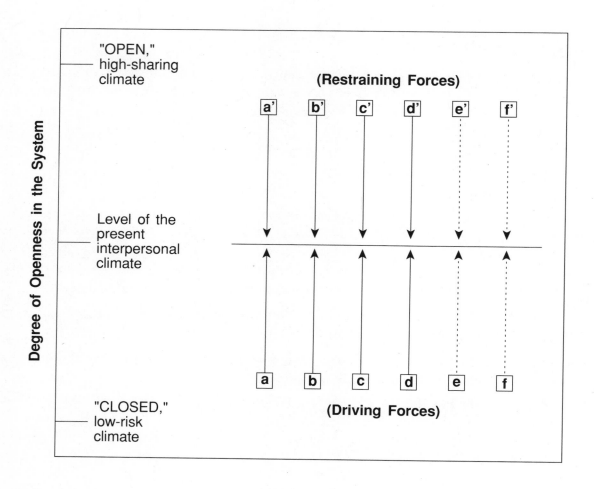

Figure 1. The Force Field

A group of forces as shown in Figure 1 may be called a "force field." The length of the arrows in the force field describes the relative strength of the forces: the longer the arrow, the stronger the force. For descriptive purposes the forces in Figure 1 are shown as equal in strength, but a force field can be made up of forces of varying strengths. Indeed, the strength of any single force may itself vary as either end of the continuum of openness is approached. A team or organization stabilizes its behavior where the forces pushing for change are equal to the forces resisting change. Lewin called the result of this dynamic balance of forces the "quasi-stationary equilibrium." The equilibrium is represented in Figure 1 by the line marked "Level of the present interpersonal climate." It is at this level of functioning that the system is not completely "closed"—in terms of a total lack of openness, feedback, and risk taking—but neither is there the degree of each needed for people to work together as effectively as they might. The arrows meeting at the line indicate that the current state is being maintained somewhere between the end points on a continuum of team functioning by a balance of discernible driving and restraining forces.

The Implementation of Change

Since the management team is interacting at its present level because of a balance of organizational and individual needs and forces, change will only occur if the forces are modified so that the system can move to and stabilize itself at a different level where the driving and restraining forces are again equal. The equilibrium can be changed in the direction of more openness by (1) strengthening or adding forces in the direction of change, (2) reducing or removing some of the restraining forces, or (3) changing the direction of the forces.

Any of the basic strategies may change the level of the team's functioning, but the secondary effects will differ depending on the method used. If a change in the equilibrium is brought about only by strengthening or adding driving forces, the new level may be accomplished by a relatively high degree of tension, which itself may reduce effectiveness. In Figure 1 the line representing the "Level of the present interpersonal climate" will move upward toward more openness under the pressure of strengthened driving forces. The additional pressures upward, however, will be met by corresponding increases in resistance. The resulting increase of tension in the system will be characterized by a lengthening of the arrows pushing upward and downward at the new level.

Attempts to induce change by removing or diminishing opposing forces will generally result in a lower degree of tension. In the example an important restraining force that requires removal is the managers' lack of experience and skills in dealing with conflict. As the managers acquire new interpersonal skills, a key restraining force will be removed. Moreover, changes accomplished by overcoming counterforces are likely to be more stable than changes induced by additional or stronger driving forces. Restraining forces that have been removed will not push for a return to old behaviors and ways of doing things. If changes come about only through the strengthening of driving forces, the forces that support the new level must be stable. For example, it often happens that during a team-building session the team members are stimulated toward new ways of working together; however, they find that soon after returning to the day-to-day job their former behaviors and habits re-emerge. If the change started by the learning and enthusiasm of a team-building experience is to continue after the session, some other driving force must be ready to take the place of the meeting's stimulation.

One of the most efficient ways to accomplish change is to alter the direction of one of the forces. If the managers in the example can be persuaded to "test" top management's support for a more open climate, they might find more encouragement than they previously thought existed. Thus, the removal of a powerful restraining force (expected top-management disapproval) becomes an additional, strong driving force (actual top-management support) in the direction of change.

Reference

Lewin, K. (1969). Quasi-stationary social equilibria and the problem of permanent change. In W.G. Bennis, K.D. Benne, & R. Chin (Eds.), *The planning of change* (pp. 235-238). New York: Holt, Rinehart and Winston.

SHOE STORE:
COMMUNICATION IN PROBLEM SOLVING

Goals

I. To offer the team members an opportunity to observe their communication patterns while they work as a team to solve a problem.

II. To allow the team members to explore interpersonal influence in problem solving.

Time Required

Approximately one hour.

Materials

Blank paper and a pencil for each team member.

Physical Setting

A room in which the team members can work without interruption. Writing surfaces and comfortable chairs should be provided.

Process

I. The leader explains to the team members that during this activity they will work together to solve a mathematical problem and that they must arrive at consensus.[1] The team members are urged to pay attention to how the team arrives at the conclusion so that they can later discuss the process that emerges. (Five minutes.)

II. The leader states the mathematical problem as follows:

"A man went into a shoe store and found a great bargain: a pair of shoes on sale for only twelve dollars, including tax. When he went to pay for the shoes, he handed the clerk a twenty-dollar bill. It was early in the day, and the clerk

---

[1] A consensus decision is one that all team members can accept, regardless of how satisfied they are with it. Each member's opinion must be heard; no "majority-rule" voting, bargaining, or averaging is allowed.

did not have any one-dollar bills. He took the twenty-dollar bill and went to the restaurant next door, where he exchanged it for twenty one-dollar bills. He then gave the customer his change. Later that morning the restaurant owner came to the clerk and said, 'This is a counterfeit twenty-dollar bill.' The clerk apologized profusely, took back the phony bill, and gave the restaurant owner two good ten-dollar bills. Not counting the cost of the shoes, how much money did the shoe store lose?"

After stating the problem, the leader distributes paper and pencils, tells the team members to begin solving the problem, and asks them to let him or her know when they have the solution.

III. When the team members indicate that they have a solution, the leader ensures that they are all in agreement, asks for the answer ($8.00), and then asks one member to explain the process of arriving at the conclusion. (If the team members become preoccupied with the answer itself or the mathematics involved, the leader should focus their attention on the team process instead.) (Five minutes.)

IV. The leader leads a discussion of the communication issues by focusing on such behaviors as the following:

1. Reacting negatively to the phrase "mathematical problem" and establishing artificial constraints;
2. Leaving the problem solving to "experts" (self-proclaimed or otherwise);
3. Adopting pressuring tactics in reaching consensus;
4. Using "teaching aids" in convincing others (scraps of paper, paper and pencil, real money);
5. Feeling distress if a wrong conclusion is reached;
6. Using listening checks and other communication-skills techniques; and
7. Refusing to set aside personal opinion in order to reach consensus.

(Twenty minutes.)

V. The leader leads another discussion, this time focusing on the patterns of communication that were reflected in the experience, such as influence behaviors, tendencies toward one- or two-way communication modes, personal or team issues that interfered with task accomplishment, and behaviors that facilitated or hindered communication. Subsequently, the implications of these patterns for the team's future functioning are considered.

Variations

I. A ground rule may be established that the team members may use *no* teaching aids. Instead, they would have to talk through the solution.

II. The leader may distribute the problem in handout form or write it on newsprint and post it on the wall.

III. The individual members may be asked to solve the problem independently prior to attending the team session.

By Amy Zelmer. Adapted from *A Handbook of Structured Experiences for Human Relations Training* (Vol. IV), edited by J.W. Pfeiffer and J.E. Jones, 1973, San Diego, CA: University Associates.

CIRCLES OF INFLUENCE: WIDENING A TEAM'S HORIZONS

Goals

I. To offer the team members a systematic approach for evaluating the forces that influence the team.

II. To assist the team members in planning ways to increase the team's strength and influence.

Time Required

One and one-half to two hours.

Materials

I. Blank paper and a pencil for each team member.

II. A newsprint flip chart and a felt-tipped marker.

III. Masking tape for posting newsprint.

Physical Setting

A room with writing surfaces and comfortable chairs for the team members.

Process

I. The leader introduces the activity by reviewing its goals.

II. The leader draws and posts the diagram shown in Figure 1 and then leads a discussion of the diagram, ensuring that the team members understand the concept of circles of influence. (Ten minutes.)

III. Each team member is given blank paper and a pencil and is asked to spend ten minutes listing the problems affecting the team at the present time. (Ten minutes.)

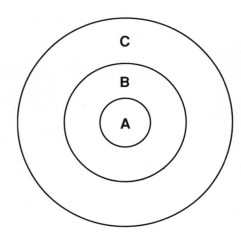

Circle A represents problems that can be solved completely by the team.

Circle B represents problems that the team can influence but cannot completely control.

Circle C represents problems or forces affecting the team that are outside its influence.

Figure 1. Diagram of Circles of Influence

IV. When the lists have been completed, they are given to the leader, who writes the problems on newsprint and asks for clarification of any vague points.

V. Each problem is discussed to determine which circle of influence it falls within. When the team members reach consensus,[1] their decision is recorded on the newsprint diagram as a brief title or code letter. (Fifteen to twenty minutes.)

VI. The team members brainstorm[2] methods for extending the boundaries of Circles A and B to increase the team's influence over the forces that exert impact on its performance. As the members contribute ideas, the leader records them on newsprint. (Ten to fifteen minutes.)

VII. The leader helps the team members to determine which of the brainstormed ideas should be pursued. The final ideas are recorded on newsprint, along with information about what specifically is to be done, who is to do it, how it is to be done, and by when. The leader asks for a volunteer to collect the newsprint generated during this step, to create a handout from the newsprint information, and to distribute this handout to all team members so that they can follow up on the established plans. (Thirty minutes to one hour.)

_____

[1] A consensus decision is one that all team members can accept, regardless of how satisfied they are with it. Each member's opinion must be heard; no "majority-rule" voting, bargaining, or averaging is allowed.

[2] Brainstorming is a technique used by groups to generate a number of creative ideas in a short time. The group members take turns contributing one idea at a time until all ideas have been exhausted. No criticism, evaluation, or judgment of ideas is allowed until the brainstorming phase has been completed. For further instructions see the activity entitled "Brainstorming: A Problem-Solving Technique."

Variations

I. To save time, the leader may draw the newsprint diagram of circles in advance and may ask the team members to prepare their lists of problems in advance.

II. The activity may be conducted again in a few months to see whether progress has been made in increasing the team's influence.

By Dave Francis and Don Young. Adapted from *Improving Work Groups: A Practical Manual for Team Building,* by D. Francis and D. Young, 1979, San Diego, CA: University Associates.

TEAM DECISIONS: EXAMINING AND CHANGING THE PROCESS

Goals

I. To examine how the team typically makes decisions.

II. To plan changes in the team's decision-making process.

Time Required

One and one-half hours.

Materials

I. A copy of the Team Decisions Information Sheet for each team member.

II. A copy of the Team Decisions Check List for each team member.

III. A copy of the Team Decisions Interpretation Chart for each team member.

IV. A pencil for each team member.

V. A newsprint flip chart and a felt-tipped marker.

Physical Setting

A room with a chair and a writing surface for each team member. Each member should be seated so that he or she can see the other team members as well as the leader and the newsprint flip chart.

Process

I. The leader introduces the activity by explaining its goals.

II. Each team member is given a copy of the Team Decisions Information Sheet and is asked to read this sheet. (Five minutes.)

III. After all members have read the information sheet, the leader leads a discussion on its content and elicits and answers questions about it. (Five minutes.)

IV. Each member is given a copy of the Team Decisions Check List and a pencil. The leader discusses the check-list instructions with the team members, eliciting and answering questions as necessary. (Five minutes.)

V. The leader asks each team member to complete the check list independently. (A minimum of five minutes.)

VI. After all team members have completed the task, the leader distributes the Team Decisions Interpretation Chart, eliciting and answering questions about the instructions on the chart. The leader then asks each team member to complete the interpretation chart. (Five minutes.)

VII. While the team members are working independently, the leader copies the Team Decisions Interpretation Chart onto newsprint. After all members have completed their task, the leader asks them to take turns reading the numbers they have circled. The leader records the numbers on the newsprint chart.

VIII. The leader identifies the decision-making style or styles that the members indicated as most typical in their team and leads a discussion on how these styles have affected the team's decisions. (Ten minutes.)

IX. The leader asks each team member to choose the decision-making process that he or she would prefer for team meetings and to share the reasons for that choice with the other members. (Three minutes per team member.)

X. While the members are presenting their preferences, the leader records them on newsprint, noting their frequency and rank ordering them.

XI. The leader instructs the team members to decide which decision-making process(es) they will use in their team meetings. If the members need help, the leader may refer them to the Team Decisions Information Sheet for clarification of the various processes. (Twenty minutes.)

XII. When the decision has been made, the leader asks the team members to identify the process they used in arriving at the decision. The leader then asks the team members to identify some actions that could be taken in the next team meeting to ensure that the selected process(es) will succeed. As the team members discuss these actions, the leader records salient items on newsprint, along with names of any members responsible for the actions. The leader then gives the sheet to a team member for reference at the next team meeting. (Even if there is unanimity from the beginning on what process should be used, the leader asks the team members to identify actions that could be taken in the next meeting to ensure that their preferred process will work.)

By Dave Francis and Don Young. Adapted from *Improving Work Groups: A Practical Manual for Team Building,* by D. Francis and D. Young, 1979, San Diego, CA: University Associates.

❖ Team Decisions Information Sheet

One of the most important questions regarding decision making is "Who actually decides?" From answers to this question, the following five decision-making processes can be clearly identified:

    1. ***Individual decision.*** One person, normally the manager, actually makes a decision. Others who are involved in the situation are expected to abide by the decision.

    2. ***Minority decision.*** A few of those involved in a situation meet to consider the matter and make a decision, and this decision is binding for all concerned.

    3. ***Majority decision.*** More than half of those involved in a situation make a decision, and it is binding for all concerned. Many political and democratic organizations use this principle.

    4. ***Consensus decision***. An entire group considers a problem on the basis of reason and discussion, with each member expressing a view. The group reaches a decision that all members can accept, regardless of how satisfied they are with it. (No "majority-rule" voting, bargaining, or averaging is allowed.)

    5. ***Unanimous decision***. Each person fully agrees on the action to be taken, and everyone concerned fully subscribes to the decision that is made.

    When people are involved in making a decision, they are much more likely to be committed to that decision than if some other person—or small group—makes a decision on their behalf. Therefore, going up the decision-making scale (from individual decisions to unanimous decisions, as outlined above) increases commitment, although it also increases the difficulty in arriving at an agreement.

❖ Team Decisions Check List

Instructions: Think about the ways in which your team typically makes decisions, and then read each of the statements below. Choose at least three and no more than five statements that are most typical of your team. Circle the number that precedes each of your choices.

1. When decision making is necessary, a few of us usually get together and take care of it.

2. The senior team member usually decides, and the question is settled.

3. All team members are encouraged to express their views, and we attempt to include something for everyone in the decision.

4. A decision typically is not made until everyone somewhat agrees with it.

5. We frequently let the majority rule.

6. The person in charge of the task makes the decisions.

7. Often all of the team members agree on a decision and support it wholeheartedly.

8. A small clique runs things in our team.

9. A decision is made only when most of the team members agree on a particular course of action.

10. We do not make a decision until every member of the team is completely in agreement with it.

11. Our team members are allowed to air their views, but our manager makes the decision.

12. A few of our team members usually dominate the group.

13. A decision is not made unless every member of the team can accept it to some extent.

14. A numerical majority is required before decisions are made.

15. A decision is not made unless every member of the team actively supports it.

❖ *Team Decisions Interpretation Chart*

Instructions: After you have marked three to five statements on the Team Decisions Check List, circle the same numbers below in the "Statement Numbers" column. Write the total number of circles in each row in the "Total Circles" column. (Be sure to count your *circles;* do not count the numbers inside the circles.) The style corresponding to the highest score in the "Total Circles" column represents a typical decision-making style among the members of your team.

Statement Numbers	Total Circles	Representative Style
2, 6, 11		Individual
1, 8, 12		Minority
5, 9, 14		Majority
3, 4, 13		Consensus
7, 10, 15		Unanimous

DECISION MAKING: LEARNING EFFECTIVE PROCESSES

Goals

I. To build the team members' awareness of decision-making processes.

II. To help the team members to recognize textbook examples in real-life decision-making processes.

III. To assist the team members in learning effective decision-making processes.

Time Required

A minimum of thirty minutes in addition to the time required for the team's regular meeting. An additional five minutes is required to discuss each additional decision made during the meeting.

Materials

I. A copy of the Decision Making Definitions for each team member.

II. One 8 ½" x 11" sign for each of the following captions: The Flop, Railroading, Self-Authorized Decision, Handclasp, Voting, Trading, and Consensus.

III. A newsprint flip chart and a felt-tipped marker.

IV. Masking tape for posting newsprint.

Physical Setting

The usual setting for the team's meetings, such as a room with a conference table and chairs. Each team member should be seated so that he or she can see the other team members as well as the leader and the newsprint flip chart.

Process

I. At the beginning of a meeting in which the team members will make decisions, the leader explains that the meeting will be combined with an activity and then explains the goals of the activity.

II. Each team member is given a copy of the Decision Making Definitions and is asked to read this handout. The leader discusses the definitions with the team members, eliciting and answering questions as necessary. (Ten minutes.)

III. The leader distributes the seven signs to seven members of the team and explains that each member should hold up his or her sign as soon as that style of decision-making process has been used in arriving at a decision. (The team member should not raise the sign until the decision has actually been made.) The leader answers any questions that the team members have about the process. If the team consists of fewer than seven members, one or more members are given more than one sign. (Five minutes.)

IV. The regular meeting is begun. Whenever a sign is held aloft, the leader asks questions such as the following and leads a discussion on the decision-making process:

1. In what ways does the sign describe this decision-making process?
2. Why was this process appropriate or inappropriate for this decision?
3. How did you feel while the decision was being made?
4. If the process was not appropriate, which process would have been appropriate and why?
5. How could we have used a different process for this decision?

During the question-and-answer session, the leader records the answers on newsprint and posts them for reference during the rest of the meeting. If no team member holds up a sign after a decision is made, the leader intervenes to bring the decision to the attention of the team. Then the first question becomes "Which sign describes this decision-making process, and how does it describe that process?" (Five minutes for each question-and-answer session.)

V. After the meeting, the leader discusses with the team members what they learned and asks for action steps to help in using appropriate decision-making processes in their meetings. The leader records the action steps on newsprint, along with the names of the members responsible and any deadline dates. The newsprint is given to one team member for reproduction and distribution to the other members.

Variations

I. The activity may be concluded after the first decision, so that scheduled business can proceed without further interruption.

II. The leader may repeat this activity at intervals to check the team's progress on learning and using different decision-making processes.

By Cyril R. Mill. Adapted from *Activities for Trainers: 50 Useful Designs,* by C.R. Mill, 1980, San Diego, CA: University Associates.

❖ Decision Making Definitions

The following definitions will help you to recognize some of the decision-making styles that a team uses:

1. *The Flop:* A suggestion is ignored.
2. *The Railroad:* A loud suggestion by one team member is acted on by the others without discussion.
3. *The Self-Authorized Decision:* A team member immediately acts on his or her own suggestion, and the team goes along without protest or discussion.
4. *The Handclasp:* Quick agreement between two members of the team moves the rest of the members to follow their suggestion.
5. *The Vote:* A tally of opinions is taken for and against a suggestion.
6. *The Trade-Off:* A team member suggests, "I will agree with this decision if you will support my proposal."
7. *Consensus:* After all team members have had a chance to contribute their individual opinions, all express willingness to go along with the decision, regardless of how satisfied they are with it. (No "majority-rule" voting, bargaining, or averaging is allowed.)

REVIEWING OBJECTIVES AND STRATEGIES: AN ACTION-PLANNING TASK

Goals

I. To review and evaluate the team's accomplishments during the past year.

II. To acquaint the team members with the basic procedure for action planning.

III. To offer the team members an opportunity to practice action planning by preparing objectives and action steps for major team efforts in the next year.

Time Required

Two hours and forty-five minutes to three hours.

Materials

I. At least six copies of the Reviewing Objectives and Strategies Sheet for each team member.

II. Blank paper and a pencil for each team member.

III. A newsprint flip chart and a felt-tipped marker.

IV. Masking tape for posting newsprint.

Physical Setting

A room with writing surfaces and chairs for the team members.

Process

I. The leader introduces the goals of the activity.

II. Explaining that planning must be based on some data, the leader invites the team members to review the team's accomplishments during the past year.

The leader leads the team in brainstorming[1] answers to the question "What has our team accomplished during the past year?" (If the team members have difficulty in getting started, the leader encourages them to think in terms of such things as new systems that have been devised and implemented, new technical resources that have been mastered, new skills that have been acquired, improvements in relations with other teams, and awards that have been received.) All answers are listed on newsprint; then the team reviews the list to eliminate items that are redundant or that do not represent general agreement. (Fifteen minutes.)

III. The leader distributes blank paper and pencils and asks each team member to rate his or her satisfaction with the team's performance during the past year on a scale of 1 (very dissatisfied) to 7 (very satisfied).

IV. The ratings are collected, and the leader records them on newsprint so that all team members can see the range. The leader elicits comments about the ratings. (Ten minutes.)

V. The brainstorming procedure is repeated for the question "What have been our team's failures or shortcomings during the past year?" (The team members may be reluctant to speak openly about failures because these often are perceived as personal weaknesses. If this proves to be the case, the leader should assure the team members that what they say will not be repeated. Another approach that is helpful is briefly explaining the value of confronting weaknesses openly.) (Ten minutes.)

VI. The team members review the list of team shortcomings, eliminating those that do not represent areas of general concern. (Ten minutes.)

VII. The leader gives each team member six copies of the Reviewing Objectives and Strategies Sheet and tells the team members that they may either work individually or consult freely with one another and that their task is to prepare as many objectives and strategies as they can, limiting themselves to *present operations and ongoing tasks*. The leader states that the emphasis of the activity is on quantity of ideas rather than on technicalities and reminds the team members that an objective is simply a statement of intention, whereas a strategy is a statement of the steps that one will take to reach an objective. (Thirty minutes.)

VIII. After thirty minutes the team members are instructed to tape their Reviewing Objectives and Strategies Sheets to newsprint and to post their newsprint on the walls so that everyone can walk around and read the recorded information. (Ten minutes.)

---

[1] Brainstorming is a technique used by groups to generate a number of creative ideas in a short time. The group members take turns contributing one idea at a time until all ideas have been exhausted. No criticism, evaluation, or judgment of ideas is allowed until the brainstorming phase has been completed. For further instructions see the activity entitled "Brainstorming: A Problem-Solving Technique."

IX. The leader helps the team to compile a list of new areas in need of planning, using data from the team's list of shortcomings, objectives generated from the activity just completed, and the team members' further reflections. A sheet of newsprint with the heading "Changes We Want to Effect" is posted, and suggestions are listed on this sheet. (Twenty minutes.)

X. The leader leads a discussion of the items on the list of desired changes. As each item is examined, a written statement of objective—along with planned action steps, the names of those responsible for the steps, deadlines for the steps, and resources needed—is compiled and posted on newsprint. (Thirty minutes.)

XI. The team reviews the statements, summarizing and categorizing wherever possible. The leader asks for a volunteer to devise a handout reflecting the information on the final newsprint list and to distribute copies of this handout to the team members so that they can use it as the team's work plan for the coming year. Arrangements are made for the first of several follow-up sessions to review progress.

Variations

I. If the team has difficulty in working through an issue during Step X, the leader may instruct the team members to form three subgroups, each of which is to prepare three charts as follows:

1. Chart I (a statement of the issue or the problem):

    a. What do we do well?
    b. What do we do poorly?

2. Chart II:

    a. Write a pessimistic statement that describes our approach to _____ _____.
    b. Write an optimistic statement that describes our approach to _____ _____.

3. Chart III:

    a. What objectives must be established to move from the pessimistic statement to the optimistic one? List three to five objectives that are clear and measurable.
    b. What strategies must be followed to accomplish each objective? List as many as are needed and indicate the necessary resources.

II. If a block of time devoted to "thinking about the future" would be more productive than Step VII, the following procedure may be used:

1. The leader comments that even though the future is unpredictable, it can be useful to ask "What might happen?" and "How would we cope?"

2. The leader divides the team members into three subgroups, gives each subgroup four sheets of newsprint and several felt-tipped markers, and presents the following instructions:

"Your subgroup's task is to spend ten minutes identifying four significant trends, internal or external to the team, that could have an impact on your operation within the next five years. Consider the four trends as future problems with which your team will have to grapple. Write a trend or problem at the top of each of the sheets of newsprint."

3. Each subgroup is directed to give two of its newsprint sheets to each of the other subgroups. Each subgroup now has four new problems with which to work. The leader then gives the following instructions:

"Identify strategies to cope with each of the problems you have received. Be as imaginative as you wish, but do not assume that you will have unlimited resources of money or personnel. Write your solutions for each problem on the sheet of newsprint." (Forty minutes.)

4. The subgroups take turns presenting their problems and strategies, and the listening members are encouraged to share their reactions.

III. The activity and instructions may be modified to meet the needs of temporary task teams by having the task-team members review their efforts to date and their strategies for the accomplishment of their task.

By Cyril R. Mill. Adapted from *The 1982 Annual for Facilitators, Trainers, and Consultants,* edited by J.W. Pfeiffer and L.D. Goodstein, 1982, San Diego, CA: University Associates.

❖ *Reviewing Objectives and Strategies Sheet*

1. Objective (What is your intention? What do you plan to achieve? What end result do you want?)

2. Strategies (What action steps will be necessary to reach the objective?)

3. Who will be responsible? (Who will take *each step* that you just identified?)

4. When will the steps be completed? (What is the deadline for *each step* of your strategy?)

5. Resources needed (If money, additional people or information, or other resources are necessary for any of the steps you have identified, indicate them here.)

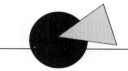

Introduction to
Stress Management

In today's organizations, team members are expected to perform accurately and quickly and to act responsibly at all times. It is certainly no surprise that these expectations can lead to stress. Periodic pressure can lead to occasional bouts of stress; prolonged pressure, if not relieved, can lead to burnout. Recovery from stress is not easy, and recovery from burnout can be extremely difficult and time consuming. Consequently, the best approach is to guard against levels of stress that are too high and/or go on for too long a period of time. Obviously, assessing a team's level of stress is a complicated endeavor. Some stress is necessary for life—any life, not just a team's success. The issue is how to keep the stress to a level that is appropriate—a level that stimulates rather than destroys.

The activities in the Stress Management section deal with this issue. They have to do with identifying energy resources and depleters, managing energy and time, managing complex tasks, and dealing with role-related stress.

ENHANCING PERSONAL ENERGY: IDENTIFYING RESOURCES AND DEPLETERS

Goals

I. To help the team members identify their own energy resources and depleters.

II. To present techniques for increasing personal energy.

Time Required

Approximately one and one-half hours.

Materials

I. A copy of the Enhancing Personal Energy Suggestion Sheet for each team member.

II. A copy of the Enhancing Personal Energy Work Sheet for each team member.

III. A pencil for each team member.

Physical Setting

A room with flexible seating to allow the team members to form dyads. Writing surfaces should also be provided.

Process

I. The leader introduces the goals of the activity, distributes copies of the Enhancing Personal Energy Suggestion Sheet, and asks the team members to read this handout. (Ten minutes.)

II. The leader leads a discussion of the handout contents, pointing out that an objective measure of energy resources and depleters is not necessary because everyone feels the existence of these elements. It is further emphasized that skills at controlling energy resources can be both learned and strengthened. (Ten to fifteen minutes.)

III. The team members are given copies of the Enhancing Personal Energy Work Sheet and pencils and are instructed to complete their work sheets. (Ten minutes.)

IV. The team members choose partners and discuss and compare their completed work sheets. (Twenty minutes.)

V. The leader reconvenes the total team and elicits comments concerning what the team members learned about their own energy. (Fifteen minutes.)

VI. The leader leads a concluding discussion, asking questions such as the following:

1. In what ways were your energy depleters similar to those of your fellow team members? In what ways were they different?

2. In what ways were your energy resources similar to those of your fellow team members? In what ways were they different?

3. What steps can we take as a team to minimize our commonly experienced energy depleters? What steps can we take to enhance our commonly experienced energy resources?

4. What steps can you take on your own to minimize your energy depleters?

5. What steps can you take on your own to enhance your energy resources?

6. What kinds of support can we give one another in stressful periods?

7. What might you do to increase the overall level of energy experienced in the team?

By Eileen F.N. Collard, Warren Sam Miller, and William Grimberg. Adapted from *Process Politics: A Guide for Group Leaders,* by E. Guthrie and W.S. Miller, 1981, San Diego, CA: University Associates and from *A Trainer's Manual for Process Politics,* by E. Guthrie, W.S. Miller, and W. Grimberg, 1981, San Diego, CA: University Associates.

❖ *Enhancing Personal Energy Suggestion Sheet*[1]

Most jobs involve a certain amount of stress from time to time. Some of this stress can be positive, giving us the impetus to strive, which, in turn, can lead to achievement and good feelings about what we have done. Stress becomes negative, however, when we experience too much of it at one time, when it continues for a long period, and/or when we have no means of dealing with it. The following "rules to live by" might help you to minimize the hassles you face and to make the best use of your personal energy.

1. ***Go with the flow.*** The key to going with the flow is to remember that life is lived in the here and now, each day at a time. Yesterday can be relived only as a memory, and tomorrow can be experienced only in anticipation. Energy spent in worry about what has happened in the past or in anxiety about what might happen in the future is energy that could be used more effectively by making the most of the present moment.

2. ***Trust your hunches***. Everyone can benefit from getting in touch with common sense and following what it dictates. This rule is helpful in getting through strategy sessions or conflict situations. It can be useful to express a hunch: "I don't know where this notion is coming from yet, but I have a hunch that we're missing the point." The other people involved can then help sort out the logic and examine whether or not the hunch is on target.

It is important not to hold back opinions because of fear of what others might think. Intuitive thinking in brainstorming[2] sessions can be very useful and can spark creativity among team members.

3. ***Learn from what you do.*** A correlation seems to exist between the degree of learning from involvements and the amount of personal energy available for use: the more a person keeps learning, the more energy he or she has.

The individual who suspects that he or she may have stopped learning from his or her work should answer the following questions:

- Am I listening carefully to what is going on around me?
- Am I talking too much?
- Am I bored?

---

[1] By Eileen F.N. Collard and Warren Sam Miller. Adapted from *Process Politics: A Guide for Group Leaders,* by E. Guthrie and W.S. Miller, 1981, San Diego, CA: University Associates.

[2] Brainstorming is a technique used by groups to generate a number of creative ideas in a short time. The group members take turns contributing one idea at a time until all ideas have been exhausted. No criticism, evaluation, or judgment of ideas is allowed until the brainstorming phase has been completed. For further instructions see the activity entitled "Brainstorming: A Problem-Solving Technique."

- How can I learn more from my present involvements?
- Are my present involvements appropriate for me, or should I consider dropping some?
- Am I saying "no" enough?

It is certainly natural and normal to become bored, to change interests, and to want to move on to new areas of concern. It is possible to lose effectiveness after being in the same arena for more than a couple of years. All of us should regularly examine how much we are learning and whether we are losing effectiveness so that we can make any needed changes.

One way to keep learning is to consider every activity as a course of study. For example, in a meeting one can study the ways in which a team operates. This approach to learning means remaining constantly aware of the variety of ways in which an experience can be viewed, with evaluation and learning happening all the time. Everyone becomes bored with activities that have been completely mastered; thus, seeking new activities generates opportunities to keep learning.

4. ***Keep your life in balance.*** Each of us needs time for family, work, socializing, and being alone. A feeling of being "off balance" is usually attributable to giving too little attention to one of these areas of life. People differ in the amount of time needed for these concerns; but everyone needs time for contact with other human beings, for feeling challenged and productive, for having fun, and for contacting his or her inner self.

The "right" balance of time spent on these concerns varies from person to person and changes over time. Everyone should determine which needs he or she tends to shelve during busy periods and what type of personal balance should be consciously planned for and achieved.

❖ *Enhancing Personal Energy Work Sheet*[3]

List below your energy resources (the things that give you energy) as well as your energy depleters (the things that take away your energy).

Energy Resources   **Energy Depleters**

List the times in your life when you have:

1. Gone with the flow (by not fretting about the past or worrying about the future).

2. Trusted your hunches.

3. Learned from experience.

4. Done something to get or keep your life in balance.

List your own rules for getting the most out of your energy:

---

[3] Developed by Betty Aldridge and Warren Sam Miller, Minneapolis, Minnesota. Used with permission.

BURNOUT REMEDIES: STRATEGIES FOR MANAGING ENERGY AND TIME

Goals

    I. To help the team members assess the ways in which they spend their time.

    II. To help the team members determine how they would rather spend their time.

    III. To introduce the team members to remedies for burnout.

Time Required

One hour and forty-five minutes.

Materials

    I. A copy of the Burnout Remedies Information Sheet for each team member.

    II. A sheet of newsprint listing the following questions (prepared in advance by the leader):

        1. Which of your current activities give you energy? Which deplete your energy?

        2. Which pertain to your job? Which have to do with your personal life?

        3. How does the amount of time you spend on each activity compare with the amount of satisfaction it provides you?

        4. In what activities not previously mentioned do you like to participate?

        5. What patterns do you see emerging?

    III. Blank paper and a pencil for each team member.

    IV. A newsprint flip chart and a felt-tipped marker.

    V. Masking tape for posting newsprint.

Physical Setting

A room large enough so that pairs of team members can work together without disturbing one another. Writing surfaces and movable chairs should be provided.

Process

I. The leader introduces the activity and its goals.

II. After instructing the team members to form pairs, the leader distributes blank paper and pencils and posts the newsprint list of questions (see Materials, IV). The partners are asked to take turns interviewing each other by asking the posted questions and making notes about responses. (Fifteen minutes.)

III. After all pairs have completed their interviews, the leader leads a discussion of what the team members learned during the previous step. (Ten minutes.)

IV. The leader asks each team member to spend ten minutes writing an answer to the question "If you had a month to do anything you wanted, what would you do?" The leader emphasizes that the answer should include detailed information about specific activities. (Ten minutes.)

V. The team members are instructed to share their answers with their partners and to discuss how they feel about the schedules they envisioned for themselves. (Fifteen minutes.)

VI. The leader reconvenes the total team, distributes copies of the Burnout Remedies Information Sheet, and leads a discussion on the contents of this handout. (Ten minutes.)

VII. The team members are instructed to rejoin their partners to discuss plans for adjusting their activity schedules for the next month so that these schedules more closely resemble their "ideal" months. (Fifteen minutes.)

VIII. The total team is again assembled for a discussion of the schedule-adjustment plans developed in Step VII. The leader emphasizes the importance of relying on a support group to help prevent or remedy burnout and then asks questions such as the following:

1. What parallels can you draw between your current work activities and the things you would spend a month doing if you could?

2. How could you modify your work activities or arrange your work schedule so that you could spend more time engaged in those activities that give you the greatest satisfaction?

3. What could the team do to help you spend more time doing what you love to do?

During the discussion the leader encourages the team members to enter into agreements to help one another as necessary. Highlights and any agreements reached are recorded on newsprint. At the conclusion of the discussion, the leader asks a volunteer to devise a handout from the newsprint and to distribute copies to all team members. (Fifteen minutes.)

IX. The leader leads a discussion of the entire activity, eliciting the team members' reactions.

Variations

I. The leader may omit the emphasis on individual burnout and focus solely on burnout as it relates to team and/or organizational activities. In this case the interview questions and the handout should be altered.

II. The leader may make arrangements with the team members to reconvene at a later date to check on progress and to discuss their current feelings about the issues of time management, stress, and burnout.

By Eileen F.N. Collard, Warren Sam Miller, and William Grimberg. Adapted from *A Trainer's Manual for Process Politics,* by E. Guthrie, W.S. Miller, and W. Grimberg, 1981, San Diego, CA: University Associates.

❖ *Burnout Remedies Information Sheet*

Individual Burnout

Symptoms

- Tendency to blame others
- Excessive complaints
- Low energy
- Boredom
- Physical illness
- Failure to see friends
- Misplaced priorities
- Feeling of being overwhelmed
- Agitation
- Denial of burnout
- Insomnia
- Feeling of being trapped
- Fatigue
- Short temper
- Chemical abuse
- Decreased creativity
- Nonproductivity while busy
- Inability to focus on matters at hand
- Dejection
- Absence of physical well-being
- Feeling of ineffectiveness
- Lack of enthusiasm

Remedies

1. Ask for help.
2. Examine priorities.
3. Choose to become burned out for a set period of time.
4. Contact support-group members for help.
5. Take a week off.
6. Engage in energizing activities.
7. Examine the balance between personal time, social time, family time, and work time.
8. Go on an enjoyable retreat.
9. Take a leave of absence.

10. Ask for feedback about personal use of chemicals.
11. Inform others of the feeling of burnout and of personal plans to take a "sabbatical."
12. Take a "mental-health" break.
13. Meditate.
14. Get more sleep.

Team/Organizational Burnout

Symptoms

- Nonproductive, nervous energy while working on tasks
- Little energy for accomplishing maintenance concerns[1]
- Tendency to blame "outside" forces
- Nonproductive meetings
- Requests for relief
- Team members exhibit one another's negative symptoms.

Remedies

1. Ask for help from fellow team members or other co-workers.
2. Ask for help from an outsider.
3. Have a team lunch outside the work setting or go on a field trip with fellow team members.
4. Suspend operations until the team feels capable of resuming.
5. Eliminate meetings held during mealtime or after work hours.
6. Recognize that everyone will lose unless an effort is made to recover.
7. Recognize that the situation is systemic and requires a major intervention.

Measures to Prevent Individual and/or Team/Organizational Burnout

1. Plan regular retreats for fun and a change of perspective.
2. Make a list every day of priority activities to be completed as well as activities that can be delayed.
3. Schedule weekly "maintenance" meetings with fellow team members.
4. Develop an awareness of the circumstances that generate burnout.
5. Say "no."

---

[1] A team has both *task* and *maintenance* concerns. The task concerns have to do with the team's goals, and the maintenance concerns have to do with the ways in which the team members interact as they accomplish their goals.

6. Avoid stressful situations or groups.
7. With the help of support-group members, examine options in various situations.
8. Meditate.
9. Include considerations of benefits, success, and visible results as part of planning processes.
10. Take a leave of absence or vacation when symptoms of burnout begin to appear.
11. Renegotiate roles.
12. Keep priorities in order.
13. Be aware of and take advantage of personal energy cycles.
14. Identify and make use of a personal support base.

THE TROUBLE WITH MARTI: MANAGING COMPLEX TASKS

Goals

I. To foster the team members' awareness of the factors that can lead to stress.

II. To offer the team members an opportunity to experience some of these factors.

III. To offer the team members an opportunity to share their feelings and ideas about coping with stress on the job and about managing complex tasks in short periods of time.

Time Required

Approximately forty-five minutes.

Materials

I. A copy of The Trouble with Marti Case-Study Sheet for each team member.

II. One sheet of blank paper.

III. A pencil for each team member.

IV. A watch or clock for the leader's use in monitoring time.

Physical Setting

A room with a table and chairs for the team members.

Process

I. The leader announces that in this session the team members will have an opportunity to practice their problem-solving skills on a case study.

II. The leader reads the following instructions aloud:

1. After receiving the case-study sheet, you and your fellow team members will read it, discuss it, and answer each of the five questions on the sheet.

2. You will have exactly fifteen minutes to complete this task.

3. Select one team member to record the team's response for each question.

4. Select one team member to keep a "participation log" that lists the names of the members who contribute during the discussion.

5. I will monitor the time for you and let you know when the time is up.

6. I will not answer any questions for you until you have completed the task. However, I will read these instructions again if anyone wishes.

III. The leader lays the case-study sheets face down on the table, along with the blank sheet of paper and the pencils, and cautions the team members not to pick up the materials until they are instructed to begin the task. After explaining that the sheet of blank paper is to be used by the team member who keeps the participation log, the leader asks the team members to begin working on the task. While the team members work, the leader makes comments such as the following every minute or so:

1. Remember your time limit.
2. Two minutes have passed, so you should have finished reading the case study and started discussing it.
3. You have only ten minutes left; that gives you two minutes per question.
4. You have only eight minutes left, so you should have completed your answer to the first question.
5. You should be moving to the third question. There are only six minutes left.
6. You have only a few minutes more. Remember that you must be done on time.
7. Four minutes to go. You should be discussing the fourth question.
8. You should be discussing the last question. Just two minutes left.
9. Sixty seconds.
10. Thirty seconds to finish up. You need to hurry.
11. Fifteen seconds.
12. Time. Stop your discussion.

During this time the leader refuses to answer any questions.

IV. At the end of the fifteen-minute period, the leader asks the team members to turn in their completed answers and their participation log.

V. The leader leads a discussion of the experience by asking questions such as the following:

1. How did you feel about the comments I made as you were working?
2. How did you feel about your fellow team members?
3. How did you feel about yourself?
4. How do you feel about the team's completed work?
5. How did the nature of the task and the way it was presented to you affect your work?
6. How did you organize yourselves to complete the task? What did you do that was effective? What did you do that was ineffective?
7. In what ways were the conditions of this activity like the conditions you experience on the job? In what ways were the conditions of this activity different from the ones you generally experience?

8. What have you learned about stress on the job? What have you learned about managing and completing complex tasks in short periods of time? How can you use what you have learned in the future?

Variation

The leader may substitute a case study that is specific to the team's area of expertise.

By Richard L. Bunning.

❖ The Trouble with Marti Case-Study Sheet

The Situation

"I'm not sure that going to the president is the right thing to do," says Frank.

"Well, we can't go on this way," wails Yvonne. "That woman is going to drive us crazy."

"I agree that we have to do something," responds Rick, "but I'm not sure that going to the president is wise, either. After all, wouldn't he be inclined to support his vice president and think we're nothing but a bunch of chronic complainers?"

These three supervisors—Frank, Yvonne, and Rick—are discussing a problem that is growing more difficult each day: the leadership approach of their boss, Marti. Eight months ago Marti was named vice president of the southwestern region of XYZ Manufacturing. She replaced a dynamic and popular executive named Ardath, who resigned to take a higher-paying job elsewhere. Shortly before Marti took her position, a new company president was appointed; the new president's mission was to return the regional manufacturing site to profitability after two years of financial decline.

Marti, who evidently was successful as a specific-projects manager at the corporate headquarters in the midwest, seems to be uncomfortable in her new role as the leader of a support-services department. Her knowledge of Frank's, Yvonne's, and Rick's specialty areas is quite limited; she also does not appear to be eager to spend the time to learn. She applauds the completion of special projects but discounts the contributions of those in her department who support these projects by filing, entering computer data, and maintaining the flow of information on paper. She further alienates her staff members by criticizing them in front of others. Several other top managers are becoming dissatisfied with Marti's performance; in fact, she has become the object of veiled ridicule throughout the organization.

Then a week ago, without previously asking for input from her staff, Marti announced a departmental reorganization. She shuffled many departmental responsibilities among Frank, Yvonne, and Rick and reassigned a number of their subordinates.

After the announcement Frank, Yvonne, and Rick spoke with Marti separately, each trying to convince her to reconsider the reorganization. Marti dismissed their concerns by informing them that if they were "just more committed," things would "work out fine." When Frank told Marti that he would do his best but would need some extra help to complete the increased work load, Marti's response was "Maybe you need a time-management course." The three supervisors agree that reorganization was needed; but they object to the way Marti handled the situation and especially to the fact that she failed to consult them beforehand. Marti's determination and single-mindedness—evidently assets in her role as a special-projects manager at the corporate headquarters—have resulted in a thoroughly demoralized department. Several department members are actively seeking other employment.

The three supervisors feel that they are at the end of their resources and have been discussing what, if anything, to do next. The options they have considered include resigning, calling a clandestine departmental meeting to discuss the situation and perhaps to decide on a group action, signing a "no-confidence" petition, just doing nothing, and making an appointment with the president to protest.

Now the three supervisors sit dejectedly, pondering their situation. "If only Ardath hadn't left," says Rick.

Questions To Be Answered

1. Why might Marti have been chosen for her position?

2. How might Frank, Yvonne, and Rick have contributed to the problem?

3. How has Marti contributed to the problem?

4. Which of the options, if any, should the supervisors pursue? What other option(s) might be more appropriate?

5. How can this situation be resolved in such a way that the organization achieves its goals and everyone concerned can live with the outcome?

ROLE MAPPING:
DEALING WITH ROLE-RELATED STRESS

Goals

I. To acquaint the team members with the relationship between roles and stress.

II. To introduce the process of role mapping, whereby the team members can identify their sources of role-related stress and then plan changes to particular roles or to the effects of those roles.

Time Required

Approximately two hours.

Materials

I. A copy of the Role Mapping Theory Sheet for each team member.

II. A copy of the Role Mapping Work Sheet for each team member.

III. A pencil for each team member.

IV. A sheet of newsprint listing the following questions (prepared in advance by the leader):

Questions to Ask the Partner You Are Helping

1. How would you describe your ideal resolution of this role situation? (Would you like to drop the role? If not, how would you describe this role if it were exactly the way you wanted it to be?)

2. If you would like to drop the role, what specific things could you do to make that happen? If you would like to change it, what specific changes could you make to bring you closer to your ideal situation?

3. If you do not choose to change or drop the role itself, how could you change the way that role affects you?

V. Masking tape for posting newsprint.

Physical Setting

A room with movable chairs for the team members. Writing surfaces should be provided. The room should be large enough so that subgroups can work on devising action plans without disturbing one another.

Process

I. The leader introduces the activity by explaining its goals.

II. The leader distributes copies of the theory sheet and pencils and asks the team members to read the theory sheet.

III. The leader leads a discussion of the contents of the theory sheet, eliciting and answering questions as necessary. (Ten to fifteen minutes.)

IV. The leader distributes copies of the work sheet, announces that for the duration of the activity the team members will be identifying and addressing sources of stress related to their *work-related* roles,[1] briefly reviews the work sheet with the team members to ensure that they understand how to complete it, and then asks them to work independently to fill out Items 1 through 6 on their work sheets. (The leader explains that later the team members will complete Item 7 in subgroups.) (Twenty minutes.)

V. After all team members have completed the first six items on the work sheet, the leader asks them to assemble into subgroups of three members each for the purpose of completing Item 7 on the work sheet. The leader explains that each subgroup is to follow this procedure:

1. The members concentrate on one member's action plan at a time;

2. The person whose action plan is the focus of the subgroup effort (called the "focus person" in these instructions) chooses *one role only* that he or she is willing to discuss with the others.

3. The focus person briefs the other subgroup members on the rating and ranking for the chosen role and any other specific information that he or she wishes to share.

4. The two members who have been briefed helped the focus person to devise an action plan for the chosen role. *[Note to leader: At this point the prepared newsprint sheet should be posted.]* This process entails asking the questions on newsprint plus any others that seem pertinent and helping the focus person to complete the four columns of Item 7 on the work sheet.

5. The subgroup members should plan to spend fifteen minutes on each person's action plan (forty-five minutes on the entire procedure).

The leader elicits and answers questions about the task, emphasizes that each team member is to write an action plan *for one role only,* and then asks the subgroups to begin. As the subgroups work, the leader keeps them apprised of the time remaining and when the fifteen-minute periods are over.

VI. After forty-five minutes the leader reconvenes the total team and asks questions such as the following:

---

[1] The leader may mention that later, on their own time, the team members might want to complete a version of the work sheet including both work-related and nonwork-related roles.

1. How do you feel at this moment about the stress you experience as a result of your work-related roles?
2. How did you feel while you were working on your own action plan with your partners? How did you feel while you were helping your partners complete their action plans?
3. What similarities or patterns did you see in your subgroup? What differences did you see? What conclusions can you draw from those similarities or differences?
4. How might you benefit as a result of completing this task? How might the team benefit?

The leader makes concluding remarks and encourages the team members to work on their own to devise action plans for other roles as they see fit.

Variation

If the team has four or fewer members, in Step V the leader may ask the members to assemble into subgroups of two or may eliminate the use of subgroups.

By Michael Lauderdale. Adapted from *Burnout: Strategies for Personal and Organizational Life; Speculations on Evolving Paradigms,* by M. Lauderdale, 1982, San Diego, CA: Learning Concepts. Used with the permission of the author.

❖ Role Mapping Theory Sheet

For each of us, life is predicated on expectations, many of which are related to the roles we fill. Yet change is inevitable in some, if not all, of our roles. Sometimes a role change comes from an external source; sometimes it comes from within, as a result of maturing or of changing interests and needs. When a role change occurs, a person's expectations regarding the role must be adjusted. Failure to make such an adjustment can lead to stress and eventually to burnout.

Role mapping is a technique for developing insight into one's roles, expectations associated with those roles, and the related situations that can be pinpointed as sources of stress. It may help to imagine yourself suspended by a network of lines radiating from you, each line representing one social role. These lines comprise your social existence; direct your actions; and provide you with support, comfort, and meaning. Stress occurs when one of these lines begins to tug at you in a way that makes you feel uncomfortable rather than comfortable. Your expectations of the role and the reality of that role are in conflict.

1. *Identify roles.* The first step in the process of role mapping is to identify all of your roles—a task that may seem simpler than it actually is. It is easy to underestimate the number of roles you fill and, thus, the sets of expectations that you have. For example, if your job requires you to supervise others, you have a separate role and set of expectations associated with each person you supervise. Although you may think of yourself as behaving in a uniform way with each person, that is probably not true. Some of your subordinates may be more energetic than others, some more dependable, some more in need of support or guidance. Each is unique, and your relationship with each person makes unique demands on you. If you do not supervise people, the same principle is true of colleagues; because each is unique, you have a different role with each. In addition, you probably have other roles in the organization: a subordinate to your supervisor, a department member, a mentor to a new employee, a task-force member, a liaison between units or departments. Each relationship means another role.

You may find that some of your roles do not include a specific other person. For example, if you live alone and do not have domestic help, you have a role as a housekeeper. Similarly, when you travel alone, you assume one or more roles that do not necessarily include a specific other person or persons. Consumer roles also may imply concrete expectations but not in connection with a particular other person.[2]

---

[2] Advertising is often based on selling new expectations. When an automobile manufacturer suggests that driving a particular car denotes success, when a cologne promises to enhance sex appeal, or when a soap is portrayed as linked with youthful vitality, we are being taught expectations. Typically what is being conveyed is that we are less than what we should be and that to achieve higher expectations (thereby becoming "more") we should purchase particular products.

Here are just a few examples of the major roles that you may fill. Remember that each of these may have other roles associated with it.

> Mother or father
> Spouse
> Employee
> Friend
> Church member
> Voter
> Neighbor
> Member of a car pool
> Concerned citizen
> Member of a special-interest group (for example, the Sierra Club, the League of Women Voters, or the Young Republicans)
> Son or daughter
> Brother or sister
> Consumer

2. *Evaluate satisfaction/frustration.* After you have identified all of your roles, the second step is to evaluate the level of satisfaction as well as the level of frustration you feel in connection with each. You do this by comparing your expectations with the current reality. If a role is not meeting expectations, you can decide how either the role or the expectations of that role might be changed. The roles that are causing you frustration or too little satisfaction are your sources of stress.

3. *Establish priorities.* The third step in the process is to establish the relative priority of each role. When you set priorities for your roles, you are actually spelling out your values. Your most important values are represented by your highest-priority roles, and things that are of minimal value to you are represented as low-priority roles.

Prioritizing your roles will help you to see with greater clarity which roles are satisfying, which are neutral, and which are sources of frustration.

This process permits you to see from a fuller perspective where you are fragmented and caught between contending roles or spread thinly across too many roles. After you complete the process, you can re-evaluate the meaning of the roles that are causing frustration; then you can work to improve those roles, to lower their priority for you, to change the effects that those roles produce, or to eliminate the roles entirely. It may be that you can trace your frustration to a single role. For example, you may be at peace with most aspects of your life but find that your role as tenant—a role you consider insignificant—is troubling you because your landlord is nosy. Once you realize that this role is the source of your irritation, you can generate options: you may make peace with your landlord; you may threaten him into avoiding you; you may learn to ignore him; you may choose another place to rent; or you may decide to buy a house (or to live with the situation temporarily until you can afford to buy).

Through this process you begin to reduce ambiguity and thus lessen stress and frustration. The personal meaning of frustration and ambiguity can be altered. One important step in changing is accepting the fact that you cannot escape by denying. Running from ambiguity does not eliminate it and may increase the potential severity of stress.

❖ *Role Mapping Work Sheet*

1. List all of your *work-related* roles and subroles.

2. Rate your satisfaction—from 1 (highly dissatisfied) to 5 (highly satisfied)—with each role you listed in the previous step. (If you need more writing space, use the back of this sheet.)

1	2	3	4	5
Highly Dissatisfied	Dissatisfied	Ambivalent	Satisfied	Highly Satisfied

(1) Role:_____ Rating_____

(2) Role:_____ Rating_____

(3) Role:_____ Rating_____

(4) Role:_____ Rating_____

(5) Role:_____ Rating_____

(6) Role:_____ Rating_____

(7) Role:_____ Rating_____

(8) Role:_____ Rating_____

(9) Role:_____ Rating_____

(10) Role:_____ Rating_____

3. Rank each role from *most important* to *least important*. Your most-important or highest-priority role will be assigned the rank of 1. (If you need more space, use the back of this sheet.)

(1) Role:_____ Rank_____

(2) Role:_____ Rank_____

(3) Role:_____ Rank_____

(4) Role:_____ Rank_____

(5) Role:_____ Rank_____

(6) Role:_____ Rank_____

(7) Role:_____ Rank_____

(8) Role:_____ Rank_____

(9) Role:_____ Rank_____

(10) Role:_____ Rank_____

4. Now combine your ratings and rankings. (If you need more writing space, use the back of this sheet.) An example follows:

Role	Rank Order	Satisfaction
Employee	1	2 (Dissatisfied)
Supervisor	2	3 (Ambivalent)
Chairman of New-Product Development Committee	3	3 (Ambivalent)
Supervisor of Fred	4	5 (Highly Satisfied)
Supervisor of Jean	5	4 (Satisfied)
Supervisor of Chris	6	1 (Highly Dissatisfied)
Co-worker of Susan	7	4 (Satisfied)
Co-worker of Sam	8	2 (Dissatisfied)
Co-worker of Terry	9	4 (Satisfied)
Co-worker of Jane	10	1 (Highly Dissatisfied)

Role	Rank Order	Satisfaction

5. List the *least-important* roles (the ones with the highest numbers in your rank order) that produce dissatisfaction or ambivalence.

6. List the *most-important* roles (the ones with the lowest numbers in your rank order) that produce dissatisfaction or ambivalence.

7. Devise an action plan for reducing your level of stress by changing some of your work-related roles or by changing the effects that these roles produce. Remember that an effective action plan specifies exactly what will be done, who will do it, when it will be done, and what resources (both people and materials) will be needed.

What Will Be Done *(List Specific Action Steps)*	**Who Will Do It**	**When It Will Be Done** *(Deadline Date)*	**Resources Needed**

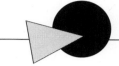

Introduction to
Team-Member Relationships

The relationships that team members share with one another have a direct bearing on the team's effectiveness. Team members must be able to involve all members in team discussions; listen to one another; freely express their ideas and feelings, including disagreement; be supportive of one another; and express commitment to the team. If poor interpersonal relationships exist—if cliques are formed, conflict is mismanaged, defensiveness is demonstrated, members participate unequally, and norms are rigid or counterproductive—the team cannot expect to reach its goals with any kind of consistency.

The activities in the Team-Member Relationships section accomplish a variety of goals connected with building stronger relationships; for example, they illustrate the phenomenon of synergy, help a team to analyze how it operates, examine the issue of team commitment, assist a team in evaluating its norms, help in identifying and correcting communication difficulties, offer a way to develop a conflict-management procedure, and assist in planning action for improving the team climate.

ALPHABET NAMES: ACHIEVING SYNERGY

Goals

I. To allow the team members to experience the effects of synergy.[1]

II. To offer the team members an opportunity to explore the relationship between team commitment to a task and synergy.

Time Required

Approximately one hour.

Materials

I. Blank paper and a pencil for each team member.

II. Newsprint and a felt-tipped marker for the team and for the leader.

Physical Setting

A chair for each team member. The chairs should be arranged in a semicircle. Writing surfaces should be provided.

Process

I. The leader distributes paper and pencils and instructs each team member to list the letters of the alphabet from "A" through "Z" in a vertical column on the left side of the paper.

II. The leader randomly selects a sentence from any written document and reads out loud the first twenty-six letters in that sentence. Each team member is instructed to write these letters in a vertical column to the right of the listed alphabet, so that all team members have twenty-six identical sets of two letters. The leader announces that the two letters in each set represent the first and last initials of a person's name.

---

[1] Synergy is the combined action of team members, which often results in a product that is greater than what any single member could have produced on his or her own.

III. The team members are told that they will have ten minutes to individually record the names of famous people whose initials correspond to any of the twenty-six sets of letters. Only one name per set of initials is permitted. The maximum score is twenty-six points, one point for each legitimate name using both initials.

IV. After ten minutes the leader instructs the team members to exchange papers and to "grade" one another's papers, checking any names they do not recognize with the person who wrote them and/or with the leader. The leader then records the individual high score and computes the team's average on newsprint.

V. The leader gives the members a newsprint flip chart and a felt-tipped marker and tells them that as a team working together they will have ten minutes to develop a second list of famous names. As the leader reads aloud a new, randomly selected sentence, a member of the team records the initial letters on the team's newsprint to the right of a column of alphabet letters. The process then continues, with the team formulating a list of up to twenty-six names and recording them on newsprint. (Ten minutes.)

VI. After ten minutes the leader reviews the team's list, checks the listed names, compares the team's scores with the average score and individual high score from the first part of the experience, and writes these scores on newsprint.

VII. The leader leads a discussion of the experience by asking questions such as the following:

1. How did you feel during the first part of the activity, while you were working on your own? How did you feel during the second part, while you were working with the team?

2. What similarities were there in the two parts of the activity and in the lists of names that were produced? What differences were there? How do you account for the similarities and differences?

3. What do the results of this activity say about:
   a. Individual work versus teamwork?
   b. Team commitment to a task?
   c. Team collaboration versus competition?
   d. Team potential versus individual potential?

4. What are the advantages of working alone (as opposed to working as a team)? What are the disadvantages? Under what conditions might working alone be preferable to working as a team?

5. What are the advantages of working as a team (as opposed to working alone)? What are the disadvantages? Under what conditions might working as a team be preferable to working alone?

The leader defines the concept of synergy for the team members, asks them for examples of synergy from their own experience, and then makes appropriate concluding remarks.

Variations

I. The nominal group technique[2] may be used for the second round, using the names generated during the first round.

II. The letters of the alphabet may be used alone, without the second set of letters, with different categories to be listed (for example, cars, food, or articles of clothing).

By Richard P. Greco. Adapted from *The 1979 Annual Handbook for Group Facilitators,* edited by J.E. Jones and J.W. Pfeiffer, 1979, San Diego, CA: University Associates.

---

[2] See the activity entitled "Nominal Group Technique: Applied Team Problem Solving."

PROCESS OBSERVATION:
ANALYZING HOW A TEAM OPERATES

Goals

I. To acquaint the team members with the various dimensions of a team's process.

II. To provide the team members with feedback concerning their team's process.

III. To offer the team members an opportunity to observe process variables in team meetings.

Time Required

Thirty-five minutes in addition to the time that the regular meeting consumes.

Materials

I. A copy of the Process Observation Report Form for each team member.

II. A pencil for the designated process observer.

Physical Setting

Any room in which the team regularly meets.

Process

I. At the beginning of a team meeting, the leader explains that it is useful to analyze the process by which a team operates and accomplishes things. The leader states that, accordingly, for the next several meetings one member will observe (but not participate), analyze the team's functioning, and report his or her observations at the conclusion of the meeting. The leader also clarifies that the members will take turns observing and that each observer will record his or her observations on a specific form for that purpose. (Five minutes.)

II. The leader distributes copies of the Process Observation Report Form and reviews the form with the team, eliciting and answering questions about it. (Fifteen minutes.)

III. The leader chooses a volunteer to serve as the first observer and gives this person a pencil. All other members are asked to put their observation forms away and to concentrate on the business of the meeting.

IV. After the business of the meeting has been concluded, the leader asks the observer to report on his or her observations about the team's process. Then the leader elicits reactions from the remaining members.

Variations

I. Sections of the report form may be assigned to different team members in advance of the meeting.

II. Two observers may be chosen so that their observations can be compared.

III. The meeting may be videotaped. Subsequently, all team members review the tape, complete the form, and then share their observations.

IV. The observer may participate in the meeting while he or she is observing.

Adapted from *A Handbook of Structured Experiences for Human Relations Training* (Vol. I, Rev.), edited by J.W. Pfeiffer and J.E. Jones, 1974, San Diego, CA: University Associates.

❖ *Process Observation Report Form*

Team_____ Date_____

Interpersonal-Communication Skills

1. Expressing (both in words and without words)

2. Listening

3. Responding

Communication Pattern

4. Direction (one person to another, one person to the whole team, all through a leader)

5. Content (expression of thoughts and ideas; expression of feelings)

Leadership

6. Major roles (record names of team members)

    _____ Information processor (requested facts, helped the team analyze and summarize what was happening)

    _____ Coordinator

_____ Evaluator (helped the team evaluate its work during the meeting)

_____ Harmonizer (sought to maintain harmony)

_____ Gatekeeper (kept communication flowing, en couraged participation and sharing)

_____ Follower (passively went along with the team)

_____ Blocker (blocked the team's progress)

_____ Recognition seeker

_____ Dominator (dominated the discussion)

_____ Avoider (avoided confrontation and difficult issues)

7. Leadership style

_____ Democratic (leader encouraged everyone to participate and to contribute to decisions)

_____ Autocratic (leader guided the entire process and made all decisions without asking for the team's input)

_____ Laissez faire (leader took a "hands-off" approach and let the members do what they wanted)

8. Response to leadership style

_____ Eager participation _____ Low commitment _____ Resistance

_____ Lack of enthusiasm _____ Holding back

Climate

9. Tone of the meeting (How did the meeting "feel"? Were the team members at ease and comfortable with one another? Did they cooperate to accomplish the purpose of the meeting?)

10. Cohesiveness (Did the team members function as a unit?)

Goals

11. Explicitness

12. Commitment to agreed-on goals

Situational Variables

13. Group size (Were all the people here who should have been here? Was anyone absent who should have been included?)

14. Time limit (Was a time limit set for the meeting? Were time limits set for specific discussions? Did the team adhere to the set limits?)

15. Physical facilities (Was the size of the room adequate? Was it equipped with everything the team members needed during the meeting?)

Observer's Reactions

16. Feelings experienced during the observation

17. Feelings at this moment

18. Hunches, speculations, and ideas about the process observed

WIDGET ENGINEERING CORPORATION: EXAMINING TEAM COMMITMENT

Goal

To offer the team members an opportunity to examine the issue of commitment to a team by analyzing the role play of a specific managerial problem.

Time Required

One and one-half hours.

Materials

One copy of the Widget Engineering Corporation Briefing Sheet for each team member.

Physical Setting

A main meeting room in which the role play takes place. Another room should be provided so that the team member who plays the role of Terry can study that role in privacy.

Process

I. The leader gives each team member a copy of the briefing sheet and asks the members to read this sheet. (Five minutes.)

II. The leader leads a discussion of the problem. (Twenty minutes.)

III. The leader asks for a volunteer to play the role of Terry and instructs the volunteer to leave the room and prepare for the role by studying the briefing sheet. In the role player's absence, the remaining team members discuss the situation and what Chris should do. The leader asks for a volunteer to play the role of Chris. (Fifteen minutes.)

IV. The team member who is role playing Terry is called back to the main meeting room to meet with the person who is role playing Chris. While the other team members silently observe, the two players attempt to work through the problem. (Ten minutes.)

V. The leader elicits comments from the observers and helps the team to review the role play. (Twenty minutes.)

VI. The leader summarizes the discussion and then asks questions such as these:

1. What have we learned about commitment in teams?
2. How would we define "commitment" for this team? What would it look like?
3. How will the rest of the organization recognize our commitment?
4. What does "commitment" mean in terms of our interactions with other teams in this organization?
5. What will we do to encourage commitment among ourselves?

By Dave Francis and Don Young. Adapted from *Improving Work Groups: A Practical Manual for Team Building,* by D. Francis and D. Young, 1979, San Diego, CA: University Associates.

❖ *Widget Engineering Corporation Briefing Sheet*

Widget Engineering Corporation has been going through a major reorganization because its basic product line has become outdated by the invention of new plastic materials. Several small production units have been closed, and the company is reorganizing its factory in Boston to handle the newly developed materials. Top management is particularly anxious about the success of this factory; overall profitability has been poor in recent years, and a failure in Boston might be disastrous for the company.

For the last four months, Terry, an advisor in the work-study department, has been assigned to the Boston factory. Terry's task is "to identify operational and training requirements and to ensure that adequate systems and training are planned and conducted." Terry's supervisor, Chris, is based at the company's administrative offices, which are thirty-five miles away. Chris visits Terry for about half a day every two weeks.

Chris, who wants to use a team approach with Terry and the three other work-study advisors, has organized meetings in which the team works through several problem-solving exercises designed to increase the department's effectiveness. Terry's behavior in these meetings is erratic. Sometimes Terry is morose and quiet, avoiding contact with the other team members; when questioned about this lack of participation, Terry withdraws further and appears hurt. On other occasions, however, Terry is positive and open, offering suggestions and actively responding to comments made by others. Chris has heard that Terry's daily interactions with people are similarly erratic.

Chris has been intimidated by the threat of Terry's withdrawal and has not dealt with the problem. It would be difficult for Chris to replace Terry with someone of equal experience. However, Chris knows that if the company's financial and technical problems are to be solved, Terry and the other work-study advisors at the Boston factory must perform in a consistently effective manner at all times.

The problem is brought to a head one day when Jim, the manager of the Boston factory, telephones Chris to complain about Terry. Jim says, "Frankly, I'm worried. Sometimes Terry's reports are on time and carefully done, and sometimes I don't get them at all. Also, I can't predict whether Terry's going to be optimistic and energetic or pessimistic and scarcely able to function. And that's not all. I've heard that Terry seems badly stressed—sometimes loses control and flies off the handle. I believe this behavior is starting to affect the morale around here. You know how important Boston is to us. I need a good work-study service, and Terry just isn't reliable."

Chris thanks Jim for the call, picks up the phone, makes an appointment with Terry, and then plans what to say.

DOS AND DON'TS:
EVALUATING TEAM NORMS

Goals

    I. To help the team members to identify team norms.

    II. To assist the team members in determining which of the identified norms have the greatest effect on the cohesiveness of their team.

Time Required

Approximately one hour and fifteen minutes.

Materials

    I. Blank paper and a pencil for each team member.

    II. A newsprint flip chart and a felt-tipped marker.

    III. Masking tape for posting newsprint.

Physical Setting

A room with writing surfaces for the team members.

Process

    I. The leader announces that during the activity the members will be identifying and evaluating team norms. The leader clarifies that a team norm is a rule—generally unwritten but understood by all—that regulates the behavior of team members. The following examples are given:

        1. When a team meeting is held, the members arrive early or on time—not a few minutes late.

        2. Team members treat customers in respectful, caring ways.

        3. When one team member is facing an imminent deadline, the other members pitch in and help.

    II. The leader distributes blank paper and pencils, asks the team members to assemble into triads, and instructs each triad to list five "dos" and five "don'ts" that represent existing team norms. (Twenty minutes.)

III. After reconvening the total team, the leader asks the triads to take turns reading their lists. As each item is announced, the leader records it on newsprint. As each sheet of newsprint is filled, the leader posts it in a prominent place so that all team members can see it. (Ten minutes.)

IV. The leader leads a discussion of all items posted on newsprint, and the team as a whole decides which three "dos" and which three "don'ts" have the greatest impact on the team's cohesiveness. (Twenty to thirty minutes.)

V. The leader asks questions such as the following:
1. What have we learned about how norms affect a team's functioning?
2. How can we use what we have learned to improve our team's cohesiveness?

Variation

If the team has fewer than six members, the leader may omit the formation of subgroups.

By David W. Johnson/Frank P. Johnson, *JOINING TOGETHER: Group Theory and Group Skills,* © 1975, pp. 61-62. Adapted by permission of Prentice Hall, Inc., Englewood Cliffs, New Jersey.

TEAM COMMUNICATIONS: IDENTIFYING AND CORRECTING DIFFICULTIES

Goals

    I. To help the team members to identify specific malfunctions in team communication.

    II. To assist the team members in planning actions to correct the identified malfunctions in communication.

Time Required

Approximately one and one-half hours.

Materials

    I. Blank paper and a pencil for each team member.

    II. A newsprint flip chart and a felt-tipped marker.

    III. Masking tape for posting newsprint.

Physical Setting

A room with wall space for posting newsprint. Writing surfaces should be provided for the team members.

Process

    I. The leader writes the following information on newsprint and displays the newsprint in such a way that all team members can see it easily.

Three Examples of Communication Malfunction in the Team

Example	Effect It Had on Me
1.	
2.	
3.	

    II. Blank paper and pencils are distributed. The leader instructs each team member to follow the newsprint format, defining three specific examples of communication difficulties within the team and describing how these incidents affected him or her. (Ten minutes.)

III. The team members take turns reporting examples and the accompanying effects. As examples and effects are cited, the leader records them on newsprint; as each newsprint sheet is filled, the leader posts it in a prominent spot. (Ten to fifteen minutes.)

IV. The leader leads a discussion of the posted examples. During this discussion the team members:

1. Identify any communication malfunctions that are similar in terms of cause or effect;

2. Prioritize the examples in terms of their importance to the team; and

3. Decide specifically what should be done to prevent the occurrence of such malfunctions in the future.

By Dave Francis and Don Young. Adapted from *Improving Work Groups: A Practical Manual for Team Building,* by D. Francis and D. Young, 1979, San Diego, CA: University Associates.

CONFLICT MANAGEMENT: DEVELOPING A PROCEDURE

Goal

To help the team members to develop a procedure for managing conflict.

Time Required

Two to two and one-half hours.

Materials

I. A copy of the Conflict Management Suggestion Sheet for each team member.
II. Blank paper for each team member.
III. A pencil for each team member.
IV. A newsprint flip chart and a felt-tipped marker.
V. Masking tape for posting newsprint.

Physical Setting

A room with a table and chairs for the team members. If a table is not available, the leader may substitute clipboards or other portable writing surfaces. Plenty of wall space should be available for posting newsprint.

Process

I. The leader distributes copies of the Conflict Management Suggestion Sheet and asks the team members to read the sheet. (Ten minutes.)
II. The leader reviews the content of the suggestion sheet with the team members, eliciting and answering questions as necessary. (Twenty minutes.)
III. The team members are asked to select partners. Each team member is given blank paper and a pencil, and each pair of team members is instructed to write a set of guidelines for conflict management that the team can use. The leader clarifies that the ideas presented in the section of their handout entitled "A Procedure for Managing Conflict" can serve as a useful starting point and that they may approach this task in any way they wish; for example, they may borrow ideas from the handout, modify these ideas, write entirely new

guidelines, or combine the handout ideas with their own. The leader stipulates that each pair of team members should be prepared to present their guidelines to the team later and to explain their reasons for including specific ideas. (Twenty to thirty minutes.)

IV. The leader asks the pairs to take turns presenting their guidelines and their reasons for choosing as they did. As this information is presented, the leader records it on newsprint and posts each newsprint sheet after it is filled. (Twenty to thirty minutes.)

V. The leader reviews the posted information with the team members and assists them in achieving consensus[1] about which guidelines they want to adopt for their team.

VI. When the team members have reached consensus, the leader records the final guidelines on newsprint. Then the leader gives the newsprint list to a volunteer to reproduce and distribute to all team members. The leader also suggests posting a copy in the room where the team usually holds its meetings.

VII. Before adjourning, the leader elicits reactions to the activity and makes concluding comments.

By Larry Porter. Adapted from *The 1991 Annual: Developing Human Resources,* edited by J. William Pfeiffer, 1991, San Diego, CA: University Associates.

---

[1] A consensus decision is one that all team members can accept, regardless of how satisfied they are with it. Each member's opinion must be heard; no "majority-rule" voting, bargaining, or averaging is allowed.

❖ *Conflict Management Suggestion Sheet*

A Procedure for Managing Conflict

1. Do not ignore something that bothers you. Work on the issue involved before the situation becomes intolerable to you. However, if needed, a cooling-off period may be established, with an agreed-on time to deal with the issue later.

2. Talk directly to the other person involved. Work with the other person to try to solve the issue yourselves.

3. If your organization has a consultant or a human resource development (HRD) specialist on staff, ask that person for suggestions on how to approach the other person or for suggestions on how to define the issue. Be sure to check back with this resource person for feedback or perspectives on the result.

4. If the solution you work out involves a potential change of work procedure, get the approval of your manager before you implement the change.

5. If someone approaches you with an issue, be willing to work on it. You may also wish to seek the help of a staff consultant or HRD person in clarifying your point of view.

6. If an individual begins to complain to you about another person who is not present, encourage that individual to talk directly with the other person instead. This approach to handling conflict is much more positive and discourages the perpetuation of rumors, false information, and so on.

7. If, after you have tried to work on the issue on your own with the other person involved—and there has been no change and the conflict still exists—ask for help from a staff consultant or HRD specialist.

Things to Keep in Mind Before Working on an Issue

1. Be sure that there is a real problem and that you are not just in a bad mood.

2. Try to identify the real issue or opportunity, not just the symptoms or personalities.

3. Be prepared to work toward a mutually agreeable solution, not just toward "winning."

4. Remember that it is all right to disagree and that the other person is not "bad" if he or she disagrees with you.

5. Keep some perspective. Relationships are not destroyed but can even be enhanced by working toward a mutually satisfactory solution to a conflict.

Things to Keep in Mind While Working on an Issue

1. Look for a "win/win" solution: an arrangement whereby both you and the other person involved "win."

2. Do your best to put yourself in the other person's shoes.

3. Be willing to "own" part of the problem as belonging to you. (Avoid thinking "That's not *my* problem.")

4. Remember that talking about your feelings is more effective than acting them out.

5. Establish a common goal and stay focused on it.

6. Be persistent in coming to a satisfactory solution if it is really important to you.

7. Use the effective feedback behaviors listed below under "Giving Feedback."

8. At the end of the discussion with the other person, summarize what has been decided and who will take any next steps.

Giving Feedback

Giving "feedback" is a way of helping another person to consider changing his or her behavior. It is communication to a person that gives that person information about how he or she affects you. Used properly, it can be a helpful "guidance-control" mechanism for an individual to use in altering his or her behavior.

Here are the criteria for useful feedback:

1. *It describes rather than judges.* Describe your *own* reaction. Avoid "judging" language so that the other person will feel less defensive.

2. *It is specific rather than general.* Don't say, "You are dominating." Say instead, "Just now when we were deciding the issue you didn't listen to what I said but kept right on talking."

3. *It takes into account the needs of both the recipient and the giver of the feedback.* Feedback can be destructive when it serves only your own needs and fails to consider the needs of the other person.

4. *It is directed toward behavior that the other person can do something about.* Frustration is only increased when a person is reminded of some shortcoming over which he or she has no control.

5. *It is requested rather than "dumped."* Feedback is most useful when the recipient has asked for it.

6. *It is well timed.* In general, feedback is most useful when it occurs as soon as possible after the given behavior.

7. *It is checked to ensure that it is clear.* Ask the recipient to try to rephrase what you have said.

TEAM-CLIMATE ASSESSMENT: ACTION PLANNING FOR IMPROVEMENT

Goals

I. To help a team to examine its working climate.

II. To assist the team members in preparing an action plan for improving the team's working climate.

Time Required

One hour and fifteen to thirty minutes.

Materials

I. A copy of the Team-Climate Assessment Form for each team member.

II. A pencil for each team member.

III. Blank paper for each team member.

Physical Setting

A room in which the team members can work without interruptions.

Process

I. The leader distributes copies of the Team-Climate Assessment Form and pencils and instructs the team members to complete their forms. (Five minutes.)

II. After asking the team members whether they want to report their individual scores orally or write them on blank paper and turn them in anonymously, the leader collects the scores according to the team members' chosen method.

III. The leader summarizes the scores on newsprint, recording the range and the mean score for each item. (Five to ten minutes.)

IV. The leader helps the team to examine and discuss the following issues:

1. The range of scores and the mean score for each item;

2. Whether the team would develop better if the members' behaviors moved more to the left or right side of the scale on each item;

3. The specific behaviors that relate to each item; and

4. The overall team climate and the members' ideas for improving it.

(Thirty minutes.)

V. The leader assists the team members in devising an action plan for improving the team climate, concentrating on *who* will do *what* and *by when*. The final plan is recorded on newsprint, and the leader asks for a volunteer to create a handout from the newsprint plan and to distribute a copy of this handout to each team member. The leader announces that at a later date the team will review its action plan, complete the form again, and compare the new scores with the scores from this session.

_____

By Dave Francis and Don Young. Adapted from *Improving Work Groups: A Practical Manual for Team Building,* by D. Francis and D. Young, 1979, San Diego, CA: University Associates.

❖ *Team-Climate Assessment Form*

Instructions: Give your candid opinions of this team by rating its characteristics on the seven-point scales shown below. Circle the appropriate number on each scale to represent your evaluation.

1. Openness

Are individuals open in their transactions with others? Are there hidden agendas? Are some topics taboo for discussion within the group? Can the team members express their feelings about others openly without fear that others will take offense?

1	2	3	4	5	6	7

Individuals are   Individuals are
very open   very guarded

2. Conformity

Does the team have rules, procedures, policies, and traditions that are preventing it from working effectively? Are the ideas of senior members considered to be "law"? Can individuals freely express unusual or unpopular views?

1	2	3	4	5	6	7

Rigid conformity to   Open team with
an inappropriate pattern   a flexible pattern

3. Support

Do the team members pull for one another? What happens when an individual makes a mistake? Do members who are strong expend energy in helping members who are less experienced or less capable?

1	2	3	4	5	6	7

High level of support   Little help for
for individuals   individuals

4. Confronting Difficulties

Are difficult or uncomfortable issues worked through openly? Are conflicts confronted or swept under the carpet? Can the team members openly disagree with the team leader? Does the team devote much energy to working through difficulties thoroughly?

1	2	3	4	5	6	7

Difficult issues
are avoided

Problems are attacked
openly and directly

5. Risk Taking

Do individuals feel that they can try new things, risk failure, and still get support? Does the team encourage its members to extend themselves?

1	2	3	4	5	6	7

Risk taking in work
is not encouraged

Experimentation and personal
exploration are the norm

6. Shared Values

Have the team members worked through their own values with others? Is time spent on considering the cause (why) as well as the effect (what)? Do the team members share specific, fundamental values?

1	2	3	4	5	6	7

No basis of
common values

Large area of
common ground

7. Energy

Do the team members put sufficient energy into working on relationships with one another? Does team membership act as a stimulus and energizer to individuals?

1	2	3	4	5	6	7

High level of positive
energy

Little energy directed
toward the team

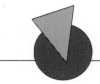

Introduction to
Meetings

Meetings constitute a common trouble spot for teams. Almost everyone who has ever worked in a team—or in an organization, for that matter—is familiar with what can go wrong with a meeting:

- Time is wasted.
- People are asked to attend when they do not really need to be there.
- Those attending do not know the reason for the meeting until they arrive (and therefore cannot prepare properly).
- The meeting leader does not plan carefully so that the purpose is accomplished efficiently.
- Those attending fail to speak up when they disagree with what is happening.
- The people attending are not allowed to put their concerns on the meeting agenda.
- After the meeting, the people who attended fail to do what they said they would do.

This list of potential problems is only a sample and cannot begin to illustrate the frustration people feel when they are "trapped" in an ineffective meeting.

On the other hand, Schindler-Rainman, Lippitt, and Cole (1988) have pointed out some of the characteristics of an effective meeting:

- The furniture is arranged so that every person attending can see all of the others.
- At the front of the room, there is a place to record ideas, preferably on a newsprint pad so that the information can be saved. (Chalkboards and "whiteboards" have to be erased.)
- An agenda is presented, amended, and agreed on.
- There are time estimates of how long each agenda item should take.

- Someone records the thinking and decisions of the meeting and agrees to prepare the notes in handout form afterward and to distribute that handout to everyone who attended.
- The meeting notes indicate who has agreed to what before the next meeting; names are underlined in the notes.
- Dates of future meetings (not just the next meeting) are set well ahead so that people can make arrangements to attend and can record the information on their individual calendars.
- At least once or twice during the meeting someone asks, "How are we doing on our meeting process today? How can we be more productive?"
- Those in attendance consider whether anyone else should be involved and, if so, who.
- At the end of the meeting, people review who will be doing what before the next meeting.

The activities in the Meetings section deal with ways in which team members can make their meetings more effective. They emphasize issues such as starting meetings appropriately, focusing the team on the subject of the meeting, warming up, increasing team members' awareness of meeting procedures, clarifying and evaluating what the team members consider to be "successful" meetings, devising meeting agendas, and creating a check list for team meetings.

REFERENCE

Schindler-Rainman, E., Lippitt, R., & Cole, J. (1988). *Taking your meetings out of the doldrums* (rev. ed.). San Diego, CA: University Associates.

RECOGNITION: STARTING MEETINGS APPROPRIATELY

Goals

I. To introduce the concept of recognizing team members at the beginning of meetings.

II. To generate ideas about how the team members would like to accomplish recognition at their own meetings.

Time Required

One hour to one hour and fifteen minutes.

Materials

I. A copy of the Recognition Theory and Idea Sheet for each team member.

II. A newsprint flip chart and a felt-tipped marker.

III. Masking tape for posting newsprint.

Physical Setting

A room with chairs for the team members. The members should be seated so that they can see the leader, the newsprint flip chart, and one another. Plenty of wall space should be available for posting newsprint.

Process

I. The leader distributes copies of the theory and idea sheet and asks the team members to read this sheet. (Ten minutes.)

II. The leader leads a discussion of the handout contents, eliciting and answering questions as necessary. (Ten minutes.)

III. The team members are asked to brainstorm[1] visual and auditory methods of accomplishing recognition at the beginning of *their own* team meetings. As ideas are contributed, the leader records them on newsprint and posts each completed sheet of newsprint. (Ten minutes.)

IV. The leader helps the team members to achieve consensus[2] about which methods they would like to try. The leader records the team's final choices on newsprint, removes the previous sheets of newsprint from the wall, and posts the final choices.

V. The team members select two methods from their final newsprint list and practice these methods. After each method is practiced, the leader elicits reactions. (Twenty minutes.)

VI. The leader asks a volunteer to reproduce the team's final choices in handout form and distribute the handout to all team members. Plans are made for the method of recognition to be used at the next team meeting.

By William R. Daniels. Adapted from *Group Power II: A Manager's Guide to Conducting Regular Meetings,* by W.R. Daniels, 1990, San Diego, CA: University Associates. Used with the permission of the author.

---

[1] Brainstorming is a technique used by groups to generate a number of creative ideas in a short time. The group members take turns contributing one idea at a time until all ideas have been exhausted. No criticism, evaluation, or judgment of ideas is allowed until the brainstorming phase has been completed. For further instructions see the activity entitled "Brainstorming: A Problem-Solving Technique."

[2] A consensus decision is one that all team members can accept, regardless of how satisfied they are with it. Each member's opinion must be heard; no "majority-rule" voting, bargaining, or averaging is allowed.

❖ *Recognition Theory and Idea Sheet*

During the first few minutes of a team's regular meeting, the team members have a strong need for social orientation; consequently, they should be *recognized* in some way. Attending to this need for recognition helps the members to know what is expected of them; this knowledge, in turn, frees them to concentrate on the subject matter of the meeting instead of on themselves and the "pecking order."

If the leader does not properly recognize and guide the members, the resulting pattern of the meeting probably will not reflect the roles that the members are expected to play. Appropriate recognition draws attention to the formal relationships that the members have with one another; it reminds them that in this setting they are not just individuals but functionaries—with specific roles within the organization's power structure.

Giving recognition at the beginning of a meeting consists of making the roles of the team members *visible* and *audible*. It is entirely appropriate, for instance, to begin regular meetings by emphasizing the differences in roles through roll calls, seating arrangements, and reminders of the rules that govern when the team members can speak and what subjects they can address. The opening of the meeting should be a process that draws attention to roles and functions rather than to the individuals fulfilling them, and the process should show the *intended* relations between those roles rather than any modifications that may have evolved informally.

Some teams begin their meetings in a very particular (and often formal) way: the members arrive in a certain order; they dress in a certain way; they sit in a certain arrangement; one particular person generally speaks first. For other teams and their leaders, such formalities and deliberate attention to status are offensive; they see such behavior as a throwback to more traditional forms of organization. They prefer a more relaxed and "friendly" atmosphere.

An organizational culture in which everyone is friendly and approachable is a definite asset. However, it is important to note that respect and affection among people at work are built on clear and successful role performance. This means that recognition (role affirmation) at the beginning of each meeting is every bit as essential in an informal atmosphere as it is in a formal one.

Ideas for Recognition

Here are some ideas to stimulate thinking about ways to accomplish recognition at the beginning of regular team meetings:

Visual

1. Any guests assemble in the meeting room first. Then the permanent team members arrive in a processional, with the meeting leader in the lead or at the end of that processional.

2. Only permanent team members are seated at the conference table, with the leader at the head. All other participants are seated in chairs surrounding the table at a short distance.

3. Only permanent team members are given binders containing copies of the meeting agenda and other meeting documents; all other participants are given the agenda and documents as unbound handouts.

4. The chairs or table locations of the permanent team members are designated with placards or brass plates bearing their titles.

5. Special styles or colors of chairs are used to denote the various ranks of the permanent team members and the guests.

6. Special styles or colors of name tags are used for the various ranks of the permanent team members and the guests.

7. During the first minutes of the meeting, the permanent team members stand for some ritual (for example, roll call, the leader's reading of the agenda, or a statement about their responsibilities as permanent members).

Auditory

1. The leader does a roll call of the permanent team members, by name and title.

2. Each permanent team member takes a minute at the start of the meeting to share some achievement (his or her own or a fellow team member's) since the last meeting.

3. The leader begins the meeting by polling only the permanent team members to see if any have guests to introduce or additions or corrections to make to the agenda.

4. The leader begins the meeting on a light note by describing a picture (perhaps of some recent and humorous event in the life of the organization)—or showing an actual cartoon depicting some aspect of organizational life—and asking each permanent team member to provide a caption for that picture or cartoon.

5. The leader begins the meeting on a light note by asking each permanent team member to answer the question "What is the title of one book on the top shelf of your bookcase?"

NEWS BULLETIN: FOCUSING THE TEAM

Goals

    I. To develop readiness for interaction at the beginning of a team meeting.

   II. To free the team members from personal concerns so that they can concentrate on team matters.

Time Required

Approximately five minutes per team member: two or three minutes for sharing of personal concerns plus another two or three minutes for team discussion of these concerns. (This time may need to be expanded in order to accomplish Goal II.)

Physical Setting

Any room in which the team regularly meets.

Process

    I. The leader introduces the activity by pointing out that occasionally television newscasters interrupt regularly scheduled programs to make announcements and then state that details will be provided later. It is explained that such interruptions are distracting in two ways: they detract from the viewers' enjoyment of the interrupted programs, and they pique curiosity about issues that are not clarified at the time. The leader then states that a similar situation sometimes occurs during team meetings; while important team business is being conducted, members interject distracting comments about personal concerns.

   II. The leader proposes a solution to this dilemma by suggesting that the team members share their personal concerns and "news items" at the outset of each meeting, before team matters are dealt with. Then the team members are invited to take turns spending two or three minutes revealing whatever personal concerns they wish. After each member's turn, interaction is encouraged. (The leader should monitor each interaction period carefully so that the team members neither stray from the subject at hand nor force attention away from the individual who has just finished sharing.)

  III. The leader directs the team members' attention to team matters.

Variations

I. The team members may be given the option of simply sharing their feelings and concerns and explaining as much as they wish without receiving responses from the other members.

II. The time requirement for the activity may be reduced by asking each team member to complete the phrase "Right now I am..." in one sentence.

III. The leader may specify that the team members share their feelings in short comments concerning a specific subject, such as issues that are presently causing confusion, irritation, or happiness.

IV. Between Steps II and III, the leader may lead a brief discussion by eliciting answers to questions such as the following:

1. What did the sharing of personal concerns accomplish for you? What did it accomplish for the team?
2. What are the advantages and disadvantages of this sharing procedure?
3. How might the procedure help our team to improve its functioning?

By Fred E. Woodall. Adapted from *A Handbook of Structured Experiences for Human Relations Training* (Vol. IX), edited by J.W. Pfeiffer, 1983, San Diego, CA: University Associates.

LOWLIGHTS AND HIGHLIGHTS: A WARMUP FOR TEAM MEETINGS

Goals

I. To offer the team members an opportunity to announce personal news at the outset of a team meeting, so that subsequently their attention can be directed toward team issues.

II. To encourage the team members to share information with one another.

Time Required

Five to fifteen minutes, depending on the number of team members.

Physical Setting

Any room in which the team regularly meets.

Process

I. The leader introduces the goals of the activity and then explains the procedure: each team member takes a turn sharing at least one "lowlight" and then at least one "highlight." A lowlight is a significant piece of bad news. This news may be a problem or a failure worth notice as a learning opportunity; or it may simply be an event or situation that the team member perceives as negative and for which he or she wants sympathy, commiseration, or understanding from the other team members. A highlight is a significant piece of good news. This news may be an accomplishment or any event or situation that the team member perceives as positive and wants the other members to know about and celebrate. After both the lowlight and the highlight, the other team members respond briefly to what has been said. No one passes; each team member contributes one or more lowlights and highlights.[1]

II. The team members take turns sharing their lowlights and highlights.

---

[1] The leader discourages passing because it leaves the other team members unequally exposed. Often this causes the other members to become more guarded in their participation. Also, it robs the procedure of its potential vitality.

III. The leader very briefly summarizes the information shared, thanks the members for their participation, and directs the team's attention to other matters.

Variations

I. The leader may encourage the team members to respond to lowlights with "boos" and to the highlights with cheers or applause.

II. The leader may offer awards on a revolving basis for the best lowlight and the best highlight.

III. A time limit may be set for each team member's turn.

IV. Each team member may share one highlight, then one lowlight, and finally another highlight so that the team members have a more positive sense of what is happening with one another.

By William R. Daniels. Adapted from *Group Power II: A Manager's Guide to Conducting Regular Meetings,* by W.R. Daniels, 1990, San Diego, CA: University Associates.

MEETING EVALUATION: INCREASING AWARENESS OF PROCEDURES

Goals

I. To increase the team members' awareness of the procedures they use in their meetings.

II. To assist the team members in finding ways to make their meetings more effective.

III. To provide the team members with an opportunity to react to new meeting procedures.

Time Required

Fifteen to twenty minutes in addition to the time required for the team's regular meeting.

Materials

A newsprint flip chart and a felt-tipped marker.

Physical Setting

Any room in which the team regularly meets. Each member should be seated so that he or she can see the other team members as well as the leader and the newsprint flip chart.

Process

I. At the end of any team meeting in which a new procedure is used, the leader introduces the activity by explaining its goals.

II. The leader draws a vertical line down the middle of a sheet of newsprint and labels the left column with a plus (+) sign and the right column with a minus (-) sign.

III. The leader asks the team members to evaluate the meeting by answering the following questions. After each question has been asked, the leader records the team members' answers in the appropriate column on the newsprint sheet:

1. What worked well? (+ column)
2. What energized you? (+ column)
3. What should we do more of? (+ column)
4. What did not work very well? (- column)
5. What did you find boring? (- column)
6. What made you feel uncomfortable? (- column)
7. What should we discontinue? (- column)
8. What should be changed? (either column)

IV. The leader asks for action steps that could make meetings more effective and records salient points on newsprint, adding the names of the people responsible and any deadline dates that are applicable. The newsprint sheet is given to one member of the team to reproduce and distribute to the team members for follow-up action.

Variations

I. This activity may follow any team meeting. If no new procedure is used, the third goal is omitted.

II. The leader may wish to repeat the activity at intervals as a check on progress.

By William R. Daniels. Adapted from *Group Power II: A Manager's Guide to Conducting Regular Meetings,* by W.R. Daniels, 1990, San Diego, CA: University Associates. Used with the permission of the author.

SUCCESSFUL MEETINGS: CLARIFYING AND EVALUATING

Goals

I. To build a definition of a "successful" meeting.

II. To identify techniques and guidelines that foster success in meetings.

III. To identify typical problems that arise during meetings and some ways of minimizing those problems.

IV. To demonstrate one technique for evaluating a meeting.

Time Required

One hour and ten minutes.

Materials

I. A newsprint flip chart and a felt-tipped marker.

II. Masking tape for posting newsprint.

Physical Setting

A room with plenty of wall space available for posting newsprint. Comfortable chairs should be provided for the team members.

Process

I. The leader introduces the activity by explaining its goals. The leader also emphasizes that although certain techniques can be used to make meetings effective, no standard rules exist regarding the ways in which meetings must be conducted. (Five minutes.)

II. The leader asks the team to brainstorm[1] indicators of success in meetings and encourages the team members to consider behavioral cues as well as personal

---

[1] Brainstorming is a technique used by groups to generate a number of creative ideas in a short time. The group members take turns contributing one idea at a time until all ideas have been exhausted. No criticism, evaluation, or judgment of ideas is allowed until the brainstorming phase has been completed. For further instructions see the activity entitled "Brainstorming: A Problem-Solving Technique."

feelings. The leader records the indicators on newsprint and posts them for reference throughout the activity. (Ten minutes.)

III. The leader leads a discussion of methods for facilitating meetings and making them successful. As the team members contribute their ideas, the leader records salient points on newsprint and posts the newsprint. (Twenty minutes.)

IV. The leader elicits comments on problems that the team members have encountered during meetings and encourages the members to discuss and determine ways to handle such problems. Any action steps are recorded on newsprint, along with the names of team members responsible for the action and deadline dates. The newsprint is given to one member of the team to reproduce and distribute to the other members for follow-up. (Twenty minutes.)

V. The team members are asked to create a short definition of a successful meeting. The leader records the suggestions on newsprint and helps the team members to reach consensus[2] on a definition. The definition is recorded and given to a team member for reproduction and distribution to the team. If no consensus is reached, the team may decide to work on a definition later; in that case, this action step should be added to the others. (Ten minutes.)

VI. To evaluate the activity and to practice one technique for evaluating a meeting, the leader asks the team members to describe what they liked or disliked about the experience and what they learned.

Variation

If the team consists of more than six members, subgroups may be formed during Step III. Each subgroup selects one member as the recorder. The leader provides each recorder with blank paper, a pencil, and a clipboard or other portable writing surface. The subgroups discuss methods for facilitating meetings and making them successful; the recorders make notes on the discussion. Subsequently, the leader reconvenes the entire team and asks the recorders to take turns sharing the subgroups' ideas. During this sharing the leader records ideas on newsprint and posts the newsprint.

By Eileen F.N. Collard, Warren Sam Miller, and William Grimberg. Adapted from *A Trainer's Manual for Process Politics,* by E. Guthrie, W.S. Miller, and W. Grimberg, 1981, San Diego, CA: University Associates.

---

[2] A consensus decision is one that all team members can accept, regardless of how satisfied they are with it. Each member's opinion must be heard; no "majority-rule" voting, bargaining, or averaging is allowed.

CREATING AGENDAS: USING A CHECK LIST

Goals

I. To assist the team members in reviewing an agenda and finding ways to improve it.

II. To assist the team members in redrafting an agenda.

Time Required

One hour.

Materials

I. A copy of the Creating Agendas Sample Agenda for each team member.

II. A copy of the Creating Agendas Check List for each team member.

III. Several sheets of blank paper and a pencil for each team member.

IV. A newsprint flip chart and a felt-tipped marker.

V. Masking tape for posting newsprint.

Physical Setting

A room with a chair and a writing surface for each team member. Each member should be seated so that he or she can see the other team members as well as the leader and the newsprint flip chart.

Process

I. The leader introduces the activity by explaining its goals.

II. Each team member is given a copy of the Creating Agendas Sample Agenda and is asked to read it and to jot down on the bottom of the sheet seven ways in which the agenda can be improved. (Five minutes.)

III. The leader asks the team members to take turns sharing their suggestions with the rest of the team. The leader records these suggestions on newsprint and posts the newsprint. When two or more members offer the same suggestion, the leader places a tick mark by the original suggestion. (Fifteen minutes.)

IV. Each team member is given a copy of the Creating Agendas Check List, several sheets of blank paper, and a pencil.

V. The leader asks the members to work together to rewrite the agenda in improved form. The leader explains that they should refer to the check list and to the suggestions that are posted as they create the new agenda. (Twenty minutes.)

VI. After the team has completed the task, the leader asks one member to read the revised agenda and leads a discussion based on questions such as these:

1. In what ways does the new agenda meet the needs of the people who will attend the meeting?
2. Which items on the check list were not addressed? Why?
3. In what ways can you use what you have learned in creating agendas for your own meetings?

The leader records any salient points on newsprint and gives the newsprint to one of the members for reproduction and distribution to the other members.

Variation

Instead of using the Creating Agendas Sample Agenda, the team members may work together to create an agenda for a particular meeting. Then they would work to improve it.

By William R. Daniels. Adapted from *Group Power I: A Manager's Guide to Using Task-Force Meetings,* by W.R. Daniels, 1986, San Diego, CA: University Associates.

❖ *Creating Agendas Sample Agenda*

Memo From: Max

Date: June 18

Subject: Monthly staff meeting, June 21

Please be on time!

We have a lot to cover. RE: Summer schedule, and we'd like to get things done quickly.

See you there.

❖ *Creating Agendas Check List*

Use this check list in creating an agenda for an effective meeting.

General Information

_____Name of team

_____Title of meeting

_____Who is calling the meeting

_____Date

_____Starting time

_____Ending time

_____Place

_____Agenda put out ahead of meeting (at least one day but not more than one week ahead of time, so it will be fresh in people's minds)

_____Desired outcomes

_____Meeting procedure (for example, any of various problem-solving techniques, presentations, discussions, etc.)

_____Decision-making method (for example, voting agreement of all members)

_____Final decision maker (team, leader, other)

_____Preparation suggestions (for example, background materials)

_____Other notes to participants

People Attending

_____Leader/chairperson

_____Team members

_____Role assignments (for example, subject-matter experts, implementation specialist, recorder, facilitator)

_____Guest resource people

Agenda Schedule

_____Sequence of items

_____Person(s) responsible for each item

_____Procedure for dealing with each item

_____Time allocated for each item

CHECKPOINTS: CREATING A CHECK LIST FOR TEAM MEETINGS

Goals

    I. To provide the team members with a check list for keeping a meeting on target and tracking their progress.

    II. To help the team members create a meetings check list that is applicable to their situation.

Time Required

Approximately one hour.

Materials

    I. A copy of the Checkpoints Sample Meetings Check List for each team member.

    II. A few sheets of blank paper and a pencil for each team member.

    III. A newsprint flip chart and a felt-tipped marker.

    IV. Masking tape for posting newsprint.

Physical Setting

A room with a chair and a writing surface for each team member. Each member should be seated so that he or she can see the other team members as well as the leader and the newsprint flip chart.

Process

    I. The leader introduces the activity by explaining its goals.

    II. Each team member is given a copy of the Checkpoints Sample Meetings Check List and is asked to read it. Explaining that this sample check list is used by a real company, the leader reviews each item on the check list and leads a discussion based on questions such as these:

        1. Why would the items on this check list be important to a team?

        2. How might some of these items be changed to be more applicable to the meetings of this team?

3. What items are missing that would be important to this team?

Salient points are recorded on newsprint and posted. (Fifteen minutes.)

III. If the team consists of more than five members, the leader asks them to work in subgroups of three or four members each. Each team member is given a pencil and a few sheets of paper. Based on the previous discussion, one or more check list items are assigned to each subgroup (depending on the number of subgroups). The subgroups work on the assigned items to word them positively, appropriately, and concisely. Each subgroup selects a spokesperson to report later to the total team. (Fifteen minutes.)

IV. After all team members have completed the task, the leader reconvenes the team and asks the spokespersons to take turns sharing their revised items. As the items are read, the leader records them on newsprint and posts the newsprint. (Five minutes.)

V. The leader helps the team members reach consensus[1] on a checklist they wish to use in their meetings. When the agreed-on checklist has been recorded on newsprint, the leader gives it to one of the members for preparing a copy for the meeting room and/or for each member of the team. (Five minutes.)

VI. The leader leads a discussion based on questions such as these:

1. How will the check list be used?
2. At which meetings will the check list be appropriate?
3. In what ways will the check list change our meetings?

(Five minutes.)

VII. The leader models the use of the team's new check list by reviewing each item in light of the current meeting.

By Mary Kitzmiller.

---

[1] A consensus decision is one that all team members can accept, regardless of how satisfied they are with it. Each member's opinion must be heard; no "majority-rule" voting, bargaining, or averaging is allowed.

❖ *Checkpoints Sample Meetings Check List*

1. Follow up the last meeting and recheck action steps.
2. Ask "Who?" and "By when?"
3. Ask "Who else needs to know what happened at this meeting? Who will inform them?"
4. Share responsibility for saying that the meeting is not working.
5. Debrief at the end of the meeting.

Introduction to
Inventories and Forms

The materials in the Inventories and Forms section can be especially useful to a team that wants to assess its effectiveness via some kind of measurement device or record-keeping system. All of the questionnaires and forms included here may be freely reproduced for educational/training activities. *Systematic or large-scale reproduction or distribution (more than one hundred copies)—or inclusion of any of these items in publications for sale—may be done only with prior written permission from the sources indicated.*

After the team members have completed an inventory or form, they should meet to discuss their responses. It is a good idea for a team to have had some experience in giving and receiving feedback before attempting such a meeting. (See the activities in the Team Effectiveness section.) Team members need to feel that they can express their true feelings and viewpoints. When this is the case, responses to inventories and forms can be evaluated in the spirit in which they were intended—to help the team to fulfill its potential as an operating unit.

The leader can do much to develop such an atmosphere of openness. For example, the leader can invite comments about his or her own leadership or facilitation of a meeting and can then accept both positive and negative feedback with statements of appreciation and enthusiasm about improvements that can be made in the future.

POSTMEETING REACTION FORM

Instructions: Circle the number on each scale that most nearly represents your opinion.

1. How well did we do today in accomplishing our task?

   Task Accomplishment

1	2	3	4	5
Poor	Fair	Satisfactory	Good	Excellent

   Suggestions for improving task accomplishment:

2. How well did we do today in working as a team and building our relationships?

   Team Cohesiveness

1	2	3	4	5
Poor	Fair	Satisfactory	Good	Excellent

   Suggestions for improving team cohesiveness:

3. How clear were we about our goals?

Clarity of Goals

1	2	3	4	5
Confused	Unclear	Fairly Clear	Clear	Very Clear

Suggestions for improving clarity of team goals:

4. How cooperatively did we work?

Team Cooperation

1	2	3	4	5
Uncoop-eratively	Independently	Somewhat Cooperatively	Cooperatively	As a Real Team

Suggestions for improving team cooperation:

5. How productive were we?

Team Productivity

1	2	3	4	5
Unpro-ductive	Not Truly Productive	Somewhat Productive	Productive	Very Productive

Suggestions for improving team productivity:

POSTMEETING EVALUATION FORM

Instructions: Following are two sets of ten statements. Rank order the statements in each of the two sets from 1 to 10, with 1 representing what the meeting or behavior was *most* like and 10 representing what the meeting or behavior was *least* like. Use this procedure: in each set, first identify the statement that you would rank as 1, then the statement that you would rank as 10, then 2, then 9, alternating toward the middle of the scale.

The meeting was like this:

_____ There was much warmth and friendliness.

_____ A lot of aggressive behavior was displayed.

_____ The team members were uninterested and uninvolved.

_____ Some team members tried to dominate and take over.

_____ The team was in need of help.

_____ Much of the conversation was irrelevant.

_____ The team was strictly task oriented.

_____ The team members were very polite.

_____ There was much underlying irritation.

_____ The team worked on its process issues.

My behavior was like this:

_____ I was warm and friendly to some.

_____ I did not participate much.

_____ I concentrated on the job.

_____ I tried to get all the team members involved.

_____ I took over the leadership.

_____ I was polite to all.

_____ My suggestions frequently were off the subject.

_____ I was a follower.

_____ I was irritated.

_____ I was eager and aggressive.

Adapted from "Postmeeting Reactions Form" in *A Handbook of Structured Experiences for Human Relations Training* (Vol. III, Rev.), edited by J.W. Pfeiffer and J.E. Jones, 1974, San Diego, CA: University Associates. This form may be freely reproduced for educational/training activities. *Systematic or large-scale reproduction or distribution (more than one hundred copies)—or inclusion of items in publications for sale—may be done only with prior written permission from University Associates.*

THE TEAM-EFFECTIVENESS CRITIQUE

Most teams exist and persist because (1) the purpose of the team cannot be accomplished by individuals working on their own, and (2) certain needs of individual members can be satisfied by belonging to the team. Of course, the mere existence of a team does not ensure that it will operate effectively; a team is effective only to the degree to which it is able to use its individual and collective resources. The measure of the team's effectiveness is its ability to achieve its objectives and satisfy the needs of the individuals in the team.

An organization is a collection of teams. The success of an organization depends on the ability of the teams within it to work together to attain commonly held objectives. Because organizations are becoming increasingly more complex, team leaders must be concerned with developing more cohesive and cooperative relationships between individuals and teams. Similarly, the development of effective teams within the organization will determine, to a large extent, the ability of the organization to attain its goals.

FACTORS CONTRIBUTING TO TEAM DEVELOPMENT AND EFFECTIVENESS

Team development is based on the assumption that any team is able to work more effectively if its members are prepared to confront questions such as: How can this collection of individuals work together more effectively as a team? How can the team better use the resources represented? How can the team members communicate with one another more effectively to make better decisions? What is impeding the team's performance?

The answers to these questions may be found by examining the factors that lead to team development and effectiveness. These factors can be measured, or inventoried, by team members with the use of the Team-Effectiveness Critique. Before the critique form is administered, however, all team members should understand the terminology used to describe the nine factors. The following descriptions can be presented to the team members prior to completion of the critique.

By Mark Alexander. Adapted from *The 1985 Annual: Developing Human Resources,* edited by L.D. Goodstein and J.W. Pfeiffer, 1985, San Diego, CA: University Associates. This critique and the accompanying explanatory information may be freely reproduced for educational/training activities. *Systematic or large-scale reproduction or distribution (more than one hundred copies)—or inclusion of the critique or its explanatory information in publications for sale—may be done only with prior written permission from University Associates.*

1. Shared Goals and Objectives

In order for a team to operate effectively, it must have stated goals and objectives. These goals are not a simple understanding of the immediate task, but an overall understanding of the role of the team in the total organization, its responsibilities, and the things the team wants to accomplish. In addition, the members of the team must be committed to the goals. Such commitment comes from involving all team members in defining the goals and relating the goals to specific problems that are relevant to team members. The time spent on goal definition in the initial stages of a team's life results in less time needed later to resolve problems and misunderstandings.

2. Utilization of Resources

The ultimate purpose of a team is to do things effectively. In order to accomplish this, the team must use effectively all the resources at its disposal. This means establishing an environment that allows individual resources to be used. Team effectiveness is enhanced when every member has the opportunity to contribute and when all opinions are heard and considered. It is the team's responsibility to create an atmosphere in which individual members can state their opinions without fear of ridicule or reprisal. It is each individual member's responsibility to contribute information and ideas and to be prepared to support them with rational arguments. Maximum use of team members requires full participation and self-regulation.

3. Trust and Conflict Resolution

In any team situation, disagreement is likely to occur. The ability to openly recognize conflict and to seek to resolve it through discussion is critical to the team's success. People do not automatically work well together just because they happen to belong to the same work team or share the same job function. For a team to become effective, it must deal with the emotional problems and needs of its members and the interpersonal problems that arise in order to build working relationships that are characterized by openness and trust. The creation of a feeling of mutual trust, respect, and understanding and the ability of the team to deal with the inevitable conflicts that occur in any team situation are key factors in team development.

4. Shared Leadership

Individuals will not function as a team if they are brought together simply to "rubber stamp" decisions made by the team's formal leader or others not in the team. The development and cohesion of a team occurs only when there is a feeling of shared leadership among all team members. This means that all team members accept some responsibility for task functions—those things necessary to do the job—and maintenance functions—those things necessary to keep the team together and interacting effectively. *Task functions* include initiating discussions or actions, clarifying issues and goals, summarizing points, testing for consensus or agreement, and seeking or giving information. Task leadership helps the team to establish its direction and assists the team in moving toward its goals. *Maintenance functions* include encouraging involvement and participation, sensing and expressing team feelings, harmonizing and facilitating reconciliation of disagreements, setting standards for the team, and "gatekeeping" or bringing people into discussions. No one person can be expected to perform all these required leadership functions effectively at all times. Teams perform better when all members perform both task and maintenance functions.

5. Control and Procedures

A team needs to establish procedures that can be used to guide or regulate its activities. For example, a meeting agenda serves to guide team activities during a meeting. Schedules of when specific actions will be taken also regulate team activities. Team development and team-member commitment are facilitated through maximum involvement in the establishment of agendas, schedules, and other procedures. Of course, the team should determine how it wishes to maintain control. In meeting situations, control most often is achieved through the appointment of a chairperson whose responsibility is to facilitate the procedure established by the team. Some teams find that they do not need a formal team leader; each member regulates his or her own contributions and behavior as well as those of others.

6. Effective Interpersonal Communications

Effective team development depends on the ability of team members to communicate with one another in an open and honest manner. Effective interpersonal communications are apparent when team members listen to one another and attempt to build on one another's contributions. Effective interpersonal communications are achieved through self-regulation by team members, so that everyone in the team has an equal opportunity to participate in discussions.

7. Approach to Problem Solving and Decision Making

Solving problems and making decisions are two critical team functions. If a team is going to improve its ability to function as a team, recognized methods for solving problems and making decisions should be studied and adopted. The lack of agreed-on approaches to problem solving and decision making can result in wasted time, misunderstandings, frustration, and—more importantly—"bad" decisions.

A generally accepted, step-by-step procedure for problem solving and decision making is as follows:

1. Identify the problem, being careful to differentiate between the real problem and symptoms of the problem.

2. Develop criteria or goals.

3. Gather relevant data.

4. Identify all feasible, alternative solutions or courses of action.

5. Evaluate the alternatives in light of the data and the objectives of the team.

6. Reach a decision.

7. Implement the decision.

Needless to say, there are variations of this procedure. However, whatever method is used, an effective team will have an agreed-on approach to problem solving and decision making that is shared and supported by all members.

8. Experimentation/Creativity

Just as it is important for a team to have certain structured procedures, it also is important that the team be prepared occasionally to move beyond the boundaries of established procedures and processes in order to experiment with new ways of doing things. Techniques such as brainstorming[1] as a means of increasing creativity should be tried periodically to generate new ways to increase the team's effectiveness. An experimental attitude should be adopted in order to allow the team greater flexibility in dealing with problems and decision-making situations.

9. Evaluation

The team periodically should examine its team processes from both task and maintenance aspects. This examination or critique requires the team to stop and look at how well it is doing and what, if anything, may be hindering its operation. Problems may result from procedures or methods or may be caused by individual team members. Such problems should be resolved through discussion before the team attempts further task accomplishment. Effective self-evaluation is probably one of the most critical factors leading to team development.

Ultimately, the strength and degree of a team's development will be measured in two ways: (1) in its ability to get things done—its effectiveness—and (2) in terms of its cohesiveness—the sense of belonging that individual members have and the degree of their commitment to one another and the goals of the team.

USE OF THE TEAM-EFFECTIVENESS CRITIQUE

The periodic review of a team's operating practices in light of the factors leading to team development is a simple and useful method for improving a team's effective-

---

[1] Brainstorming is a technique used by groups to generate a number of creative ideas in a short time. The group members take turns contributing one idea at a time until all ideas have been exhausted. No criticism, evaluation, or judgment of ideas is allowed until the brainstorming phase has been completed.

ness. The Team-Effectiveness Critique can be used as an observational tool by an independent observer or as an intervention device for the entire team. In this case, the critique should be completed by each individual team member, who will then share his or her assessment with the entire team. This sharing can be expanded to a consensus activity by asking team members to reach a common assessment for each of the nine factors. Agreement about areas in which improvements could be made would then lead to team action planning.

THE TEAM-EFFECTIVENESS CRITIQUE

Instructions: Rate your team on each of the following nine dimensions using a scale of one to seven, indicating your assessment of your team and the way it functions by circling the number on each scale that you feel is most descriptive of your team.

1. Goals and Objectives

1	2	3	4	5	6	7

There is a lack of commonly understood goals and objectives.

The team members understand and agree on goals and objectives.

2. Utilization of Resources

1	2	3	4	5	6	7

All resources of team members are not fully recognized and/or utilized.

The resources of all team members are fully recognized and utilized.

3. Trust and Conflict Resolution

1	2	3	4	5	6	7

There is little trust among team members, and conflict is evident.

There is a high degree of trust among team members, and conflict is dealt with openly and worked through.

By Mark Alexander. Adapted from *The 1985 Annual: Developing Human Resources,* edited by L.D. Goodstein and J.W. Pfeiffer, 1985, San Diego, CA: University Associates. This critique and the accompanying explanatory information may be freely reproduced for educational/training activities. *Systematic or large-scale reproduction or distribution (more than one hundred copies)—or inclusion of the critique or its explanatory information in publications for sale—may be done only with prior written permission from University Associates.*

4. Leadership

1	2	3	4	5	6	7

One person dominates, and team-leadership roles are not carried out or shared.

There is full participation in leadership; leadership roles are shared by team members.

5. Control and Procedures

1	2	3	4	5	6	7

There is little control, and there is a lack of procedures to guide team functioning.

There are effective procedures to guide team functioning; team members support these procedures and regulate themselves.

6. Interpersonal Communications

1	2	3	4	5	6	7

Communications between team members are closed and guarded.

Communications between team members are open and participative.

7. Problem Solving/Decision Making

1	2	3	4	5	6	7

The team has no agreed-on approaches to problem solving and decision making.

The team has well-established and agreed-on approaches to problem solving and decision making.

8. Experimentation/Creativity

1	2	3	4	5	6	7

The team is rigid and does not experiment with how things are done.

The team experiments with different ways of doing things and is creative in its approach.

9. Evaluation

1	2	3	4	5	6	7

The team never evaluates its functioning or process.

The team often evaluates its functioning and process.

SURVEY OF TEAM DEVELOPMENT

Instructions: For each of the following thirteen items, place a check mark to the left of the statement that most nearly describes the team.

1. ***Unity:*** the extent to which the team feels a sense of unity, cohesion, or "we-ness."

   _____ a.   The team is just a collection of individuals or subgroups; there is little team feeling.

   _____ b.   There is some team feeling, but unity stems more from external factors than from real friendship.

   _____ c.   The team is very close, and there is little room or need felt for other contacts and experience.

   _____ d.   The team experiences a strong common purpose and spirit based on real friendship; the team usually sticks together.

2. ***Self-Direction:*** the extent to which the team creates its own motivation.

   _____ a.   The team experiences little drive from anywhere, either from its members or from its formal leader.

   _____ b.   The team has some self-propulsion but needs considerable pushing from its formal leader.

   _____ c.   The team is dominated by a strong single member, a clique, or its formal leader.

   _____ d.   Initiating, planning, executing, and evaluating come from the whole team.

3. ***Team Climate:*** the extent to which the team members feel free to be themselves.

   _____ a.   The team climate inhibits good fun; behavior; and the expression of desires, fears, and opinions.

   _____ b.   The team members express themselves but without observing the interests of the total team.

   _____ c.   The team members freely express needs and desires; they joke, tease, and argue to the detriment of the team.

   _____ d.   The team members feel free to express themselves but limit their expression to the welfare of the total team.

By Hedley G. Dimock. Adapted from *Groups: Leadership and Group Development,* by H.G. Dimock, 1987, San Diego, CA: University Associates. This survey may be freely reproduced for educational/training activities. *Systematic or large-scale reproduction or distribution (more than one hundred copies)—or inclusion of the survey in publications for sale—may be done only with prior written permission from University Associates.*

4. **Distribution of Leadership:** the extent to which team-leadership roles are distributed among the team members.

_____ a. A few team members always take the team-leadership roles; the rest of the team members are passive.

_____ b. Some of the team members take the team-leadership roles, but many remain passive followers.

_____ c. Many team members take team-leadership roles, but one or two are continually followers.

_____ d. Team leadership is shared by all members of the team.

5. **Distribution of Responsibility:** the extent to which responsibility is shared among the team members.

_____ a. Everyone tries to get out of jobs.

_____ b. Responsibility is carried by a few team members.

_____ c. Many team members accept responsibilities but do not carry them out.

_____ d. Responsibilities are distributed among and carried out by nearly all the team members.

6. **Problem Solving:** the extent to which the team is able to think clearly, make use of everyone's ideas, and decide creatively about its problems.

_____ a. The team does not do much thinking as a team; decisions are made hastily, or the team lets its formal leader do most of the thinking.

_____ b. The team does some cooperative thinking, but gets tangled up in pet ideas; the result is confused movement toward solutions.

_____ c. The team does some thinking as a team, but not as yet in an orderly process.

_____ d. The team experiences good pooling of ideas and orderly thought; everyone's ideas are used to reach a final plan.

7. **Resolving Disagreements:** the extent to which the team members work together to resolve disagreements.

_____ a. The team waits for its formal leader to resolve disagreements.

_____ b. The strongest subgroup dominates through a vote and majority rule.

_____ c. Compromises come about when each subgroup gives up something.

_____ d. The team as a whole arrives at a solution that satisfies all of the team members and that is better than any single suggestion.

8. **Basic Needs:** the extent to which the team gives a sense of security, achievement, approval, recognition, and belonging.

_____ a. The team experience does little to meet most members' needs.

_____ b. The team experience contributes to some degree to meeting the basic needs of most team members.

_____ c. The team experience contributes substantially to meeting the basic needs of most members.

_____ d. The team experience contributes substantially to meeting the basic needs of all members.

9. **Variety of Activities:** the extent to which the team is open to new and varied activities.

_____ a. There is little variety in activities; the team members stick to the same things.

_____ b. The team experiences some variety in activities.

_____ c. There is considerable variety in activities; the team tries out some new activities.

_____ d. There is great variety in activities; the team is continually trying out new activities.

10. **Depth of Activities:** the extent to which activities allow the team members to use their full potentials, skills, and creativity.

_____ a. There is little depth in activities; the team members just scratch the surface.

_____ b. There is some depth of activities, but team members are not increasing their skills.

_____ c. There is considerable depth in activities; team members are able to utilize some of their abilities.

_____ d. There is great depth in activities; team members find each activity a challenge that develops their abilities.

11. **Leader-Member Rapport:** the extent to which relations between the team and its formal leader are productive.

_____ a. The team members are generally antagonistic or resentful toward the formal leader.

_____ b. The team members are generally indifferent or noncommunicative toward the formal leader; friendship is neither sought nor rejected.

_____ c. The team members are generally friendly toward and interested in the formal leader; they are attentive to the leader's suggestions.

_____ d. The team members have close relationships with the formal leader; there is strong rapport, openness, and sharing.

12. ***Role of the Formal Leader:*** the extent to which the team is centered around the formal leader.

_____ a. Activities, discussion, and decisions revolve around the interests, desires, and needs of the formal leader.

_____ b. The team looks to the formal leader for suggestions and ideas; the formal leader makes decisions when a member is blocked.

_____ c. The formal leader acts as a stimulus, suggesting ideas or other means of doing things; the formal leader helps the team to find ways of making its own decisions.

_____ d. The formal leader stays out of discussions and makes few suggestions, letting the team members decide for themselves.

13. ***Stability:*** the extent to which the team feels a sense of security.

_____ a. The team experiences high absenteeism and turnover, which have a great deal of influence on the team.

_____ b. The team experiences high absenteeism and turnover, which have little influence on team growth.

_____ c. The team experiences some absenteeism and turnover, with minor influence on the team.

_____ d. The team experiences low absenteeism and turnover; the team is very stable.

TEAM-PROFILE QUESTIONNAIRE

Instructions: For each of the statements in this questionnaire, refer to the following scale and decide which number corresponds to your level of agreement with the statement; then write that number in the blank to the left of the statement.

Strongly Disagree	Disagree	Do Not Know	Agree	Strongly Agree
1	2	3	4	5

_____ 1. The present goals and objectives of this team are clear and relevant to its overall mission.

_____ 2. Role definitions are clear so that misunderstandings seldom arise about who is responsible for what.

_____ 3. Decisions are made on a timely basis, with adequate opportunity for input and consideration by those affected.

_____ 4. The team members enjoy a relatively high level of disclosure, believing that the facts are usually friendly and that in the long run it is better to deal with reality than to deny, avoid, or distort it.

_____ 5. The team members have a high awareness of the impact of their behavior on their environment and have open lines of communication with each other.

_____ 6. The team members are skilled at diagnosing and working on team problems; the team members attend to the process as well as to the content of their meetings.

_____ 7. Mistakes are not punished but rather are viewed as opportunities to learn; risk is accepted as a condition of growth and change.

_____ 8. The team leadership is flexible, shifting in style to suit the needs of the situation and the people involved.

_____ 9. Collaboration is entered into freely, and ways of helping one another are highly developed.

By Glenn H. Varney. Adapted from *Building Productive Teams* (pp. 29-30), by G.H. Varney, 1989, San Francisco: Jossey-Bass. Used with permission from Jossey-Bass. This questionnaire may be freely reproduced for educational/training activities. *Systematic or large-scale reproduction or distribution (more than one hundred copies)—or inclusion of this questionnaire in publications for sale—may be done only with prior written permission from Jossey-Bass.*

Strongly Disagree	Disagree	Do Not Know	Agree	Strongly Agree
1	2	3	4	5

_____10. The team is able to focus energy on appropriate priorities, not merely respond to the most urgent crisis or follow the plan simply because it exists.

_____11. Relationships are honest; interpersonal issues are confronted rather than swept under the rug.

_____12. The team members are highly aware of available resources and make effective use of them.

_____13. The team members are aware of their interdependencies, and collaboration rather than competition predominates.

_____14. The team norms foster creativity; members are not locked into past traditions and are able to bring fresh perspectives to present problems.

_____15. Conflicts are considered a normal part of working together and are dealt with openly and honestly.

_____16. Problem solving is pragmatic and informal; the team leader is frequently challenged, and status and territorial rights take a back seat to the requirements of the problem.

_____17. Planning is considered an essential activity, and all the team members participate actively in the process.

_____18. The team provides a supportive environment for its members to realize their uniqueness by allowing for and encouraging individual differences.

_____19. The overall trust level is high, as evidenced by a healthy amount of confronting, spontaneity, and risk taking in meetings.

TEAM-DEVELOPMENT RATING FORM

Instructions: Rate your team on each of the following eight dimensions using a scale of one to five, indicating the team's position on each continuum with a circle.

1. *The Team's Purpose*

1	2	3	4	5

I am uncertain about the team's purpose.   I am clear about the team's purpose.

2. *Team Membership*

1	2	3	4	5

I am out.   I am in.

3. *Elbow Room*

1	2	3	4	5

I am crowded.   I am comfortable.

4. *Discussion*

1	2	3	4	5

Discussion is cautious and guarded.   Discussion is open and free.

By Marvin R. Weisbord. Adapted from *Productive Workplaces: Organizing and Managing for Dignity, Meaning, and Community* (p. 302), by M.R. Weisbord, 1987, San Francisco: Jossey-Bass. Used with permission from Jossey-Bass and Marvin R. Weisbord. This rating form may be freely reproduced for educational/training activities. *Systematic or large-scale reproduction or distribution (more than one hundred copies)—or inclusion of this rating form in publications for sale—may be done only with prior written permission from Jossey-Bass and Marvin R. Weisbord.*

5. *Use of Skills*

1	2	3	4	5

Use is poor.   Use is full.

6. *Support*

1	2	3	4	5

Team members support   Team members support
themselves only.   all members.

7. *Conflict*

1	2	3	4	5

Conflict is avoided.   Conflict is worked on.

8. *Influence on Decisions*

1	2	3	4	5

Few team members   All team members
have influence.   have influence.

TEAMWORK SURVEY

Team leader's name_____

Your name_____

Your age_____ Date survey is completed_____

Your education level: High school_____ B.S./B.A._____ Master's_____ Ph.D._____

Your length of service (years)_____

Location_____

Instructions: You and the other members of your team have been asked to fill out this survey to assist your team in improving its productivity. For each item in the survey, the statement on the left is the opposite of the statement on the right. The circles represent ranges of agreement with those statements, as follows:

O	O	O	O	O
I strongly agree with the statement on the left.	I agree with the statement on the left.	I am neutral.	I agree with the statement on the right.	I strongly agree with the statement on the right.

Rate your team on each dimension by filling in the appropriate circle. As you fill in your responses, think of your team as a whole and the way the team members work together. If you are a team leader, think of yourself as a part of the team when you respond to the statements.

1. O   O   O   O   O

Communications in my team are generally guarded.				Communications in my team are generally open.

By Glenn H. Varney. Adapted from *Building Productive Teams* (pp. 33-36), by G.H. Varney, 1989, San Francisco: Jossey-Bass. Used with permission from Jossey-Bass. This survey may be freely reproduced for educational/training activities. *Systematic or large-scale reproduction or distribution (more than one hundred copies)—or inclusion of this survey in publications for sale—may be done only with prior written permission from Jossey-Bass.*

I strongly agree with the statement on the left.	I agree with the statement on the left.	I am neutral.	I agree with the statement on the right.	I strongly agree with the statement on the right.
2. O	O	O	O	O

I do not know what my team's objectives are.   I know what my team's objectives are.

3. O	O	O	O	O

I am rewarded for innovating or making improvements that benefit my team.   I am not rewarded for innovating or making improvements that benefit my team.

4. O	O	O	O	O

Members of my team do not have confidence in one another.   Members of my team have confidence in one another.

5. O	O	O	O	O

My team's objectives are not attainable.   My team's objectives are attainable.

6. O	O	O	O	O

My team has no set procedures for solving problems.   My team has set procedures for solving problems.

7. O	O	O	O	O

My team does not have a well-defined system for communicating with other team members.   My team has a well-defined system for communicating with other team members.

I strongly agree with the statement on the left.	I agree with the statement on the left.	I am neutral.	I agree with the statement on the right.	I strongly agree with the statement on the right.
8. O	O	O	O	O
My team leader and I do not agree on my job objectives.				My team leader and I agree on my job objectives.
9. O	O	O	O	O
My team spends much of its time "fighting fires."				My team takes time to plan ahead and thereby avoids "fighting fires."
10. O	O	O	O	O
My team leader tends to dominate decision making.				My team leader encourages team participation in decision making
11. O	O	O	O	O
My abilities, knowledge, and experience are not utilized by my team.				My abilities, knowledge, and experience are fully utilized by my team.
12. O	O	O	O	O
Members of my team do not trust one another.				Members of my team trust one another.
13. O	O	O	O	O
I do not understand my role on this team.				I clearly understand my role on this team.

I strongly agree with the statement on the left.	I agree with the statement on the left.	I am neutral.	I agree with the statement on the right.	I strongly agree with the statement on the right.

14.   O   O   O   O   O

My team pressures members to conform to certain norms.	My team encourages individual differences.

15.   O   O   O   O   O

I do not understand my job objectives relative to my team's objectives.	I understand my job objectives relative to my team's objectives.

16.   O   O   O   O   O

The work climate in my team is relaxed.	The work climate in my team is tense.

17.   O   O   O   O   O

Team meetings are poorly organized.	Team meetings are well organized.

18.   O   O   O   O   O

I am committed to my job objectives.	I am not committed to my job objectives.

19.   O   O   O   O   O

Members of my team are loyal to the team.	Members of my team are not loyal to the team.

20.   O   O   O   O   O

Team members generally do not listen to one other.	Team members generally listen to one another.

I strongly agree with the statement on the left.	I agree with the statement on the left.	I am neutral.	I agree with the statement on the right.	I strongly agree with the statement on the right.
21. O	O	O	O	O

When an interpersonal issue is raised in the team, we avoid it.   When an interpersonal issue is raised in the team, we have procedures for resolving it.

22. O	O	O	O	O

I receive feedback frequently.   I receive feedback infrequently.

23. O	O	O	O	O

My job objectives are challenging.   My job objectives are not challenging.

24. O	O	O	O	O

I agree with my role on my team.   I do not agree with my role on my team.

25. O	O	O	O	O

There is little evidence of conflict between team members.   There is much evidence of conflict between team members.

26. O	O	O	O	O

My team leader is open to suggestions on how to improve his or her performance.   My team leader is not open to suggestions on how to improve his or her performance.

27. O	O	O	O	O

I am satisfied with my team's productivity.   I am not satisfied with my team's productivity.

I strongly agree with the statement on the left.	I agree with the statement on the left.	I am neutral.	I agree with the statement on the right.	I strongly agree with the statement on the right.

28. O   O   O   O   O

I am not given enough authority to do my job.

I am given sufficient authority to do my job.

29. O   O   O   O   O

I do not feel that my team leader considers my input when making decisions.

I feel that my team leader considers my input when making decisions.

30. O   O   O   O   O

I do not understand the roles of my fellow team members.

I understand the roles of my fellow team members.

31. O   O   O   O   O

My team's productivity is generally low.

My team's productivity is generally high.

32. O   O   O   O   O

I hesitate to be candid with my fellow team members.

I feel free to be candid with my fellow team members.

33. O   O   O   O   O

My performance evaluations are based on my performance.

My performance evaluations are not based on my performance.

34. O   O   O   O   O

Consensus is rarely reached within my team.

Consensus is usually reached within my team.

I strongly agree with the statement on the left.	I agree with the statement on the left.	I am neutral.	I agree with the statement on the right.	I strongly agree with the statement on the right.

35. O   O   O   O   O

| Team members are generally uncooperative. | | | | Team members are generally cooperative. |

36. O   O   O   O   O

| Team members are unclear about how they are expected to make decisions. | | | | Team members are clear about how they are expected to make decisions. |

37. O   O   O   O   O

| My job objectives are not attainable. | | | | My job objectives are attainable. |

38. O   O   O   O   O

| Decisions often are not explained to members of my team. | | | | Decisions usually are explained to members of my team. |

39. O   O   O   O   O

| Praise is seldom provided for a job well done. | | | | Praise is usually provided for a job well done. |

40. O   O   O   O   O

| My team encourages me to improve my skills. | | | | My team does not encourage me to improve my skills. |

41. O   O   O   O   O

| Feedback in my team is usually negative and destructive. | | | | Feedback in my team is usually positive and helpful. |

	I strongly agree with the statement on the left.	I agree with the statement on the left.	I am neutral.	I agree with the statement on the right.	I strongly agree with the statement on the right.
42.	O	O	O	O	O

Team meetings are generally unproductive, with few conclusions drawn or decisions made.

Team meetings are generally productive, with conclusions drawn and decisions made.

| 43. | O | O | O | O | O |

My team does not have a sense of direction.

My team has developed a clear sense of direction.

TEAM-DEVELOPMENT SCALE

Instructions: For each of the first ten questions in this inventory, refer to the scale provided and decide which number corresponds to your response; then circle that number on the scale. The eleventh item is an open-ended question; feel free to respond openly and completely.

1. To what extent do I feel a real part of the team?

1	2	3	4	5
Completely a part, all of the time.	A part most of the time.	On the edge; sometimes in, sometimes out.	Generally outside, except for one or two short periods.	On the outside, not really a part of the team.

2. How safe is it in this team to be at ease, relaxed, and myself?

1	2	3	4	5
I feel perfectly safe to be myself; they will not hold mistakes against me.	I feel most people would accept me if I were completely myself, but there are some I am not sure about.	Generally, you have to be careful what you say or do in this team.	I am quite fearful about being completely myself in this team.	A person would be a fool to be himself or herself in this team.

3. To what extent do I feel "under wraps," that is, having private thoughts, unspoken reservations, or unexpressed feelings and opinions that I have not felt comfortable bringing out in the open?

1	2	3	4	5
Almost completely under wraps.	Under wraps many times.	Slightly more free and expressive than under wraps.	Quite free and expressive much of the time.	Almost completely free and expressive.

4. How effective are we, in our team, in getting out and using the ideas, opinions, and information of all team members in making decisions?

1	2	3	4	5
We do not really encourage everyone to share ideas, opinions, and information with the team in making decisions.	Only the ideas, opinions, and information of a few members are really known and used in making decisions.	Sometimes we hear the views of most members before making decisions, and sometimes we disregard most members.	A few are somewhat hesitant about sharing their opinions, but we generally have good participation in making decisions.	Everyone feels his or her ideas, opinions, and information are given a fair hearing before decisions are made.

5. To what extent are the goals the team is working toward understood, and to what extent do they have meaning for you?

1	2	3	4	5
I feel extremely good about the goals of our team.	I feel fairly good, but some things are not too clear or meaningful.	A few things we are doing are clear and meaningful.	Much of the activity is not clear or meaningful to me.	I really do not understand or feel involved in the goals of the team.

6. How well does the team work at its tasks?

1	2	3	4	5
Coasts, loafs, makes no progress.	Makes a little progress; most members loaf.	Progress is slow; spurts of effective work.	Above average in progress and pace of work.	Works well, achieves definite progress.

7. Our planning and the way we operate as a team is largely influenced by:

1	2	3	4	5
One or two team members.	A clique.	Shifts from one person or clique to another.	Shared by most of the members; some left out.	Shared by all members of the team.

8. What is the level of responsibility for work in our team?

1	2	3	4	5
Each person assumes personal responsibility for getting work done.	A majority of the members assume responsibility for getting work done.	About half assume responsibility; about half do not.	Only a few assume responsibility for getting work done.	Nobody (except perhaps one) really assumes responsibility for getting work done.

9. How are differences or conflicts handled in our team?

1	2	3	4	5
Differences or conflicts are denied, suppressed, or avoided at all costs.	Differences or conflicts are recognized, but remain unresolved mostly.	Differences or conflicts are recognized; some attempts are made to work them through by some members, often outside the team meetings.	Differences and conflicts are recognized, and some attempts are made to deal with them in our team.	Differences and conflicts are recognized, and the team usually is working them through satisfactorily.

10. How do people relate to the team leader?

1	2	3	4	5
The team leader dominates the team, and people are often fearful or passive.	The team leader tends to control the team, although people generally agree with the team leader's direction.	There is some give and take between the team leader and the team members.	Team members relate easily to the team leader and usually are able to influence the team leader's decisions.	Team members respect the team leader, but they work together as a unified team with everyone participating and no one dominant.

11. What suggestions do you have for improving our team's functioning?

TEAM-OBSERVATION GUIDE

Name of Team_____ Date of Meeting_____

Time_____ Observer _____

Instructions: Use the following words, phrases, and questions to prompt your observations of the climate, involvement, interaction, cohesiveness, and productivity of the team.

CLIMATE

1. Is the physical setup conducive to interaction?

2. Distractions

3. Ventilation

4. Lighting

5. Time limit (pressure) on space?

6. Emotional climate (cooperative; competitive)

7. Formal/informal support

8. Pride in team (accepting; judgmental)

9. Expressed feelings (fears; desires; concerns)

General Notes on Climate:

INVOLVEMENT

1. Why are team members here?

2. Lateness/absenteeism

3. Interest in team talk

4. Stake in problems

5. Commitment to team

6. Attentive (list names)

7. Restless (list names)

8. Withdrawn (list names)

General Notes on Involvement:

INTERACTION

1. Lines of communication (one to one; one to team; all through leader)

2. Participation (What percentage of the team is doing half of the talking?)

3. Overparticipators

4. Underparticipators

5. Who has the power in the team?

6. Pairings, subgroups

7. Impact of team size on interaction

8. Balance of task and team-building roles:

   Task _____ %
   Team _____ %

9. To what extent are team members listening and building on the ideas of others?

General Notes on Interaction:

COHESIVENESS

1. Degree of team solidarity

2. Team versus individual interests

3. Team norms observed

4. Who does not conform?

5. Pressure to conform

6. Readiness to accept majority decisions

General Notes on Cohesiveness:

PRODUCTIVITY

1. Were the goals stated?

2. Did the team members contribute to goal statements?

3. Are the goals clear?

4. Are the goals realistic?

5. Are the goals understood by all?

6. Is the effectiveness of procedures evaluated regularly?

7. Are outcomes evaluated regularly?

8. What steps does the team use in making decisions?

9. At what points (or under what circumstances) does the team's decision-making procedure get offtrack?

10. Are decisions from the previous session being carried out?

11. How is the team going about planning the next session?

12. Effects of roles of (a) leader or chairperson, (b) advisor, and (c) recorder or secretary.

13. Style of leadership

14. Impact of leadership style on participation

General Notes on Productivity:

BEHAVIOR-FREQUENCY OBSERVATION GUIDE

Team_____ Observer_____ Date of Rating_____

Instructions: Rate the frequency of each team member's behavior using this scale:

0 = Not Observed
1 = Once or Twice
2 = A Few Times
3 = Frequently

Members' Names							
• Initiated activities							
• Assumed leadership in team							
• Made friendly approaches to others							
• Acted withdrawn or out of team							
• Got angry and shouted or sulked							
• Showed enthusiasm for activity							
• Showed off, sought attention							
• Disrupted or disturbed team							
• Fidgeted, appeared nervous							
• Helped others to participate or learn							
• Helped team assess its performance							
• Praised or supported others							

By Hedley G. Dimock. Adapted from *Groups: Leadership and Group Development,* by H.G. Dimock, 1987, San Diego, CA: University Associates. This observation guide may be freely reproduced for educational/training activities. *Systematic or large-scale reproduction or distribution (more than one hundred copies) may be done only with prior written permission from University Associates.*

TEAM-BEHAVIOR QUESTIONNAIRE

Instructions: Answer each question with the *first names only* of two team members. Base your nominations on interactions in the team. Be sure to choose two people for each question. *Do not include yourself.*

1. Which team members can most easily influence others to change their opinions? _____ _____

2. Which team members are least able to influence others to change their opinions? _____ _____

3. Which team members have clashed most sharply with others in the course of team meetings? _____ _____

4. Which team members are most highly accepted by the team? _____ _____

5. Which team members are most ready to support other team members? _____ _____

6. Which team members try to keep themselves in the limelight? _____ _____

7. Which team members are most likely to put personal goals above team goals? _____ _____

8. Which team members have most often introduced topics not directly related to the team task? _____ _____

9. Which team members have shown the greatest desire to accomplish something? _____ _____

10. Which team members have wanted to avoid conflict in team discussions? _____ _____

Adapted from "Group-Behavior Questionnaire" in *A Handbook of Structured Experiences for Human Relations Training* (Vol. III, Rev.), edited by J.W. Pfeiffer and J.E. Jones, 1974, San Diego, CA: University Associates. This questionnaire may be freely reproduced for educational/training activities. *Systematic or large-scale reproduction or distribution (more than one hundred copies)—or inclusion of this questionnaire in publications for sale—may be done only with prior written permission from University Associates.*

11. Which team members tend to withdraw from active discussion when strong differences begin to appear? _____ _____

12. Which team members have sought to help in the resolution of differences between other team members? _____ _____

13. Which team members have wanted the team to be warm, friendly, and comfortable? _____ _____

14. Which team members have competed most with others? _____ _____

15. Which team members have done the most to keep the team lively? _____ _____

16. With which team members would you choose to work? _____ _____

17. With which team members have you talked least? _____ _____

INTERPERSONAL-SKILLS QUESTIONNAIRE

Instructions: This questionnaire is to be used in describing a fellow team member. For each of the statements that follow, refer to the scale provided and decide which number corresponds to your level of agreement with the statement; then write that number in the blank to the left of the statement.

Rarely	Sometimes	Often	Most of the Time	Almost Always
1	2	3	4	5

_____ 1. This person is clear in describing his or her preferences and expectations for me and others.

_____ 2. This person is prepared to listen attentively to me when I am expressing my thoughts and feelings.

_____ 3. I can trust this person with my private ideas and opinions.

_____ 4. This person is sensitive and aware of how I am feeling in our mutual activities.

_____ 5. This person is open and flexible in implementing new ideas and proposals of others.

_____ 6. This person helps me to feel included and supported in the team.

_____ 7. This person is open to receiving feedback on his or her behavior and its impact on me.

_____ 8. This person discloses to me personal concerns and problems related to work.

_____ 9. It is quite easy for me to talk with this person whenever I have the desire or need.

By Hedley G. Dimock and Doug Scott. Adapted from *Groups: Leadership and Group Development,* by H.G. Dimock, 1987, San Diego, CA: University Associates. This questionnaire may be freely reproduced for educational/training activities. *Systematic or large-scale reproduction or distribution (more than one hundred copies)—or inclusion of this questionnaire in publications for sale—may be done only with prior written permission from Hedley G. Dimock.*

Rarely	Sometimes	Often	Most of the Time	Almost Always
1	2	3	4	5

_____10. When I go to this person with a problem about my work, I know I will get thoughtful criticism and constructive help.

_____11. This person's manner makes it easy for me to tell him or her when things are not going as well as expected.

_____12. This person gives me commendation and recognition for a job well done.

_____13. This person is ready to confront me and others and to deal with any possible conflicts.

_____14. When we are discussing team problems, this person asks for my ideas and opinions.

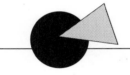

Introduction to
Supplemental Materials

The pieces that form the contents of the Supplemental Materials section are intended to supplement the activities in this volume and to provide the team leader and members with useful information about teams, how they operate, and related subjects. All of these materials may be freely reproduced for educational/training activities. *Systematic or large-scale reproduction or distribution (more than one hundred copies)—or inclusion of any of these items in publications for sale—may be done only with prior written permission from the sources indicated.*

Specific events or circumstances in a team's life often generate the leader's and/or the members' interest in a particular subject matter. At such times the leader can refer to this section and choose an appropriate list, handout, or article to read and/or to distribute and discuss with the team members. The team leader may find that these materials do more than generate lively discussion, however; they also may provide valuable insights in how to get the team successfully past various hurdles. The materials cover a wide variety of subjects: the characteristics of effective team leaders and members, symptoms of team problems, win-lose situations, responsibility in communication, how to communicate in a supportive rather than defensive manner, how to resolve conflict, the power of conflict in team discussions, various decision-making styles, how to deal with disruptive people in meetings, and viewing resistance from a positive perspective.

CHARACTERISTICS OF AN EFFECTIVE TEAM

1. The team members share a sense of purpose or common goals, and each team member is willing to work toward achieving these goals.

2. The team is aware of and interested in its own processes and examining norms operating within the team.

3. The team identifies its own resources and uses them, depending on its needs. The team willingly accepts the influence and leadership of the members whose resources are relevant to the immediate task.

4. The team members continually try to listen to and clarify what is being said and show interest in what others say and feel.

5. Differences of opinion are encouraged and freely expressed. The team does not demand narrow conformity or adherence to formats that inhibit freedom of movement and expression.

6. The team is willing to surface conflict and focus on it until it is resolved or managed in a way that does not reduce the effectiveness of those involved.

7. The team exerts energy toward problem solving rather than allowing it to be drained by interpersonal issues or competitive struggles.

8. Roles are balanced and shared to facilitate both the accomplishment of tasks and feelings of team cohesion and morale.

9. To encourage risk taking and creativity, mistakes are treated as sources of learning rather than reasons for punishment.

10. The team is responsive to the changing needs of its members and to the external environment to which it is related.

11. Team members are committed to periodically evaluating the team's performance.

12. The team is attractive to its members, who identify with it and consider it a source of both professional and personal growth.

13. Developing a climate of trust is recognized as the crucial element for facilitating all of the above elements.

By Philip G. Hanson and Bernard Lubin. Adapted from "Team Building as Group Development," © 1986 *Organizational Development Journal,* Spring. Adapted with permission from the *Organizational Development Journal.* This list may be freely reproduced for educational/training activities. *Systematic or large-scale reproduction or distribution (more than one hundred copies)—or inclusion of this list in publications for sale—may be done only with prior written permission from the Organizational Development Journal.*

CHARACTERISTICS OF EFFECTIVE TEAM LEADERS

Effective team leaders:

1. Communicate
2. Are open, honest, and fair
3. Make decisions with input from others
4. Act consistently
5. Give the team members the information they need to do their jobs
6. Set goals and emphasize them
7. Keep focused through follow-up
8. Listen to feedback and ask questions
9. Show loyalty to the company and to the team members
10. Create an atmosphere of growth
11. Have wide visibility
12. Give praise and recognition
13. Criticize constructively and address problems
14. Develop plans
15. Share their mission and goals
16. Display tolerance and flexibility
17. Demonstrate assertiveness
18. Exhibit a willingness to change
19. Treat team members with respect
20. Make themselves available and accessible
21. Want to take charge
22. Accept ownership for team decisions
23. Set guidelines for how team members are to treat one another
24. Represent the team and fight a "good fight" when appropriate

By M.M. Starcevich and S.J. Stowell. Adapted from *Teamwork: We Have Met the Enemy and They Are Us,* by M.M. Starcevich and S.J. Stowell, 1990, Bartlesville, OK: The Center for Management and Organization Effectiveness. Used with permission of the publisher. This list may be freely reproduced for educational/training activities. *Systematic or large-scale reproduction or distribution (more than one hundred copies)—or inclusion of this list in publications for sale—may be done only with prior written permission from The Center for Management and Organization Effectiveness.*

CHARACTERISTICS OF EFFECTIVE TEAM MEMBERS

Effective team members:

1. Support the team leader
2. Help the team leader to succeed
3. Ensure that all viewpoints are explored
4. Express opinions, both for and against
5. Compliment the team leader on team efforts
6. Provide open, honest, and accurate information
7. Support, protect, and defend both the team and the team leader
8. Act in a positive and constructive manner
9. Provide appropriate feedback
10. Understand personal and team roles
11. Bring problems to the team (upward feedback)
12. Accept ownership for team decisions
13. Recognize that they each serve as a team leader
14. Balance appropriate levels of participation
15. Participate voluntarily
16. Maintain confidentiality
17. Show loyalty to the company, the team leader, and the team
18. View criticism as an opportunity to learn
19. State problems, along with alternative solutions/options
20. Give praise and recognition when warranted

Items 1 through 21 by M.M. Starcevich and S.J. Stowell; Items 22 through 29 by Roger G. James and Aaron J. Elkins. Items 1 through 21 adapted from *Teamwork: We Have Met the Enemy and They Are Us* (pp. 118-119), by M.M. Starcevich and S.J. Stowell, 1990, Bartlesville, OK: The Center for Management and Organization Effectiveness. Used with permission from the publisher. Items 22 through 29 adapted from *How to Train and Lead a Quality Circle,* by R.G. James and A.J. Elkins, 1983, San Diego, CA: University Associates. The entire list may be freely reproduced for educational/training activities. *Systematic or large-scale reproduction or distribution (more than one hundred copies)—or inclusion of the items in publications for sale—may be done only with prior written permission from the respective publishers.*

21. Operate within the parameters of team rules
22. Confront the team leader when his or her behavior is not helping the team
23. Share ideas freely and enthusiastically
24. Encourage others to express their ideas fully
25. Ask one another for opinions and listen to them
26. Criticize ideas, not people
27. Avoid disruptive behavior such as side conversations and inside jokes
28. Avoid defensiveness when fellow team members disagree with their ideas
29. Attend meetings regularly and promptly

SYMPTOMS OF TEAM PROBLEMS

Symptoms	Description	Explanation
Backbiting and complaining	Members of the team openly complain about and find fault with one another.	Team members are not clear about standards, leading to a loss of control over the team members.
Presence of a "spy of the owner"	Members of the team suspect and distrust new members.	New members have difficulty breaking into the established team.
Two coalitions	The team has two factions, one of which has very little influence or power.	The team experiences a lack of cohesiveness.
Personal stress	Stress shows up in the team members, evidenced by "blowing up" and physical symptoms.	Team members feel threatened and thus become less efficient and more dissatisfied.
Combative behavior	Team members resort to yelling and to combative behavior in the name of playing the devil's advocate.	Team members express conflict through the use of threats, attacks, and so on.
Infinite details	Team members scrutinize every detail and check on all aspects of minor or major decisions.	Team members distrust one another and fear being penalized for errors.
Amount of time to make decisions	Decisions on minor issues are brought to the top of the organization, requiring excessive time.	Team members feel a lack of trust directly related to team problem solving.
Shifting and changing decisions	Decisions often are changed shortly after being made.	Team members are not willing to commit the team to a unified course of action.

By Glenn H. Varney. Adapted from *Building Productive Teams* (p. 101), by G.H. Varney, 1989, San Francisco: Jossey-Bass. Used with permission from Jossey-Bass. This table may be freely reproduced for educational/training activities. *Systematic or large-scale reproduction or distribution (more than one hundred copies)—or inclusion of this table in publications for sale—may be done only with prior written permission from Jossey-Bass.*

TEAM-BUILDING AGENDA

1. ***Goals***

   What should the goals be for the team-building session?
   What should the overall goals be for our team?
   What should the goals be for yourself?

2. ***Strategic Planning***

   Where do we want to be in 1, 3, 5 years?

3. ***Expectations***

   What do we expect of others on the team? The management?
   What are the team leader's expectations of team members?

4. ***Decision Making***

   Who makes what decisions?
   How should decisions be made?

5. ***Organization***

   Are we organized appropriately?

6. ***Morale***

   What is the current level of morale in our team?
   How could it be improved?

7. ***Relations with Other Units***

   How well are we working with other departments? With headquarters?

8. ***Strengths and Weaknesses***

   What do we see as our strengths as a team? Our weaknesses?
   How do we correct our weaknesses?

9. ***Current Problems***

   Are there any current problems or concerns not listed that we need to address?

HIDDEN AGENDAS

Any team works on two levels: (1) the level of the surface task with which the team is immediately concerned and (2) the level of the hidden, undisclosed needs and motives of its individual members. The team members' aspirations, attitudes, and values affect the way they react to the team's surface task. Such individual "hidden agendas" siphon off valuable energy that could be used for accomplishing the task at hand and for team maintenance. Understanding how these hidden agendas work in the life of a team helps the team members to achieve their common goal more efficiently.

INDIVIDUAL NEEDS

A person joins a team in order to fulfill or express certain personal needs. That person's behavior as a member of that team is neither random nor haphazard: it is keyed to his or her personal motivations, which may be social or emotional, explicit or hidden from the team, known or unknown to the individual.

Needs, of course, take different forms and can be satisfied in different ways for different people. Physical and security needs are basic: an individual must have food, shelter, and warmth in order to maintain life; in order not to be overwhelmed by anxiety, he or she must also achieve some security and stability in the environment.

When such basic survival needs are met, other needs press for satisfaction. An individual has social, ego, and self-fulfillment requirements as well. These are the needs that can best be fulfilled in a team situation; thus, their satisfaction is often the individual's motivation for joining and/or staying on a team.

As individuals seek acceptance from others, social needs become apparent; when these are filled, the ego presses for its satisfaction. Finally, as individuals begin to understand their own unique identities, they can become fully themselves.

Hidden beneath the surface of the team's life are many individual, conflicting currents: its members' needs for belonging, acceptance, recognition, self-worth, self-expression, and productivity. Such needs are personal and subjective, but they are not necessarily "selfish." Looking for the satisfaction of personal needs through team membership is both "normal" and "natural." The question is not how or whether these needs should be satisfied, but how they affect the team as a whole.

By J. William Pfeiffer and John E. Jones. Adapted from *The 1974 Annual Handbook for Group Facilitators,* edited by J.W. Pfeiffer and J.E. Jones, 1974, San Diego, CA: University Associates. This article may be freely reproduced for educational/training activities. *Systematic or large-scale reproduction or distribution (more than one hundred copies)—or inclusion of this article in publications for sale—may be done only with prior written permission from University Associates.*

If one individual's needs block another from achieving his or her needs, or if such personal needs hinder the team from accomplishing its goals, then there is cause for concern. It is possible for individuals to fulfill their needs in ways that do not raise obstacles for other members of the team.

SOME SUGGESTIONS FOR TEAM LEADERS

The team leader should keep in mind the fact that a team continually works on both the hidden and the surface levels. Hidden agendas may prevent the team from moving as fast as team members would like or expect.

Hidden agendas can be addressed in the following ways:

1. The team leader can look for hidden agendas and learn to recognize their presence.

2. A team member may help to surface hidden agendas by making comments such as "I wonder if we have said all that we feel about the issue. Maybe we should take time to go around the table and ask for individual comments so that we can open up any further thoughts."

3. Hidden agendas can be brought into the open and discussed. But not all hidden agendas can be confronted successfully by a team; some are best left under the surface.

4. The team leader should not criticize the team for the presence of hidden agendas; they are legitimate and must be worked with just like the surface task. The amount of attention that should be given to the hidden agendas depends on the degree of their influence on the team's task.

5. The team leader should help the team to find the means of solving hidden agendas. Problem-solving methods are needed, though techniques vary.

6. The team should spend some time evaluating its progress in handling hidden agendas. The last fifteen minutes of a meeting devoted to such evaluation is often very helpful.

Better and more open ways of dealing with hidden agendas should become apparent through experience. As a team matures, hidden agendas are often reduced, thus increasing the amount of energy the team has to devote to its surface tasks.

WIN-LOSE SITUATIONS

Win-lose situations pervade the culture. Law courts use an adversarial system; political parties strive to win elections and to win points in legislatures; debates are common in schools, universities, and in the media; put-downs are generally regarded as wit. Competing with and defeating an opponent is the most widely publicized aspect of many sports and recreational activities.

The language of business, politics, and even education is marked with win-lose terms. One "wins" a promotion, "beats" the competition, and obtains "the racer's edge" for an automobile. Students strive to "top the class" or "outsmart" the teacher. Although cooperative effort and collaboration are recognized, the culture emphasizes "healthy" competition.

In an environment that stresses winning, it is not surprising that competitive behavior persists where it is not appropriate. In many team meetings, members interrupt one another to introduce their own ideas, proposals are made that other members do not even acknowledge, and partnerships and power blocs are formed to support one program over another. When team members analyze the operation of the meeting, they commonly agree that they were not listening to one another because they were thinking of ways to state a case or to counter someone else's proposal or interrupting to make a point before the speaker clinched the sale of an idea. In these ways they acted as competing individuals rather than as a collaborating team. They started out to reach the best decision but slipped into a win-lose contest. Very often the team's original purpose is completely overshadowed by the struggle to win. This is a common failing of teams.

Win-lose contests frequently occur in organizational life. Individuals may strive for dominant position, and battles can rage discreetly—or not discreetly—between departments. For example, a planning department may develop a new assembly procedure. When the procedure is introduced to the assembly department, the workers may resent it and lock horns with the planners. It is easy to interpret such a situation in win-lose terms. The planners are trying to show that they know more and can design a procedure better than the workers on the job. If the new procedure works well, the planners "win." On the other hand, if the innovation does not improve production, the planners "lose." In a sense, the assemblers "win" because their usual operation proved superior. Seen in this light, it should be

---

By Gerry E. Wiley. Adapted from *The 1973 Annual Handbook for Group Facilitators*, edited by J.E. Jones & J.W. Pfeiffer, 1973, San Diego, CA: University Associates. This article may be freely reproduced for educational/training activities. *Systematic or large-scale reproduction or distribution (more than one hundred copies)—or inclusion of this article in publications for sale—may be done only with prior written permission from University Associates.*

expected that the workers will not be committed to giving the innovation a fair trial. In extreme cases, they may even sabotage it. In fact all efforts to plan for others are plagued by win-lose traps. In some companies and institutions, internal win-lose rivalries absorb more effort than the main production or service.

POTENTIAL RESULTS OF WIN-LOSE SITUATIONS

Although in some instances a win-lose attitude is a positive factor, it is generally destructive to interpersonal relations and organizational effectiveness. If two friends argue over how to spend an evening, the one who wants to see a movie may "win out" over the one who wants to go to a horse race. However, the horse-racing fan can retaliate by being sullen or obnoxious, thus turning a win-lose situation into a miserable ordeal for both of them. Often win-lose "victories" become losses for both parties; this has been termed a "lose-lose" result.

Some of the negative results of win-lose situations have been shown in the preceding examples. Following is a list of problems that may arise from win-lose confrontations; these problems are not listed in any particular order, nor are they comprehensive. Win-lose situations:

1. Divert time and energy from the main issues;
2. Delay decisions;
3. Create deadlocks;
4. Drive nonaggressive members of a team or committee to the sidelines;
5. Interfere with listening;
6. Obstruct exploration of more alternatives;
7. Decrease or destroy sensitivity;
8. Cause members to drop out or resign from committees;
9. Arouse anger that can disrupt a meeting;
10. Interfere with empathy;
11. Leave losers resentful;
12. Incline underdogs to sabotage;
13. Provoke personal abuse; and
14. Cause defensiveness.

ADJUSTING WIN-LOSE SITUATIONS

Because win-lose events are common, it is important to know how to cope with them. Knowing that the predominant trend of win-lose contests is toward lose-lose outcomes, it becomes imperative to redirect them toward "win-win" results. In a "win-win" result, everyone comes out on top.

One-on-one, a single individual can often deflect a contest because it takes two to fight. However, it is extremely difficult for one person to re-orient a win-lose situation in a team. Although it would be ideal to have all parties committed to avoiding win-lose results, the efforts of a significant segment of a team can usually be effective. The more team members in a win-lose situation who recognize the dangers in such a struggle and want to adjust the situation, the more likely it is that they will succeed. If such a subgroup exists in a team, its members might use any of the following means of adjustment:

1. Identify clear goals, ones that are understood and agreed on. Use the goals to test whether or not the issues are relevant.

2. Be on the lookout for win-lose situations, which can develop subtly. If team members feel under attack or feel they need to line up support, they are likely to be in a win-lose situation.

3. Listen empathically to others. Avoid working on counter-arguments while another person is speaking. Take the risk of being persuaded. Try the other person's reasoning on for size.

4. Avoid absolute statements that leave no room for modification. "I think this is the way..." is better than "This is *the only* way...."

5. When engaged in planning for others, provide some means for the others' involvement. The doers need to feel that they can have influence on decisions that affect them.

6. Try to make decisions by consensus[1] rather than by victory of the majority.

7. Test to see that trade-offs and compromises are truly accepted by all.

8. Draw a continuum line and have members place themselves on it regarding the issue at hand. It often occurs that the different "sides" are not far apart.

9. Be alert to selling or winning strategies in others, and avoid using them. A comment such as "Any intelligent person can see the advantages..." is a danger signal.

This list is not exhaustive, but it may provide a start toward more productive relationships. The key idea in adjusting win-lose situations is to strive for what is best for all rather than to try to get one's own way.

---

[1] A consensus decision is one that all team members can accept, regardless of how satisfied they are with it. Each member's opinion must be heard; no "majority-rule" voting, bargaining, or averaging is allowed.

RESPONSIBILITY IN COMMUNICATION

It is a characteristic of human nature to try to assess or "make sense of" human behavior. However, the assumptions a person makes about the behavior of others are not necessarily what those others are; instead, these assumptions are reflections of that person's own values and beliefs. When conversing with another person, it is important to remember this fact, to clarify assumptions, and to be willing to accept at least some of the responsibility for any ambiguity in the communication. Following are some suggestions about ways to take responsibility and to clarify assumptions when communicating with another person:

1. Specify the behavior(s) on which the assumption is based: "Your facial expression suggests to me that you're confused" rather than "Are you following what I'm saying?"

2. If a person's assumption compares the listener's behavior with that of other members of a reference group, state what that group is and exactly how the behavior compares: "The other members of the department always submit their weekly production reports on Monday, and each of your last four reports wasn't submitted until Thursday" rather than "You don't submit your weekly production reports promptly."

3. If a person's assumption is based on his or her own expectation of the listener's behavior, state that expectation specifically; do not assume that the listener knows the details of the expectation: "I'm expecting that report next Monday at 4:00. Can we agree on that?" rather than "Is that report going to be done on time?"

4. Elicit feedback about the assumption; ask the listener to indicate whether the assumption is accurate: "Am I correct in assuming that you've already begun writing the report that's due next Monday?"

By Gilles L. Talbot. Adapted from "Taking Responsibility Theory Sheet," by G.L. Talbot, in *A Handbook of Structured Experiences for Human Relations Training* (Vol. X), edited by J.W. Pfeiffer, 1985, San Diego, CA: University Associates. This handout may be freely reproduced for educational/training activities. *Systematic or large-scale reproduction or distribution (more than one hundred copies)—or inclusion of this handout in publications for sale—may be done only with prior written permission from University Associates.*

COMMUNICATING COMMUNICATION

One of the most important ingredients of team development is clear communication. Nevertheless, clarity alone is insufficient; therefore, the purpose of this article is to examine *effective* ways of communicating.

As Lull, Funk, and Piersol (1955) describe it,

> Effectiveness of management personnel of all grades is very dependent upon the ability to *communicate* orally not only the policy of the company but suggestions as to how work should be done, criticism of poor work, and the application of discipline, and of course the general field of human relationships. (p. 17)

And in the words of Redding and Sanborn (1964),

> It seems safe to conclude from research studies that by and large, the better supervisors (better in terms of getting the work done) are those who are more sensitive to their communication responsibilities. They tend to be those, for example, who give clear instructions, who *listen empathically,* who are accessible for questions or suggestions, and who keep their subordinates properly informed. (p. 60)

Research leads to the conclusion that there is a positive correlation between effective communication and each of the following factors: employee productivity, personal satisfaction, rewarding relationships, and effective problem solving. Two major components of effective communication are sending and receiving messages. Techniques of listening and verbalizing help in both of these dimensions.

FACTORS AFFECTING THE SENDER

Self-Feelings

In the context of each communicating situation, the sender's feelings about himself or herself will affect how the message is encoded. The following questions are conscious and subconscious trade winds that affect the effectiveness of the message: "Do I feel worthwhile in this situation?"; "Am I safe in offering suggestions?"; "Is this the right time (place)?"; "Am I the subordinate or the boss in this situation?" In

By J. Ryck Luthi. Adapted from *The 1978 Annual Handbook for Group Facilitators,* edited by J.W. Pfeiffer and J.E. Jones, 1978, San Diego, CA: University Associates. This article may be freely reproduced for educational/training activities. *Systematic or large-scale reproduction or distribution (more than one hundred copies)—or inclusion of this article in publications for sale—may be done only with prior written permission from University Associates.*

everyday jargon, these questions might be "Am I O.K.?" and "Do I count?" Usually, the more comfortable or positive the self-concept, the more effective the sender is in communicating.

Assertive Rights

Linked to self-concept is the belief that one has some rights, such as the right to change one's mind, the right to say "I don't understand" or "I don't know," the right to follow a "gut feeling" without justifying it, the right to make mistakes and be responsible for them, and the right to say "I am not sure now, but let me work on it." Believing in such rights can help strengthen the sender's self-concept and avoid the defensive maneuvering that hinders communication in exchanging information. It would be wise to remember that assertive rights are not complete without responsibility. For example, one has the right to say "I don't know," but one probably also has the responsibility to find out.

The Sender's Perception of the Message

"Do I feel the information I have is valuable? Is it something I want to say or do not want to say? How do I feel it will be received? Is the topic interesting or not interesting to me? Do I understand the information correctly, at least well enough to describe it to others, and do I know the best way to say it?"

The Sender's Feelings About the Receiver

The probability of effective communication is increased if the sender feels positive or respectful toward the receiver. Positive or respectful feelings usually carry a built-in commitment and/or desire to share communication. Negative or nonrespect-ful feelings require conscious effort to communicate effectively. For the sender it is important to know it is all right not to like everyone—or, for the optimist, to like some people less than others. It is also important to know that we live in a world in which not everyone is going to like or respect us, and that is all right too.

Suggestions for Effective Expression

In order to communicate messages effectively, the sender should consider the following points:

1. *Become aware of thoughts and feelings.* Do not be quick to brand them "good," "bad," "wrong," or "right." Accept them as a reflection of the present "you," and let them become best friends by giving support and feedback to your effectiveness and to your needs; consider what they are whispering or shouting to you. By increasing your awareness of your feelings, you can better decide what to do with them.

2. *Feel comfortable in expressing your feelings.* Such expression, when it is congruent with the situation and appropriate, can enhance communication.

3. *Be aware of the listener.* Try to verbalize your message in terms of the listener's understanding, and indicate why you feel the message is important to him or her. Does it have a specific significance for the listener, or is it just "general information"?

4. *Focus on the importance of the message.* Repeat key concepts and essential aspects of the information.

5. *Use as few words as possible to state the message.*

POINTS FOR THE LISTENER

Effective listening is as important to communication as effective sending. Effective listening is an active process in which the listener interacts with the speaker. It requires mental and verbal paraphrasing and attention to nonverbal cues like tones, gestures, and facial expressions. It is a process of listening not to every word but to main thoughts and references.

Nichols (1952) listed the following as deterrents to effective listening: (1) assuming in advance that the subject is uninteresting and unimportant; (2) mentally criticizing the speaker's delivery; (3) getting overstimulated when questioning or opposing an idea; (4) listening only for facts, wanting to skip the details; (5) outlining everything; (6) pretending to be attentive; (7) permitting the speaker to be inaudible or incomplete; (8) avoiding technical messages; (9) overreacting to certain words and phrases; and (10) withdrawing attention, daydreaming.

The feelings and attitudes of the listener can affect what he or she perceives. How the listener feels about himself or herself, how the message is perceived, and how the listener feels about the person sending the message affect how well the recipient listens. The listener should keep in mind the following suggestions:

1. **Be fully accessible to the sender.** Being preoccupied, letting your mind wander, and trying to do more than one thing at a time lessen your chances of hearing and understanding effectively. Interrupting a conversation to answer the phone may enhance your perceived ego, but the interrupted speaker feels of secondary importance.

2. **Be aware of your feelings as a listener.** Emotions such as anger, dislike, defensiveness, and prejudice are natural; but they cause us not to hear what is being said and sometimes to hear things that are not being said.

According to Reik (1972), listening with the "third ear" requires the listener to do the following things: (1) suspend judgment for a while; (2) develop purpose and commitment to listening; (3) avoid distraction; (4) wait before responding; (5) develop paraphrasing in his or her own words and context, particularly to review the central themes of the message; (6) continually reflect mentally on what the speaker is trying to say; and (7) be ready to respond when the speaker is ready for comments.

Blocks to Effective Communication

Responses that can block effective communication are as follows:

1. ***Evaluation response.*** The phrases "You should...," "Your duty...," "You are wrong," "You should know better," "You are bad," and "You are such a good person" create blocks to communication. There is a time for evaluation, but if it is given too soon, the speaker usually becomes defensive.

2. ***Advice-giving response.*** "Why don't you try...," "You'll feel better when...," "It would be best for you to...," and "My advice is..." are phrases that give advice. Advice is best given at the conclusion of conversations and generally only when requested.

3. ***Topping response.*** "That's nothing; you should have seen...," "When that happened to me, I...," "When I was a child...," and "You think you have it bad..." are phrases of one-upmanship. This approach shifts attention from the person who wants to be listened to and leaves him or her feeling unimportant.

4. ***Diagnosing, psychoanalytic response.*** "What you need is...," "The reason you feel the way you do is...," "You don't really mean that," and "Your problem is..." are phrases that tell others what they feel. Telling people how they feel or why they feel the way they do can be a two-edged sword. If the diagnoser is wrong, the speaker feels pressed; if the diagnoser is right, the speaker may feel exposed or cornered. Most people do not want to be told how to feel and would rather volunteer their feelings than have them exposed.

5. ***Prying-questioning response.*** "Why," "who," "where," "when," "how," and "what" are responses common to us all. But such responses tend to make the speaker feel "on the spot" and therefore resist the interrogation. At times, however, a questioning response is helpful for clarification, and in emergencies it is needed.

6. ***Warning, admonishing, commanding response.*** "You had better...," "If you don't...," "You have to...," "You will...," and "You must..." are used constantly in the everyday work environment. Usually such responses produce resentment, resistance, and rebellion. There are times, of course, when this response is necessary, such as in an emergency situation when the information being given is critical to human welfare.

7. ***Logical, lecturing response.*** "Don't you realize...," "Here is where you are wrong...," "The facts are...," and "Yes, but..." can be heard in any discussion with two people of differing opinions. Such responses tend to make the other person feel

inferior or defensive. Of course, persuasion is part of the world we live in. In general, however, we need to trust that when people are given correct and full data they will make logical decisions for themselves.

8. ***Devaluation response.*** "It's not so bad," "Don't worry," "You'll get over it," or "Oh, you don't feel that way" are familiar phrases used in responding to others' emotions. A listener should recognize the sender's feelings and should not try to take away those feelings or deny them to the owner. In our desire to alleviate emotional pain, we apply bandages too soon and possibly in the wrong places.

Whenever a listener's responses convey nonacceptance of the speaker's feelings, the desire to change the speaker, a lack of trust, or the sense that the speaker is inferior or at fault or being "bad," communication blocks will occur.

AWARENESS OF ONE'S OWN FEELINGS

For both senders and listeners, awareness of feelings requires the ability to stop and check what feelings one is presently experiencing and the ability to consciously decide how to respond to the feelings. At first it may be uncomfortable and easy to forget, but only by using it will this technique become second nature. The individual should picture three lists (1) the feelings being experienced, (2) the behaviors that may have generated those feelings, and (3) possible responses to the experienced feelings.

To use this technique, one stops at any point in time and mentally asks, "What am I feeling?" One usually experiences a kaleidoscope of emotions simultaneously but can work on focusing on one present, dominant feeling. After that feeling is identified, the second self-question is "What perceived behaviors are causing that feeling?" Other mental questions then follow: "Is it what the other person is saying, or how he or she is saying it? Is it because I do not want to be bothered?" The next step is for the person to choose how he or she wants to respond to the feeling.

There is much written about the importance of letting others know one's feelings so that one's actions and words can be congruent. One can choose, however, not to express a feeling because of inappropriate time, place, or circumstances. For example, I may identify a feeling of annoyance at being interrupted. To share that feeling may not be worthwhile in the situation. The main thing is that I am aware of my annoyance and what caused the feeling and can now choose whether or not to let it be a block to my listening. I may tell myself that I am annoyed but that my feeling is not going to get in the way of my listening. I can determine whether my feeling is likely to be a listening block, and I can prevent it from becoming one if I so choose.

Another way of becoming aware of feelings is "hindsight analysis." After any given situation, the individual can mentally recheck his or her responses and/or feelings: "What happened to cause those feelings? What was I feeling during my responses? Why do I tend to avoid certain people, and why do I enjoy being around others?" Asking "Why?" is very helpful in identifying feelings and the behaviors that cue those feelings. As a person works with this technique, identification and decision making will become better, resulting in more effective communication.

CONCLUSION

The communication process is complex but vital to effective problem solving and meaningful personal relationships. It is a process that is never really mastered; one can continually improve on it. It requires certain attitudes, knowledge, techniques, common sense, and a willingness to try. Effective communication happens when we have achieved sufficient clarity or accuracy to handle each situation adequately.

REFERENCES

Lull, P.E., Funk, F.E., & Piersol, D.T. (1955). What communications means to the corporation president. *Advanced Management, 20,* 17-20.

Nichols, R.G. (1952). *Listening is a ten part skill.* Chicago: Enterprise Publications.

Redding, W.C., & Sanborn, C.A. (Eds.). (1964). *Business and industrial communication: A sourcebook.* New York: Harper & Row.

Reik, T. (1972). *Listening with the third ear.* New York: Pyramid.

DEFENSIVE AND SUPPORTIVE COMMUNICATION

For team leaders, team members, teachers, parents—indeed, for most of us—much time is devoted to social influence. People continually attempt to modify the views of others and to move them to action. The quality and effectiveness of people's efforts to influence one another depend on their styles of interaction.

The following prescriptions have been suggested for communicating effectively:

- "Speak clearly and thoughtfully";
- "Avoid stereotyping";
- "Maintain an attentive posture";
- "Be honest and timely";
- "Listen carefully"; and
- "Repeat for emphasis and retention."

These principles are important and useful for improving the skills of expression and listening, but climate is more fundamental to successful communication. Supportive climates promote understanding and problem solving; defensive climates impede them.

DEFENSIVE COMMUNICATION

Communication climates are like weather climates; they represent more forces than can readily be seen. The dominant motive behind defensive communication climates is control. Although control can take many forms, it is often manifested by communication designed to persuade. The speaker may be friendly, patient, and courteous; but the goal, nevertheless, is to convince the listener.

The speaker's conscious or unconscious desire to prevail in the situation elicits a characteristic set of results: evaluation, strategy, superiority, and certainty (Gibb, 1961). As the interaction continues, these behaviors become increasingly pronounced. Each party becomes less able to hear the other or to accurately perceive

By Gary W. Combs. Adapted from *The 1981 Annual Handbook for Group Facilitators*, edited by J.E. Jones and J. W. Pfeiffer, 1981, San Diego, CA: University Associates. This article is based on "Barriers and Gateways to Communications," by C.R. Rogers and F.J. Roethlisberger, in *Harvard Business Review,* 1952, *30,* 46-52, and on "Defensive Communication," by J.R. Gibb, in *Journal of Communications, 1961, 11,* 141-148. This article may be freely reproduced for educational/training activities. *Systematic or large-scale reproduction or distribution (more than one hundred copies)—or inclusion of this article in publications for sale—may be done only with prior written permission from University Associates.*

the other's motives, values, and emotions. In short, communication breaks down. An example of defensive communication follows:

Bob Wheeler, director of finance, is talking with Nancy Russell, director of administrative services. Bob asks Nancy to prepare an additional weekly report summarizing selected financial data. Nancy balks at Bob's request and lists several reasons why an additional summary is unnecessary. Bob, who is determined that such a report be prepared, patiently answers Nancy by explaining why he needs the supplementary data. Nancy responds by defending her position.

What is likely to happen?

1. *Evaluation.* If Nancy continues to question the validity of Bob's request, one or both of them will inwardly or outwardly become critical of the other. Their dialog may appear calm and friendly, and they may or may not be aware of their own judgmental feelings; but these feelings will become obvious. The longer the conversation goes on, the greater their frustration will become until each begins to evaluate the other as stubborn, unreasonable, or downright stupid.

2. *Strategy.* As the conversation progresses, each will strategize and prepare rebuttals while the other is speaking. Energy will be focused on winning and overcoming rather than on listening and problem solving.

3. *Superiority.* One or both of the speakers will begin to feel superior to the other. Inwardly or outwardly each will start to question why the other cannot see the logic or "correctness" of his or her views and begin to think of the other as being inferior in intelligence and savvy.

4. *Certainty.* The energy of their arguments will lock the opponents into the correctness of their original views. Any feeling of tentativeness either may have had about his or her position gradually will be replaced with convictions of certainty.

One can predict that eventually one of the parties will withdraw or capitulate, that a compromise will be negotiated, or that the individuals involved will leave in anger. Regardless of the outcome, their feelings about each other are likely to be negative; commitment to following through with agreed-on action will be low. In all likelihood, their feelings about each other will be manifested in future encounters. The "loser" will admit to having lost the battle, but not the war.

SUPPORTIVE COMMUNICATION

The dominant goal underlying supportive communication climates is understanding. Supportive communication climates often facilitate a synergistic resolution to conflict. Synergy describes outcomes that combine elements of contrasting positions into a new and meaningful solution that satisfies the needs of both parties (a "win-win" situation). It differs from compromise, which results in each party's receiving only part of what is desired (a "lose-lose" strategy). In synergy, the emphasis is on integration; the speakers seek to establish a dialog, to listen, and to appreciate and explore differences of opinion.

The results characteristic of such communication are empathy, spontaneity, problem solving, and synergy. As each speaker listens to and attempts to understand the other's position, he or she, in turn, becomes free to fully hear and appreciate the other speaker's views of a particular situation. A supportive climate allows both to seek a creative resolution of their differences. A supportive communication climate could be illustrated by the earlier example, except that Bob could choose to explore Nancy's objections. What is likely to happen now?

1. *Empathy.* If Bob listens and discusses Nancy's reasons for not wanting to do an additional report, he naturally will come to understand her position better. His willingness to talk about their differences will convey to Nancy his respect for her thoughts and his evaluation of her importance. If Nancy feels understood and respected, her need to defend herself will diminish and she will feel free to hear what Bob has to say. The net result will be that each party will gain an appreciation of the other's point of view.

2. *Spontaneity.* If Bob and Nancy are open and responsive, less energy will be focused on strategic rebuttal. Both will be able to concentrate on what is being said, and each will feel free to express his or her own thoughts and feelings.

3. *Problem Solving.* Bob's willingness to explore their differences will imply that he is open to collaborative resolution, and Nancy will respond in kind. Once both are less concerned with winning, they will be more inclined to tolerate each other's perspectives and to settle the conflict in a way that is mutually satisfying.

4. *Synergy.* There is a good chance that Bob and Nancy will find a way to satisfy Bob's concern for additional data and Nancy's desire to keep down the number of reports produced, if they communicate in a way that allows them to appreciate, scrutinize, and fuse their respective—and respected—views into a new whole that is pleasing to both (Jones, 1973).

BARRIERS TO CREATING SUPPORTIVE COMMUNICATION CLIMATES

Supportive communication seems simple, but it is very difficult for those who are not in the habit of developing supportive climates. Cultural training is a major barrier to creating such climates because people are often rewarded for developing skills of argument and persuasion. Little or no time is given to teaching the attitudes and skills of listening and understanding. Therefore, it is necessary to practice the skills of supportive communication until they become second nature.

Lack of time and energy is also a barrier to supportive communication. Creating a positive milieu takes work! At least one speaker must assume responsibility for developing an atmosphere that permits both to understand and to respond to what is actually being said. It is often more convenient to respond superficially or inappropriately.

Supportive communication also involves risk. A willingness to see reality as others perceive it means running the risk of being changed oneself (Rogers & Roethlisberger, 1952). But such risks must be taken in order to share thoughts and feelings with one another authentically.

In addition, it is difficult for one person to give positive support to another when he or she feels angry and hostile. The inclination under these circumstances is to attack and hurt. Yet it is at such times that empathic communication can be most helpful. Sharing the other person's perspective defuses otherwise hostile environments and increases an appreciation for each other's points of view.

FACILITATING SUPPORTIVE COMMUNICATION

A genuine desire to define situations through interaction with others is the most important ingredient for supportive communication. If this desire is not genuine and a pretense of openness is made, it will be easily detected, others will no longer feel free to express themselves openly, and communication will break down.

Active listening is also essential to supportive communication. This requires making an effort to grasp the full meaning—both fact and feeling—of what others are saying and testing that understanding by clarifying and checking.[1]

People also need to share their perspectives with others; when there is conflict, they need to search for an end result that will satisfy both their own and the other person's objectives. This requires a shift of thinking from "me versus you" to "how we can both gain in this situation." Pragmatically, supportive communication means moving from thinking in terms of preconceived answers to thinking in terms of the desired end results and then seeking solutions that satisfy those ends (Filley, 1975).

CONCLUSION

Supportive communication requires a sharing and understanding attitude. When speaking and listening supportively, people become less defensive and more open to their experiences and the experiences of others. They become more ready to integrate other points of view and to seek solutions to conflict that satisfy the needs of both parties.

REFERENCES

Filley, A.C. (1975). *Interpersonal conflict resolution.* Glenview, IL: Scott, Foresman.

---

[1] In active listening, the listener listens carefully to the speaker and then restates, in his or her own words, what the speaker said. Then the speaker either confirms or corrects the listener's understanding.

Gibb, J.R. (1961). Defensive communication. *Journal of Communication, 11,* 141-148.

Jones, J.E. (1973). Synergy and consensus-seeking. In J.E. Jones & J.W. Pfeiffer (Eds.), *The 1973 annual handbook for group facilitators.* San Diego, CA: University Associates.

Rogers, C.R., & Roethlisberger, F.J. (1952). Barriers and gateways to communication. *Harvard Business Review, 30,* 46-52.

CONFLICT-RESOLUTION STRATEGIES

Conflict is a daily reality for everyone. Whether at home or at work, an individual's needs and values constantly and invariably come into opposition with those of other people. Some conflicts are relatively minor, easy to handle, or capable of being overlooked. Others of greater magnitude, however, require a strategy for successful resolution if they are not to create constant tension or lasting enmity in home or business.

The ability to resolve conflict successfully is probably one of the most important social skills that an individual—and particularly a member of a work team—can possess. Yet there are few formal opportunities in our society to learn it. Like any other human skill, conflict resolution can be taught; like other skills, it consists of a number of important subskills, each separate and all interdependent. These skills need to be assimilated at the cognitive level (by developing an understanding of how conflict can be resolved) as well as at the behavioral level (by developing the ability to resolve specific conflicts).

RESPONSES TO CONFLICT SITUATIONS

Children develop their own personal strategies for dealing with conflict. Even if these preferred approaches do not resolve conflicts successfully, they continue to be used because of a lack of awareness of alternatives.

Conflict-resolution strategies[1] may be classified into three major categories—avoidance, defusion, and confrontation. Figure 1 illustrates that avoidance is at one extreme and confrontation is at the other.

Avoidance

Some people attempt to avoid conflict situations altogether or to avoid certain types of conflict. These people tend to repress emotional reactions, look the other way, or

---

[1] For further information on conflict-resolution strategies, see the *Thomas-Kilmann Conflict Mode Instrument,* by K.W. Thomas and R.H. Kilmann, 1974, Tuxedo, NY: XICOM.

By Joan A. Stepsis. Adapted from *The 1974 Annual Handbook For Group Facilitators,* edited by J.W. Pfeiffer and J.E. Jones, 1974, San Diego, CA: University Associates. This article may be freely reproduced for educational/training activities. *Systematic or large-scale reproduction or distribution (more than one hundred copies)—or inclusion of this article in publications for sale—may be done only with prior written permission from University Associates.*

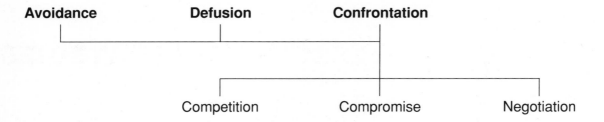

Figure 1. A Continuum of Responses to Conflict Situations

leave the situation entirely. When they choose to avoid conflicts, it is either because they cannot face up to certain situations effectively or because they do not have the skills to negotiate them effectively.

Although avoidance strategies do have value—for example, when survival is the issue and escape is possible—they may leave an individual feeling dissatisfied, facing doubts and fears about meeting the same type of situation in the future.

Defusion

This tactic is essentially a delaying action. Defusion strategies are used to "cool off" the situation, at least temporarily, or to keep the issues so unclear that attempts at confrontation are improbable. Resolving minor points while avoiding or delaying discussion of the major problem, postponing a confrontation until a more auspicious time, and avoiding clarification of the salient issues underlying the conflict are examples of defusion. Often the person who seeks to defuse a conflict wishes to accommodate—to meet the needs of the other people involved at the expense of his or her own needs.

Defusion works when delay is possible or desirable, such as when two people are too angry to discuss a problem effectively and agree to resolve that problem at a specific later time. However, if those people then fail to discuss the problem later, they may end up with feelings of dissatisfaction, anxiety about the future of their relationship, and doubts about themselves.

Confrontation

The third major strategy involves an actual confrontation of conflicting issues or persons. Confrontation can further be subdivided into competition, compromise, and negotiation.

Competition indicates a desire to meet one's own needs and a lack of concern for the needs of the others involved. The competitor uses some form of power, persuasion, or coercion. Competitive strategies include the use of physical force (a punch in the nose, war); bribery (money, favors); and punishment (withholding love, money, job promotions). Such tactics are often very effective from the point of view of the "successful" party in the conflict: that person wins; the others who are involved lose. Unfortunately, however, for the losers the real conflict may have only just begun. Hostility, anxiety, and actual physical damage are the by-products of these "win-lose" power tactics.

Compromise reflects a desire to find a resolution that will partially meet the needs of everyone involved. The individual who seeks a compromise expects the outcome to be mutually acceptable and somewhat satisfying to all of the parties; he or she also expects to give up something for the sake of achieving a resolution that everyone can live with.

Negotiation is based on a desire to meet the needs of all people involved in a conflict. With negotiation strategies, everyone can win. The negotiator works to see that everyone's needs are acknowledged as important, that several possible resolutions and their consequences are identified, and that the alternative that meets each party's goals is chosen and implemented. Because of its "win-win" emphasis, negotiation has the potential to provide the most positive and the least negative by-products of all conflict-resolution strategies.

NEGOTIATION SKILLS

Successful negotiation requires a set of skills that must be learned and practiced. These skills include (1) the ability to determine the nature of (to diagnose) the conflict, (2) effectiveness in initiating confrontations, (3) the ability to hear the other's point of view, and (4) the use of problem-solving processes to bring about a consensus decision.[2]

Diagnosing

Diagnosing the nature of a conflict is the starting point in any attempt at resolution through negotiation. The most important issue that must be decided is whether the conflict is an ideological (value) conflict or a "real" (tangible) conflict—or a combination of both. Value conflicts are exceedingly difficult to negotiate. If, for example, I believe that people's jobs should come first in their lives and that whatever personal sacrifices they make for the sake of their jobs are entirely appropriate, whereas you believe that people's personal lives should come first and that no personal sacrifices are appropriate for the sake of jobs, it would be very difficult for us to come to a position on this issue that would satisfy us both.

A difference of values, however, is really significant only when the opposing views affect people in some real or tangible way. For example, if a manager believes that work should come first and one of that manager's subordinates believes that one's personal life should come first, then there is a negotiable conflict. If both the manager and the subordinate stand on their individual principles—maintaining their value conflict—they probably will make little headway. But if, instead, they

---

[2] A consensus decision is one that all team members can accept, regardless of how satisfied they are with it. Each member's opinion must be heard; no "majority-rule" voting, bargaining, or averaging is allowed.

both concentrate on the "real" problem—the tangible effects, which concern the use of the subordinate's time—they may be able to devise a realistic, mutually acceptable resolution that does not require either of them to change his or her values. For example, the manager may agree to honor the subordinate's decision to refuse all overtime work, and the subordinate may agree to make or receive personal phone calls at work only in the case of an emergency. This resolution illustrates that the ideological differences do not need to be resolved; instead, the tangible element has been shown to be amenable to a negotiated settlement.

It is important to determine whether a conflict is a real or a value conflict. If it is a conflict in values resulting in intangible effects on either party, then it is best tolerated. If, however, a tangible effect exists, that element of the conflict should be resolved.

Initiating

A second skill necessary to conflict resolution is effectiveness in initiating a confrontation. It is important not to begin by attacking or demeaning the other party or parties involved. A defensive reaction on the part of one or more parties usually blocks a quick resolution of differences. The individual who confronts another party does so effectively by stating the tangible effects that the conflict has on him or her. For example, the individual who is confronting may say, "I have a problem. Due to your stand on placing work above everything else, I feel that to be seen by you as a valuable employee, I must work overtime even though my home life is my top priority." The meaning is clear, and it has been communicated without resorting to name calling or provoking a venomous exchange. In other words, confrontation is not synonymous with verbal attack.

Listening

After the confrontation has been initiated, a confronter must be capable of hearing the other point(s) of view. If the initial statement made by another person involved is not what the confronter was hoping to hear, a defensive rebuttal, a "hard-line" approach, or an explanation often follows. Argument-provoking replies should be avoided. Confronters should not attempt to defend themselves, explain their positions, or make demands or threats. Instead, they must be able to engage in the skill *active* listening. They should listen and reflect and paraphrase or clarify the other person's stand. When confronters have interpreted the opposition's position to the satisfaction of the other person, they should again present their own points of view, being careful to avoid value statements and to concentrate on tangible outcomes. Usually, when confronters listen to the other person, that person lowers his or her defenses and is, in turn, more ready to hear another point of view. Of course, if both persons are skilled in active listening, the chances of successful negotiation are much enhanced.

Problem Solving

The final skill necessary to successful negotiation is the use of the problem-solving process to negotiate a consensus decision. The steps in the process that follows are simply stated and easy to apply:

1. *Clarifying the problem.* What is the tangible issue? Where does each party stand on the issue?

2. *Generating and evaluating a number of possible solutions.* Often these two substeps should be done separately. First, all possible solutions should be raised in a brainstorming[3] session; then each proposed solution should be evaluated.

3. *Deciding together (not voting) on the best solution.* The one solution that is most acceptable to all parties should be chosen.

4. *Planning the implementation of the solution.* How will the solution be carried out? By whom? By what deadline?

5. *Planning for an evaluation of the solution after a specified period of time.* This last step is essential because the first solution chosen is not always the best or most workable. If the first solution has flaws, the problem-solving process should be begun again at Step 1.

REFERENCES

Gordon, T. (1971). *Parent effectiveness training.* New York: Wyden.

Wiley, G.E. (1973). Win/lose situations. In J.E. Jones and J.W. Pfeiffer (Eds.), *The 1973 annual handbook for group facilitators* (pp. 105-107). San Diego, CA: University Associates.

---

[3] Brainstorming is a technique used by groups to generate a number of creative ideas in a short time. The group members take turns contributing one idea at a time until all ideas have been exhausted. No criticism, evaluation, or judgment of ideas is allowed until the brainstorming phase has been completed.

CONSTRUCTIVE CONFLICT IN DISCUSSIONS

Many cases of ineffective decision making on a national level can be cited: the lack of preparation for the attack on Pearl Harbor, the repeated and unsuccessful escalations in the Vietnam War, the decision to cover up the Watergate break-in, and the failure to secure the timely release of the hostages in Iran. The faulty decisions reached in these instances were the result of an inadequate process of discussion that did not allow the people involved to voice disagreements and to engage in significant conflict of ideas. If conflict is stifled in teams of national policy makers, it is even more likely to be so in the teams that exist within companies.

To understand why conflict is so often suppressed when a team is engaged in the process of problem solving, it is necessary to consider our conceptions of conflict. Webster (1967) defines conflict as "disagreement...war, battle, collision, emotional tension...the opposition of persons...." Some typical student definitions of conflict concur:

- "Conflict happens when members of a group are too closed-minded to compromise."
- "It occurs when someone wants his own way in the group."
- "Hostility among members."
- "When there is conflict in a group, somebody loses and somebody else wins."

These definitions suggest that conflict is regarded as somewhat negative in nature and, perhaps, as something to be avoided. It is unfortunate that such negative connotations have become associated with conflict because when conflict is well managed, it is highly constructive; in fact, it is essential to effective problem-solving discussions.

There are, of course, both constructive and disruptive methods of dealing with conflict. Its value in a team's problem-solving discussion is realized or defeated by the members' skills in managing it. Learning how to disagree productively is a primary consideration for the training of effective team members.

By Julia T. Wood. Adapted from *The 1977 Annual Handbook for Group Facilitators*, edited by J.E. Jones and J.W. Pfeiffer, 1977, San Diego, CA: University Associates. This article may be freely reproduced for educational/training activities. *Systematic or large-scale reproduction or distribution (more than one hundred copies)—or inclusion of this article in publications for sale—may be done only with prior written permission from University Associates.*

CONFLICT AS A POSITIVE FORCE

Reaching consensus on a solution to a shared problem is a major goal of problem-solving discussions. Before a team can achieve consensus,[1] however, the views of different members must be heard, given fair consideration, and critically evaluated. Conflict or disagreement is a natural and essential part of this process. The very idea of discussion, in fact, presupposes the existence of differing viewpoints regarding the "best" method of resolving a common problem or concern.

Although many textbooks have drawn a distinction between argumentation (which is claimed to be appropriate for public speaking) and cooperative, reflective talk (which is associated with problem-solving discussions) (Brilhart, 1967; Wagner & Arnold, 1965), such a separation is misleading. Argumentation in discussion is important, indeed essential. Sound decisions, the goal of problem-solving discussions, depend on an atmosphere that is conducive to the expression of differing opinions, to the rigorous scrutiny of evidence and implications, and to the thorough consideration of all possible alternative courses of action. A team should encourage these activities, which include disagreements, in order to increase its chances of making sound and well-considered decisions. If a team discourages these activities and muffles disagreements, it is more likely to make superficial or unwise decisions.

Most decisions must be made under uncertain conditions. Relevant information may be unavailable; knowledge about future consequences or implications of the problem and its possible solutions may be, at best, speculative. Making decisions under these conditions is difficult. However, it is possible to increase the probability of making sound choices by realizing that good decisions must grow out of the clash and conflict of divergent ideas and out of the serious consideration of differing alternatives.

The traditional dictum for reflective cooperative talk is, of course, useful, but to rule out the argumentative aspects of discussion is to deny the intensity of deliberation that is necessary for sound decision making.

OUTGROWTHS OF CONFLICT

The following three noteworthy reasons exist for encouraging conflict in problem-solving discussions:

1. By entertaining diverse ideas and perspectives, team members can gain a broadened understanding of the nature of the problem and its implications.
2. By encouraging the expression of different ideas, a team has potentially more alternatives from which to select a final solution.
3. The excitement that comes from conflicting ideas stimulates healthy interaction and involvement with the team's task.

---

[1] A consensus decision is one that all team members can accept, regardless of how satisfied they are with it. Each member's opinion must be heard; no "majority-rule" voting, bargaining, or averaging is allowed.

The first two reasons affect the team product—decisions; the third reason affects the team process.

A Broadened Understanding

In a problem-solving discussion the first objective is to agree on the problem or concern that prompted the team meeting. Although many people assume that this is a simple matter, it is a significant phase in the process of decision making. Superficial attention to this first phase often leads to backtracking later or to conclusions that are based on an inaccurate assessment of the problem and that do not address the real problem.

Thus, in the process of determining the problem, conflict should be urged. It allows for differing perceptions and opinions and, thus, results in a broadened perspective on the problem. Walter and Scott (1973) strongly advocate disagreement during the initial stage of problem solving:

> Disagreement is a prerequisite for purposive discussion, and it may often contribute important junctures during discussion from which the participants can build toward better understanding of problems.... Disagreements represent various interpretations to weigh and choose; potentially, therefore, they provide profitable inquiries to pursue. (p. 253)

Only when diverse ideas are encouraged can the team hope to achieve the maximally broad understanding of its problem, and this is fundamental to the remainder of the problem-solving process.

Increased Alternatives

A second reason for encouraging conflict in discussions—perhaps the most recognized and accepted rationale—is that through disagreements team members can develop more possible solutions from which to make a final selection. Premature commitment to a solution without adequate awareness or consideration of alternative possibilities is all too frequent—it characterized the national fiascos mentioned at the beginning of this article. A team whose norm precludes disagreement is not likely to have an array of possible solutions from which to select. In this case the team's decision or solution is not one that grows out of serious and open-minded deliberation; rather, it is a careless gamble resulting from superficial discussion. Peter Drucker (1973), who has studied decision making in organizations, maintains that one of the most important functions of disagreement is that it alone can provide alternatives to a decision, and alternatives are necessary for anything other than rash decision making. When a team does not have alternatives, it cannot make a reasoned decision; instead, it simply ratifies the only idea that has been allowed to surface. Sound decisions grow out of the consideration—earnest, reflective consideration—of alternatives, and this may occur only when disagreement and conflict are accepted as a constructive part of the discussion process.

Member Interaction and Involvement

The final reason for advocating conflict in discussions is that it serves to stimulate members' interest in the team and the shared problem. Conflict implies vigorous interaction over ideas, and this increases team members' involvement with the task and enhances the process of decision making. A frequently cited value of discussion as a means of making decisions is that it allows for greater creativity in considering and solving problems. This value, however, rests on the assumption that various opinions and values will be invited and seriously considered by all team members so that creative combinations of ideas may occur. Healthy, noncombative disagreements provide a free and open atmosphere for discussion; therefore, members' creative energies are loosed for the good of the process. Extensive observation of organizational decision-making teams has led Hoffman, Harburg, and Maier (1962) to conclude that conflict results in more creative thinking, greater member commitment to a decision, and a higher-quality decision. Creativity seems to thrive on constructive conflict.

Thus, it should be clear that conflict is not to be avoided in discussions. On the contrary, it seems to be a positive force that can enhance both the process and the products of problem-solving discussion.

MANAGING CONFLICT EFFECTIVELY

Despite the fact that conflict has some significant values for discussion, everyday experience also shows that conflict can be dangerous—it can destroy a team, lead to stalemates rather than decisions, and cause major interpersonal hostilities. Whether conflict enhances or subverts discussion depends on how the conflict is managed. There are both ineffective and effective methods of dealing with it.

Disruptive Conflict

Distributive or disruptive conflict occurs when team members do not understand the value of conflict and do not have or do not use constructive means of channeling it into deliberations. In a distributive situation there is a competitive climate; members perceive the disagreement as a game in which someone will win and others must lose. There is no integration toward a common goal, no sense of team spirit in which all ideas belong to all team members. "Getting my own way" is more important than finding the best understanding of and solution for the team's common problem. In distributive situations members tend to employ such defense mechanisms as aggression, withdrawal, repression, or projection of blame onto others. Members also tend to become locked into their own viewpoints and are unwilling even to consider the possible value of others' ideas. Frequently, in distributive situations, members will resort to personal attacks instead of focusing their disagreement on the issues.

In this type of situation there are naturally some undesirable effects. The team may form cliques or subgroups. Members will be less likely to understand (or even to try to understand) one another's motives and opinions because hostility and distrust are high. When disruptive conflict penetrates discussion, it may be impossible to reach any decision because the team becomes deadlocked and no member is willing to shift position. Even if the team does manage to reach a decision, members will seldom be satisfied with it. Distributive conflict, then, is negative in its nature and its effects: it is the kind of conflict that should be avoided since it leads to nothing constructive in the process or products of discussion.

Constructive Conflict

By contrast, integrative or constructive conflict develops when team members understand the utility of disagreement and when they have acquired methods of managing conflict effectively. In integrative situations there is high team spirit and commitment to team goals. Members assume that their disagreements stem from sincere involvement with the common problem and that by discussing the differing ideas they will eventually come to an agreement that is better than any one individual's initial suggestions. In integrative situations members are cooperative toward one another. They tend to be supportive of others' ideas and open to considering the merits of opinions different from their own. Disagreements are confined to the issues and do not involve personalities.

The effects of integrative conflict are desirable. Team cohesion is usually increased because members have survived some "rough waters" and have emerged with a sound solution; they also have learned that they can trust one another to be fair and open minded. Through integrative conflict, members usually are able to reach decisions that they are proud of; the cumulative result is a process and a product that satisfies the whole team. Integrative conflict, then, is highly positive in nature because it improves not only the decisions of a team but also the process by which those decisions are made.

SUMMARY

Conflict is a necessary and integral part of realistic and effective problem-solving discussions. It is the essence of sound decision making because disagreement is the best vehicle for broadening perspectives, discovering alternatives, and stimulating creative interaction among team members. The effects of disagreement, however, depend on how it is managed by team members. Conflict can be distributive and disruptive or it can be integrative and constructive. When mismanaged, conflict can destroy a team's effectiveness; when handled well, it can greatly increase the quality of a team's work and make members feel proud of their work in the team.

Training in the nature of conflict and the methods of managing it is a pressing need for all people who participate in problem-solving groups, such as those that constitute work teams. The negative associations of conflict need to be dispelled and replaced with more realistic conceptions that make the legitimate distinction between constructive and disruptive conflict. When team members see that conflict can be a positive force in discussion, they are better prepared to adopt effective personal attitudes and behaviors in problem-solving situations. Furthermore, the differences between distributive and integrative conflict can help them learn how their own behavior contributes to the climate of the team to which they belong.

REFERENCES

Brilhart, J.K. (1967). *Effective group discussion.* Dubuque, IA: William C. Brown.

Drucker, P.F. (1973). *Management: Tasks, responsibilities, practices.* New York: Harper & Row.

Hoffman, L.R., Harburg, E., & Maier, N.R.F. (1962). Differences and disagreements as factors in creative group problem solving. *Journal of Abnormal and Social Psychology, 64,* 212.

Wagner, R.H., & Arnold, C.C. (1965). *Handbook of group discussion* (2nd ed.). Boston: Houghton Mifflin.

Walter, O.M., & Scott, R.L. (1967). *Thinking and speaking.* New York: Macmillan.

Webster's Seventh New Collegiate Dictionary. (1967). Springfield, MA: Merriman.

DECISION-MAKING STYLES

Maier's (1963) research in the area of problem solving revealed two dimensions that correlate reliably with a decision's effectiveness: quality and acceptance. The *quality* of a decision is dependent on the decision maker's grasp and utilization of the known facts. The *acceptance* of a decision is dependent on the reactions of the people who must implement that decision.

The levels of quality and acceptance required vary from decision to decision; an effective decision is one that meets the *predetermined* levels of quality and acceptance required for that particular decision. Maier developed a decision-making model based on his research. This model, which is illustrated in Figure 1, suggests that four decision-making styles—consultative, command, consensus, and convenience—are characterized by different levels of quality and acceptance, as follows:

Consultative	=	high quality, high acceptance
Command	=	high quality, low acceptance
Consensus	=	low quality, high acceptance
Convenience	=	low quality, low acceptance

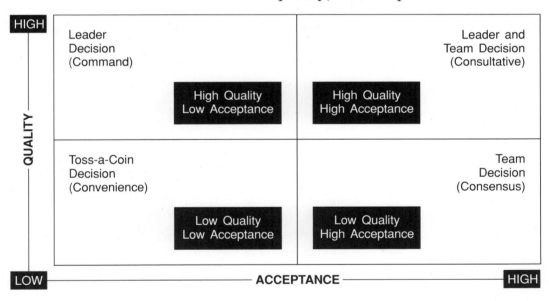

Figure 1. Decision-Making Style Model

This model for decision making provides team leaders with some basic guidelines for determining which decision-making style is appropriate for a particular situation. The four styles are described below.

THE FOUR DECISION-MAKING STYLES

1. The Consultative Decision: High Quality, High Acceptance

The team leader who determines in a particular situation that both high quality and high acceptance are required opts for a consultative decision. An example of a decision that requires both high quality and high acceptance might be reorganizing the distribution and flow of work in a team. The leader may possess a great deal of information with which to make a high-quality decision, but the acceptance of that decision on the part of the team members who must implement it is critical to the success of the decision. If the team members do not fully understand the decision and/or are not committed to it, they may inadvertently (or perhaps even purposely) hinder the implementation process.

In the case of a consultative decision, the leader consults with all team members, either individually or as a group, about the decision; subsequently, the leader carefully considers the team members' thoughts and feelings and then makes the decision. Because the leader has a firm grasp of the facts surrounding the decision, high quality is likely. Because each team member has an opportunity to voice his or her ideas and opinions, it is also likely that the decision will be highly acceptable to the team members, who must implement the decision. The team members' contributions also serve another useful purpose: they increase the amount of information to which the leader has access in making the decision.

2. The Command Decision: High Quality, Low Acceptance

If, after assessing a situation, the team leader decides that high quality is required but high acceptance on the part of the team members is not, the leader opts for a command decision. The leader makes the decision based on information that he or she has collected; the team members are not consulted. An example of a command decision might be setting the price of a product that the work team produces. When making that decision, the leader must take into account facts about production and distribution costs, competition, marketing opportunities, and profit margin. The team members who produce the item may lack the information necessary to analyze the cost of the product and probably are not concerned with the selling price; consequently, their acceptance is not an issue.

3. The Consensus Decision: Low Quality, High Acceptance

When the quality of a decision is of minor importance but high acceptance is essential, the leader opts for a consensus decision. The leader assembles the team members and assists them in the consensus process. The basic requirement of a consensus decision is that it must be one that all team members can accept, regardless of how satisfied they are with it. Each member's opinion is heard; no "majority-rule" voting, bargaining, or averaging is allowed. The outcome evolves from shared information, ideas, and feelings.

Maier (1963) offered an excellent example of a team situation in which consensus was the appropriate style of decision making. He cited the case of three women whose team leader told them to decide which two of them would work the following Saturday. These women were of equal rank on their team, and the leader deemed them to be of equal ability; the leader did not care which two of them completed the necessary work, so the quality of the decision was not an issue. Because acceptance was important, the women were asked to make the decision themselves. All had dates that Saturday: one with her husband, one with her fiance, and one with a man she had just met. The women decided that the date with the new man was most important because that relationship was still developing, so the first two women agreed to work so that the third could have the day off. Thus, the acceptance dimension was met; the women were able to tailor the decision to fit their own values, attitudes, and personalities.

4. The Convenience Decision: Low Quality, Low Acceptance

Sometimes neither the quality nor the acceptance of a decision is important. The decision is a matter of choosing between approximately equal alternatives, and the outcome is not of concern to anyone involved. In such a case, the team leader opts for a convenience decision, deciding by whatever method is most convenient at the time. No special consideration is given to selecting the "best" method. For example, if a management team is responsible for deciding which of several similarly priced brands of coffee to buy for the organization's coffee machine, the leader of that team may simply choose one brand (a "command" decision, in a sense, except that decision quality is not an issue), may ask the management team to vote, or may assign the decision to a subordinate.

CONCLUSION

When choosing a decision-making style, a team leader must consider not only the levels of quality and acceptance required of that decision but also such factors as time, the team members' capabilities, and the team's level of trust. For example, time constraints may require the use of the command decision; or if the level of trust in the team is low, a consensus decision may be difficult or impossible to achieve. Nevertheless, Maier's model offers team leaders a good place to start when trying to match a situation with an appropriate decision-making style.

REFERENCE

Maier, N.R.F. (1963). *Problem-solving discussions and conferences: Leadership methods and skills*. New York: McGraw-Hill.

ENCOURAGING OTHERS TO CHANGE
THEIR BEHAVIOR

The idea of "getting others to do what you want them to do" raises uncomfortable feelings for many people. Yet in many situations, managers, leaders of work teams, health professionals, teachers, parents, counselors, and others are expected to be able to encourage others to change certain aspects of their behavior. The following model suggests one way to help individuals make decisions about whether, when, and how to help others change their behavior. Although there are no guaranteed ways to change another's behavior, it is possible to increase the likelihood that others will change by the strategy chosen.

ASSUMPTIONS

This model is based on the following assumptions:

- People are capable of changing their behavior; they can lose weight, learn to climb mountains, and so on.
- People cannot be made to change; they must have a part in deciding if they will change—and, if so, how.
- People like and need to make their own decisions and solve their own problems, and they have a right to do so.
- Intervening is one way of expressing care and respect for others.
- In some cases, people have a right to impose their will on those around them.
- The interpersonal relationship is a tool that can be used to assist others in considering behavior change.

DEFINITIONS

The following three basic terms are essential to understanding the model:

1. *Intervention.* This is the process by which a person enters into a situation for the purpose of assisting one or more others to consider changing behavior.

By Judy Corey Morton and D.M. Blair. Adapted from *The 1979 Annual Handbook for Group Facilitators,* edited by J.E. Jones and J.W. Pfeiffer, 1979, San Diego, CA: University Associates. This article may be freely reproduced for educational/training activities. *Systematic or large-scale reproduction or distribution (more than one hundred copies)—or inclusion of this article in publications for sale—may be done only with prior written permission from University Associates.*

2. ***"Must" intervention.*** A "must" intervention is one that people feel they must perform for one or both of these reasons: (1) someone else is doing something that concretely and tangibly affects the intervenor, and/or (2) it is part of the intervenor's job to encourage others to change aspects of their behavior. For example, a teacher may feel it necessary to intervene in a situation in which students converse loudly during class. In such a case, the behavior may affect the teacher's ability to hear questions from students and may make it difficult for other students to hear the teacher.

In a must intervention, the intervenor must be satisfied with whatever alternative behavior is decided on. Even though a situation requires a must intervention, it can be discussed at a time convenient to both parties.

3. ***"Can" intervention.*** A "can" intervention is one that people feel they can perform because (1) they have a strong enough relationship with the other person to have a reasonable chance of being heard, (2) they have information that may be helpful to the other person, or (3) they want to help the other person. For example, an employer may notice that an employee is standing so close to a client that the client is uncomfortable. An employer who has a strong enough relationship with the employee may feel able to intervene because this information may be helpful to the employee.

In a can intervention, it is up to the other person to decide how or if the information will be used. It is not necessary that the intervenor know or approve of the behavior that takes place after the intervention occurs.

It is important to remember that there is no situation that inherently requires either type of intervention. If three people observe the same situation, one might decide that it calls for a must intervention, another might feel that a can intervention is most appropriate, and the third might feel that no intervention is required. It is important for the intervenors, however, to understand which type of intervention they feel the situation requires. This decision determines the strategy that will be most effective in making the intervention. If the intervenor believes that a must intervention is called for, he or she should use a must strategy; a can strategy would be much less effective.

GUIDELINES FOR A "MUST" INTERVENTION

The proposed strategy for an intervenor in a must intervention is as follows:

1. ***Initiate the communication.*** In a must situation, the situation affects the intervenor enough that he or she must assume the responsibility for changing it. Although the intervenor must initiate the communication, the other individual can be encouraged to share in deciding when and where the intervention will take place.

2. ***State the concern.*** When doing so, it is helpful to be as descriptive as possible and to include a statement about feelings. If there is a question of whose business it is to intervene, the intervenor might make a brief statement about why

it is part of his or her job to be concerned or how what is happening concretely affects that person.

It is very easy to describe concern in a damaging way. Consider the following statements, none of which specifically describes what is happening or why it is bothersome to the speaker: "Your brother would never do that!" "Stop that or you'll get a spanking!" "Mommy doesn't like it when you behave badly!" "I'm telling your father tonight!"

3. ***Involve the other person in the solution.*** Statements or questions that involve the other person in the solution increase the chances that the proposed solution will be implemented and that the intervenor may learn a new solution to a problem. It is important to enter into this solution-finding stage without knowing how the problem will be resolved.

4. ***Ensure a satisfactory solution.*** Although ideally the intervenor will enter into the negotiating stage with an open mind, he or she must ensure that the outcome of the negotiation is personally satisfactory. The intervenor who is aware of the minimal result that he or she desires has an advantage in ensuring personal satisfaction.

Being satisfied with the solution also means a willingness to follow the situation to its logical conclusion(s) should the other person choose not to define a mutually acceptable solution. An example is the patient who decides to seek another medical opinion because he or she is not satisfied with the physician's response to his or her concern. It is important to remember that all interventions do not work. If the situation is truly a "must," the intervenor must be prepared to carry the intervention to its logical consequences and have the power to do so.

5. ***In the face of resistance, shift to active listening.*** Active listening[1] shows the individual not only that what was said is being heard, but also that the feeling associated with what was said is recognized. When the person talking feels resistant, it is difficult for him or her to consider alternative solutions. Active listening helps that person to express further how he or she is feeling. Once the person has expressed these feelings and feels that he or she has been heard, problem solving is easier. To complete the must intervention, however, the intervenor must then return the focus to finding a satisfactory solution.

Other Helpful Hints

Because attempting to change behavior is likely to be stressful for both parties, it is important for the intervenor to be as descriptive as possible and to avoid language

---

[1] In active listening, the listener listens carefully to the speaker and then restates, in his or her own words, what the speaker said. Then the speaker either confirms or corrects the listener's understanding.

that labels the other person's behavior. It is also important to avoid creating a situation in which other individuals feel that they have to defend their behavior.

Harmful	Better
"What did I tell you yesterday?"	"Please follow the instructions I gave you yesterday."
"That was a bad thing to do."	"I'm upset with you for being thirty minutes late."

GUIDELINES FOR A "CAN" INTERVENTION

Although a can intervention is not vital to the intervenor's needs, it may allow the other person to increase his or her options. The intervenor, in this case, chooses to intervene because he or she:

- Cares about the other person;
- Feels he or she has information that may be helpful to the other person; and
- Has a strong enough relationship with the other person to have a reasonable chance of being heard.

The proposed strategy for a can intervention is as follows:

1. ***Ensure that a relationship is built with the other person before attempting to intervene.*** A strong relationship increases the likelihood that whatever information the intervenor has to share will be carefully considered. One of the best ways to build a relationship with others is to use listening skills. Showing other people that what they are saying and the feelings behind what they are saying are being heard is an extremely effective way to build a relationship.

2. ***State the general nature of the concern and ask the person's permission to share some information.*** Signaling the nature of one's intent and allowing the other person some control over whether he or she wants to talk about it—as well as where and when to talk about it—increase the chances that the other person will be ready and receptive at the time of the intervention.

3. ***Wait until the other person gives permission to go on.*** It is important to refrain from intervening unless it is clear that permission has been granted. Sometimes the other person may nonverbally show reluctance to discuss the issue. If there is any sense of reluctance, assume that permission has not been given.

4. ***Share personal concern(s).*** This kind of information not only can help the intervenor feel more comfortable but also decreases the likelihood that the other person will feel threatened and therefore helps him or her to focus on the content of what is being said.

5. ***Be specific.*** The more specifically the behavior or circumstance is described, the more likely it is that the other person can do something to change.

6. ***If resistance arises, shift to active listening.*** This approach allows the other person to say more about his or her concern. It also lets that person know that the intervenor is trying to understand what he or she is saying. Remember that if the situation is truly a "can," the intervention does not need to be made at all.

7. ***Be brief and state the concern only once.*** This helps avoid the appearance of nagging, and it also allows the other person to assume the responsibility for asking for more information—if it is wanted.

8. ***Allow the other person to decide how or if he or she wants to act on the intervention.*** With a can intervention, it is not necessary to know how or if the other person decides to act on the information. If the person wants to discuss it further, he or she will do so.

If the intervenor encounters resistance and/or notices no significant change in behavior, three things might be considered:

1. The intervenor's assessment of the strength of the relationship was inaccurate.
2. The intervenor could have improved the manner in which the information was presented.
3. The individual considered the information and decided not to do anything about it. (This also includes the possibility that he or she might be right.)

SUMMARY

The key to this model is for the intervenor to understand how he or she feels about a given situation. There is no situation that inherently requires a must or a can intervention. Whether a must or a can strategy should be used is based on the intervenor's set of values and/or work situation. The wrong strategy could put the intervenor in a worse position than he or she was in originally. For example, assume that Jim is stepping on Mary's toe. If Mary asks Jim for permission to speak, and he says "No," what does Mary do?

The act of intervening implies personal risk. Possible negative consequences that could occur as a result of ineffective interventions include no behavior change on the part of the other person and/or a worsening of the relationship between the two individuals. However, if done appropriately, intervening can result in behavior change and a deepening of the relationship between the intervenor and the other person.

The two strategies suggested here are ways of increasing the likelihood that other people will consider changing their behavior. Ultimately, people will decide for themselves how and if they will change. Thus, these strategies will not guarantee behavior change; they can only increase the chances that it will occur.

DEALING WITH DISRUPTIVE INDIVIDUALS IN MEETINGS

People who conduct meetings often are troubled by the behavior of a person in attendance who is disrupting the proceedings. It is important for those who conduct meetings, such as team leaders or designated team members, to have a repertoire of responses in such situations in order to maintain control and to accomplish the objectives of the meeting. This discussion will enumerate several methods that can be used to prevent, and to respond effectively to, attempts by individuals to dominate meetings at the expense of the meeting leader. The basic theme in this approach is that the leader should take initiatives to minimize disruptions and to maintain control over meetings when dominating behavior occurs.

Individuals can initiate many forms of disruptive behavior in meetings. Some of the more common ones are the following:

- Interrupting, cutting people off while they are talking;
- Speechmaking, especially repetitious discourse;
- Sidetracking, topic jumping, changing issues, multiplying concerns;
- Polarizing, pushing people to take sides, attempting to co-opt people into agreement with one point of view;
- Emotionalizing issues, expressing fear or anxiety about probable outcomes;
- Challenging the leader and others with regard to data sources, rights, legalities;
- Expressing sarcasm, claiming that "The sky is falling" or "They won't let us do what you propose";
- Complaining about the system, meeting, leader, agenda;
- Threatening to withhold support, resign, deny responsibility, seek retribution;
- Accusing the leader of being political, impugning motives;
- Pouting, withdrawing from active participation or controversial topics;
- Saying "Yes, but..." a lot, discounting the contributions of others;

By John E. Jones. Adapted from *The 1980 Annual Handbook for Group Facilitators*, edited by J.W. Pfeiffer and J.E. Jones, 1980, San Diego, CA: University Associates. This article may be freely reproduced for educational/training activities. *Systematic or large-scale reproduction or distribution (more than one hundred copies)—or inclusion of this article in publications for sale—may be done only with prior written permission from University Associates.*

- Throwing a "wet blanket" over the proceedings by pointing out all possible failures; and
- Personalizing issues and agenda topics, taking all remarks as directed toward people rather than ideas.

Many of these disruptive behaviors constitute attempts to take over or subvert the leadership of the meeting. Whenever possible the leader needs to anticipate these dominating postures and prevent their occurrence. In addition, the leader needs to be able to respond to disruptions when they occur within a meeting, whether they were anticipated or not; and there are some situations in which the leader needs to resort to drastic methods.

It is assumed in this treatment that the leader establishes the agenda, designs the meeting, and facilitates the meeting process. All of these prerogatives are sources of authority and power for the leader, and it is critical for the leader to have a broad power base from which to deal with disruptive behavior. Of course, that includes maintaining high rapport with the majority of those in attendance at the meeting. It is a good rule not to have meetings for which specific goals cannot be articulated and to avoid having meetings that are highly likely to produce negative results. The leader, then, has objectives; what are needed are strategies, tactics, and techniques to ensure that those objectives are not jeopardized by the disruptive behavior of a dominating individual.

PREVENTING DISRUPTIONS

A number of political moves can be made prior to the meeting to attempt to preclude an individual's domination of the event. These tactics are meant to keep intact the leader's ability to conduct a productive interchange among team members. They are "power plays" in the sense that they are designed to erode the other person's base of support and courage and make it possible to carry out leadership functions. These methods are not necessarily "nice," but neither is the disruption of an honest meeting. Eight tactics can be considered by the leader in advance of the meeting:

1. Get the dominator's cooperation for this one meeting. Ask the person to agree not to argue from a fixed (and often familiar) position.
2. Give the person a special task or role in the meeting, such as posting the viewpoints of others.
3. Work out your differences before the meeting (possibly with a third-party facilitator) to present a united front to all other members.
4. Structure the meeting to include frequent discussion of the process of the meeting itself.
5. Take all of the dominator's items off the agenda.
6. Set the person up to be concerned about what might be the consequences of disruption. For example, "It has come to my attention that a number of people are angry with you, and I am thinking about opening up their discussion in the meeting."

7. Set up other people who will attend the meeting to support you in dealing with the disruptive behavior of the individual. For example, they can be asked to refuse to argue with the person, give feeling reactions to the dominating behavior, and confront the dysfunctional behavior directly.

8. Make the person's behavior a published agenda item.

Obviously, these methods are manipulative in that they involve deliberate attempts to influence the behavior of another person or persons. People who attempt to dominate meetings have energy that can sometimes be channeled productively, and the best outcome of these preventive postures would be that the person who is often disruptive becomes an effective meeting participant. If these methods are not feasible, the leader needs to have options for keeping control during the meeting itself.

DURING THE MEETING

The leader has two major methods for dealing with disruptive individuals during the course of the meeting: (1) to work with that person "head-on," that is, to confront and otherwise attempt to change behavior, and (2) to use the people present to work with the domination. The important consideration is that the leader has to maintain control over what is done and must initiate change. Nine tactics can be used in a direct exchange with the disruptive individual:

1. Interview the person, modeling effective listening. The leader may learn something that is significant to the goals of the meeting by developing the dominating individual's perspective, and that person may learn how to contribute to the exchange in a productive manner.

2. Turn all of the dominator's questions into statements. This forces the person to take responsibility for expressing a point of view rather than blocking the process through questions.

3. Point out the win-lose character of debates and refuse to argue.

4. Suggest a role reversal. The person can chair the meeting while the leader attempts to dominate. The person may also be invited to argue the other side of the issue for a time or may be asked to be silent for ten minutes and report the gist of the interchange.

5. Reflect the dominator's feelings, and ignore the person's content input. "You seem particularly upset today, especially when I disagree with you. How are you feeling about my interaction with you right now?"

6. Give emotional responses to the dominator. "I feel powerless to accomplish anything here with you, and I get angry when you try to take over by attempting to ramrod through your procedural suggestions."

7. Reduce the person's position to absurdity by interviewing the dominator to the logical extremes of the argument.

8. Agree with all of the person's presentation that is not directly germane to the issue or problem. Agree with the individual's need to be heard and supported.

9. Draw out the motives of the dominator, and respond to these aims rather than to the content of the presentation.

The leader must be careful to remember that the "audience" for such exchanges can be made anxious by these techniques. The leader can inadvertently put the dominator in an underdog position, gaining sympathy from the other team members who are attending the meeting. There is a good chance that the other members are just as annoyed as the leader is about the disruptive behavior, and there are ways to use that situation to maintain control. Five interventions can be considered to that end:

1. Have the team members in attendance establish ground rules to avoid polarization. For example, the word "issue" can be made illegal; people have to couch their discussions in terms of problem solving rather than right-wrong, either-or dichotomies.

2. Post all points raised on a given topic, without names. This makes the information available to all and can lessen repetition.

3. Post all contributions made by the dominator and set the expectation that everyone has a responsibility to avoid "axe grinding."

4. Create small audiences. Give the dominator only one or two people to influence. Instruct subgroups to generate statements by consensus. Pair people with differing points of view, instruct them to interview each other, and have individuals report to the entire meeting.

5. Structure an agreement between the dominator and a major opponent. Pick the person whose position is most dissimilar to the dominator's (or ask the dominator to do this). Have this pair discuss the topic for three to five minutes and come to an agreement about one piece of the problem. Others sit in a circle around the pair, observe their process, and give them feedback afterward.

A leader can use the "audience" to control disruptive behavior by encouraging others to be open about their responses to the domination. Sometimes, however, these strategies do not succeed completely; and the leader needs more drastic approaches to consider.

WHEN ALL ELSE FAILS

When the leader feels that the meeting's purposes are being successfully thwarted by the dominator, it is important to be able to intervene in such a way as to protect the objectives. Three options are available:

1. Create a chaotic condition in the meeting, exaggerating if necessary, and show a way out. This often-used political ploy capitalizes on people's need for closure and order, and the dominator's position can often be lost in the process.

2. Adjourn the meeting when the dominator takes over.

3. Leave the meeting when the dominator takes over, disavowing responsibility for what is done.

These three methods are, of course, bold; they should not be chosen unless the situation is clearly dangerous for the leader. The final one, sometimes called the "Gromyko Intervention," because of that leader's penchant for walking out of United Nations sessions, requires follow-through in order to maintain the leader's power.

CAVEATS

All of these methods require that the leader adopt a cool, unruffled posture. Becoming angry means giving away power, and the leader of a meeting needs to focus detached attention on managing the situation in the light of the purposes established for the event. Using many of these techniques in rapid succession can result in "overkill," and the leader needs to make certain that the motive is not to punish an individual but to promote functional behavior.

Leaders who use these tactics as a matter of routine style even when they are inappropriate become sources of disruption themselves in that they prevent team members in attendance from having the opportunity to influence the discussion. Too-frequent use of these methods can intimidate members who are less bold than dominators, and the result can be that they contribute less to the meeting out of fear of being confronted.

Disruptive behavior in meetings is almost always a symptom of some defect in the organizational system that the meeting is designed to support. Leaders need to consider that every meeting is, in reality, a team-development or organization-development session; and they should facilitate it in ways that isolate problems for remedial action.

SUGGESTED ACTIVITIES

If a work team is interested in increasing its skill in dealing with disruptive individuals, the following activities should be considered:

1. Team members can be instructed to discuss with one another examples of meetings they have attended in which individuals have disrupted the proceedings. The focus should be on how the meeting leader handled the situation.

2. Team members can add from their own experiences to the twenty-five tactics listed in this article.

3. The team can make a list of behaviors that the leader should avoid in responding to disruptions, such as put-downs and arguing.

4. The team can be asked to imagine being in all of the twenty-five situations and to record their probable emotional responses as (a) meeting leaders, (b) dominators, and/or (c) other team members.

5. Team members can role play various situations to attain skill in using the suggested methods.

A POSITIVE APPROACH TO RESISTANCE

In most modern organizations there is a strong value system that stresses the need for collaboration, cooperation, and trust. Although this viewpoint certainly has much to recommend it, a problem has arisen in that this emphasis on "positive" reactions leads to a tendency to discount "negative" reactions such as competition, anger, and resistance. The reality is that there are no inherently negative reactions.

Given the proper circumstances, every human reaction has the potential to be expressed in an appropriate and effective manner. To discount any reaction—where human interaction is concerned—is to limit resources and to reduce the range of alternatives that are available. Such limitation is hardly a prescription for team building or team development—or any type of individual or organizational growth and effectiveness. There is a time to listen and a time not to listen, a time for contemplation and a time for action, and a time to grow and a time to stand firm. It is always the situation that determines what is appropriate, what is effective, and sometimes even what is ethical.

The reaction that probably is most under fire today is resistance. Frequently in a team environment, cooperation is seen as a universally good reaction; therefore, resistance—as its opposite—is often seen as bad or negative. Everyone has heard admonitions such as "Don't be defensive," "You've got to learn to compromise," or "You're thinking of your own welfare." Team members need to know when to express resistance, how to express it appropriately so that the results are positive for all of those concerned, and how to deal with another person's resistance.

The ability to resist can be seen as a personal asset in that it keeps one from being hurt and from overloading oneself. It also allows one to make clearer choices about what is good for oneself, and it helps in blocking out unimportant distractions that would hinder the achievement of one's goals. Resistance also can be seen as a team asset in that it allows the team to differentiate talent, provides new information about what might not work well, and produces a lot of needed energy.

Because resistance has traditionally been disvalued, many managers and team leaders—as well as other team members—tend to use one or more of the following low-yield strategies to deal with it:

1. *Breaking it down.* The attempt to break down resistance is usually carried out by threatening, coercing, selling, or reasoning.

By H.B. Karp. Adapted from *The 1988 Annual: Developing Human Resources,* edited by J.W. Pfeiffer, 1988, San Diego, CA: University Associates. This article may be freely reproduced for educational/training activities. *Systematic or large-scale reproduction or distribution (more than one hundred copies)—or inclusion of this article in publications for sale—may be done only with prior written permission from University Associates.*

2. *Avoiding it.* This strategy is pursued through deflection, "not hearing," or attempting to induce guilt.
3. *Discounting it.* This approach involves dismissing the resistance as unimportant, promoting tradition as the alternative to the resistance, or appealing to the resister's need to conform.

Although the low-yield strategies may work to some degree in that they may evoke positive responses from resisters for the moment, they rarely provide lasting solutions and are often quite costly. In some cases, such as with threats and attempts to induce guilt, they may even produce more and deeper resistance at a later time.

DEALING POSITIVELY WITH RESISTANCE

Dealing appropriately with resistance is a skill that is important for all members of any team. Two basic assumptions underlie a positive approach to dealing creatively with resistance:

1. *Resistance is.* People will always resist, knowingly or not, those things that they perceive as not in their best self-interest.
2. *Resistance needs to be honored.* It must be dealt with in a respectful manner.

If resistance is handled from a perspective that incorporates these two assumptions, it becomes a team asset and can enhance rather than injure a relationship between any two employees, be they supervisor and subordinate, peers, or line and staff. Another condition must exist in order for the positive approach to work: the demander—the individual who confronts the resister—must be absolutely clear about what he or she wants from the resister and must be as specific as possible in relating this information to the resister. When the demand is stated in terms of time frames, specific outcomes, potential benefits, concrete behaviors that are needed, and so forth, the probability that the demander will achieve compliance from the resister is great. Even if compliance is not possible, the resistance will become more workable.

The positive approach consists of four separate steps: (1) surfacing, (2) honoring, (3) exploring, and (4) rechecking. When the demander and the resister meet, they should complete each step before moving to the next step.

Surfacing the Resistance

After the demander has clearly stated what he or she wants from the other party, the first—and probably most difficult—step is to get the resistance out in the open. Many people intentionally withhold their resistance for a number of reasons: experience with a past heavy emphasis on the low-yield strategies, mistrust, a poor interpersonal relationship, or a lack of awareness of their own resistance. The surfacing of resistance can be approached easily and effectively by keeping two guidelines in mind:

1. ***Make the expression of resistance as "safe" as possible.*** The demander should state clearly—and publicly, if possible—that he or she wants to hear the resistance. It is a good idea to include an explanation of why the resistance is important and to be straightforward. Once the resister is aware that he or she is not going to be attacked, punished, or "sold" on what the demander wants, the demander has a much greater chance of exposing the real source of the resistance.

2. ***Ask for it all.*** Listening to a resister's statement of what he or she does not like about the very thing that the demander wants is rarely a pleasant experience for the demander. Nevertheless, it is the best approach to resistance. When the resistance exists, it is much better to hear all of it than to try to work through the situation in partial ignorance.

Honoring the Resistance

Honoring involves the following process:

1. ***Listen.*** When a person states resistance openly, he or she provides the demander with a vital source of information about what the demander wants and the potential pitfalls in achieving what is wanted. In addition, the resister is making a personal statement about who he or she is. Any attempt to discount the information not only stops the information but also carries a clear message to the resister that his or her opinion does not matter; the resister will interpret this to mean that he or she does not matter. It is of critical importance at this stage that the demander make no attempt to reinforce his or her original position, to sell, to reason, or in any way to imply that the resister should not feel as he or she does. The correct approach is simply to listen.

2. ***Acknowledge the resistance.*** The act of acknowledgment does not imply that the demander agrees with the point of resistance. It is a simple affirmation of the resister's right to resist. Statements such as "I see how that could be a problem for you" or "You certainly have a right to be concerned" allow the demander to respond to the resister's concern without relinquishing anything. The demander should acknowledge the resistance but not agree with it.

3. ***Reinforce the notion that it is permissible to resist.*** The demander should keep in mind that openly resisting in a safe environment may be a new experience for the resister. Periodically reinforcing that the resistance is valuable and that the resister is safe and appreciated for stating his or her resistance creates a positive atmosphere. Statements such as "It's really all right that you don't like all of this" or "I can see why you are angry" maintain the demander's control of the situation while making the environment continually safe for the resister.

Exploring the Resistance

Exploring involves the following tasks:

1. ***Distinguish authentic resistance from pseudo resistance.*** Authentic resistance is directed toward the specific demand that has been made; pseudo resistance is real but has nothing to do with the demand. Pseudo resistance usually originates in feelings such as resentment of authority, old grudges, the need for attention, or lack of clarity about one's desires. The demander's task is to uncover the authentic resistance. If the demander is having difficulty determining which kind of resistance is manifesting itself, he or she can simply ask the resister, "What is your objection?" The resister either will or will not be able to state clearly what the specific objection is. It is best to address the cause of the pseudo resistance later rather than at the moment unless it is blocking progress.

2. ***Probe the resistance.*** Once the resistance has been surfaced, honored, and judged authentic and the resister has realized that he or she is safe, the demander can help the resister to assume a proactive stance by simply asking, "What would you prefer?" In responding to this question, the resister works with the demander toward the objective rather than against it. The resister will suggest alternative approaches to meeting the demand in ways that provide the demander with what is wanted and permit the resister to obtain something for himself or herself at the same time. At this point it is a good idea to encourage negotiation and to keep in mind that something must change positively for the resister in order for the resistance to be permanently reduced. The end point of probing should be the development of some kind of agreement about the action to be taken.

Rechecking

Before the meeting is over, the last step is to recheck the status of the current resistance and the agreements that have been made. This step is essential because it provides closure to the issue and ensures that no agreement will be forgotten. If there is to be a second meeting, rechecking provides a basis on which to start the next meeting so that the entire process of dealing with the resistance does not have to be repeated.

CONCLUSION

The demander should always keep the following points in mind when confronted with a resister:

1. The objective is not to eliminate *all* resistance because it is not possible to do so. Instead, the objective is to work with and reduce the *needless* resistance. The reduction is usually enough to allow proceeding with the demand effectively.

2. Always keep paper and pencil handy to make notes during the process. When the problem is recorded, the resister's objection is honored and there is less chance that important points will be forgotten. Making notes also facilitates the last step, rechecking.

3. Once the resistance is at a workable level, thank the resister and move on. It is important not to try to persuade the resister to *like* the demand. It is enough that the resister is willing to agree to it.

This approach has universal application. It is valuable not only in team building and team development but also in any situation in which resistance is an issue, such as in managing conflict, scheduling work, or raising teenagers.

HUMOR AND THE EFFECTIVE TEAM

In a 1980 survey of 480 chief executive officers (Shrift, 1981), the majority of those corporate leaders felt that a sense of humor was essential to their work. Many of them agreed that they are more inclined to hire qualified job candidates with a sense of humor than more serious candidates who are equally qualified. In addition, those surveyed believed that humor is an essential means of communication and influence.

There is a growing belief on the part of top managers that business can be more enjoyable and productive when humor is a part of daily functioning. The ways in which humor relates to group dynamics that affect a team—including communication, problem solving, and conflict management—are discussed in the remainder of this article.

HUMOR AND COMMUNICATION

With regard to its role in communication, humor has been described as a "social lubricant." We tend to be attracted to and to like people who make us laugh. Consequently, humor plays a valuable role in the support of team harmony and in the communication of information. For instance, using humor can be a relatively safe way of raising risky issues and of calling attention to areas in which people have become inflexible. In his study of joking at work, Ullian (1976) says:

> Often the aim of the joker is simply to implant the consideration of a socially risky intention in the mind of the target without being attacked. While the uncertainty about the existence of an ulterior intent in joking protects the joker, the consideration of the intent even as a possibility by the target to the joke accomplishes the joker's aim. (p. 130)

For the team leader who wishes to establish a climate of trust and candor, humor can be an asset. Humor and a cheerful presentation of self are frequently perceived as indications that one enjoys relating to others and wishes to communicate good will and intentions (Tedeschi, 1974).

Humor also can be an aid to communication in a teaching or learning situation. When used effectively, humor can support the understanding and retention of information and can assist in establishing rapport. As Robinson (1977) states:

The use of humor is a mechanism which does not destroy one's self-image, but provides a way to criticize, show mistakes, express values yet save face for the individual in doing so. (p. 95)

Humor, when used while giving feedback, should not be an alternative to honesty.

HUMOR AND GROUP DYNAMICS

Humor can make a significant contribution to the effectiveness of a team. Among the many potential benefits of humor in team situations are (1) more open, less defensive communication; (2) greater team cohesiveness; and (3) feelings of belonging.

Studies of the functions of humor in work teams suggest that humor helps to release tension and to reduce boredom. Regardless of whether the team leader or a team member initiates the humor, a work team seems to create it (and not necessarily in support of organizational goals). The instinct for creativity and play becomes most evident in the most monotonous jobs; joking and playful behavior appear to be frequent solutions to the problem of "psychological survival" in routine jobs (Roy, 1960).

Humor and Creative Problem Solving

Humor can be an important resource in the managing of problem-solving meetings. It can be used as a means of reducing a problem to a more manageable size. When a team begins to work on a problem, certain norms and patterns of behavior are present; the most prevalent norm is the attitude that problem solving is serious business and is no time for fun. On the contrary, an occasion of problem solving may be a fine time for fun. Even though the team needs to address issues of importance, humor can support more creative and flexible approaches to solutions. When it is used well, humor is a support for directly encountering, rather than avoiding, difficult issues.

Problems are situations in need of changing. If solutions were readily available, those problems probably would not exist. Creativity is called for in generating solutions. Research on creativity supports the idea that humor and play are helpful. When asked how they generate creative ideas, many teams credit humor-related activities. For example, some people report that these ideas arise when they are "just playing around" or not taking themselves too seriously (Von Oech, 1982).

Von Oech also describes the work of a satellite-design team in which the members were in a playful mood and started joking about the satellite that they were working on at the time. That meeting proved to be the team's most productive one in months. At a subsequent meeting, the team returned to its more usual seriousness; and the availability of new ideas was greatly reduced. Von Oech (1982) states:

I've noticed that a fun working environment is much more productive than a routine environment. People who enjoy their work will come up with more ideas. The fun is contagious and everybody works harder to get a piece of that fun. (p. 110)

What frequently happens in a problem-solving situation is that the team members feel defensive and wonder if they are at fault or if they will be blamed for the existence of the problem at hand. Given those fears, an understandable response is to withhold information and to behave in a guarded and cautious fashion when exploring the problem. The question for the team leader thus becomes "How can I create a climate that will support open discussion and creative approaches to problem solving?"

The creation of such a climate certainly requires that the leader possess skills in team leadership, and an ability to use humor can enhance those skills. At its best the leader's use of humor in a problem-solving meeting indicates a willingness to laugh at himself or herself. When asking others not to take themselves too seriously, the leader does well to demonstrate the desired behavior.

Humor and Conflict Management

Laughter can effectively relieve tension in conflict situations. A well-timed joke can refocus negotiations in a more positive direction. The relief of laughter can give team members a chance to rethink their approaches and to see alternatives that may not have been obvious before.

There is an interesting and useful relationship between laughter and anger. It is impossible to laugh heartily and to be angry at the same time. No doubt many of us have experienced or observed the use of laughter and humor in alleviating a hostile attitude or in averting a potentially destructive incident.

As is the case with other uses of humor, sensitivity is essential. The use of humor in a conflict situation is a potentially "high-risk/high-payoff" intervention. It can be especially helpful to use oneself as the target of humor. Roberts (1980, p. 90) suggests that in a hostile situation in which no resolution seems apparent, it may be helpful to say something absurd about one's inability to respond effectively: "Hostility doesn't come easily to me; I think I'll need a little more practice before continuing" or "If things don't get better, I may have to stop helping."

SUMMARY: GUIDELINES FOR THE EFFECTIVE USE OF HUMOR

Humor can have a number of positive effects when used by a team. It can support effective communication, contribute to positive team interaction, promote creative problem solving, and facilitate conflict management. The following guidelines for using humor are appropriate for all members of a team:

1. *Start with yourself.* Ethel Barrymore suggests, "You grow up the day you have your first real laugh at yourself."

2. *Be able to take your work seriously but yourself lightly so that you can perceive and appreciate the humor in everyday encounters.* Probably the best source of humor is personal experience.

3. *Be an observer.* Be aware that you are surrounded by humor and notice that humor. For example, you can find it in signs that are displayed, in typographical errors, and in slips of the tongue.

4. *Think of humor as being of two kinds: public and private.* Public humor is shared the moment it occurs. Private humor occurs when a person sees or hears something funny and realizes that laughing would be inappropriate or harmful. Both kinds are useful.

5. *Use humor as a support for competence rather than as a means of masking a lack of competence.* Humor at its best is one aspect of an individual's communication repertoire; its use should not be an alternative to giving direct feedback or to dealing with an issue.

6. *Use humor with sensitivity and care so that it is likely to be appreciated.* Otherwise, there are few useful generalizations about situations in which humor is clearly appropriate or inappropriate.

REFERENCES

Roberts, M. (1983). *Managing conflict from the inside out.* San Diego, CA: Learning Concepts.

Robinson, V. (1977). *Humor and the health professions.* Thorofare, NJ: Charles B. Stack.

Roy, D.F. (1960). Job satisfaction and informal interaction. *Human Organization, 18,* 158-168.

Shrift, G. (1981, Summer). Laughter with confidence. *Squibbline,* pp. 2-4.

Tedeschi, J.T. (1974). Attributions, liking and power. In T. Huston (Ed.), *Foundations of interpersonal attraction* (pp. 74-81). New York: Academic Press.

Ullian, J.A. (1976). Joking at work. *Journal of Communication, 26,* 129-133.

Von Oech, R. (1982). *A whack on the side of the head.* Menlo Park, CA: Creative Think.